THE SENSATIONAL SOUTH ISLAND

New Zealand's Mountain Land

An expanded and updated version of the second part of the 2018 award finalist, *A Maverick New Zealand Way*.

A companion volume, *The Neglected North Island,* has just been judged 'Best Antipodean Cultural Travel Book 2021' by *Lux Life* magazine (**lux-review.com**).

TRAVELLER

MARY JANE WALKER

A MAVERICK
NEW ZEALAND
WAY
INTERNATIONAL
BOOK AWARDS
FINALIST
IntlBookAwards.com
Mary Jane Walker

THE SENSATIONAL SOUTH ISLAND

'Best Antipodean Cultural Travel Book 2021'

MARY JANE WALKER

A few reviews of other titles by Mary Jane Walker

"Read one of New Zealand author Mary Jane Walker's informed and richly entertaining travel books and the thirst for more adventures leads to searching for additional volumes."

Grady Harp, Amazon Hall of Fame reviewer, from a review of *A Maverick Traveller Anthology,* 20 April 2019

'Do take a walk with Mary Jane Walker!'

"In the tradition of Gertrude Bell, Freya Stark, Isabella Bird and other adventurous women, Mary Jane Walker's relationship with the world is one of insatiable curiosity. She is driven to immerse herself in experience. I was happy to walk with Walker around the world, and was pulled in by her prose."

Brooklyn Stooptalk, from an Amazon review of *A Maverick Traveller,* 20 April 2018

'Marvellous Information!!!!'

"Just an enriching book on a place I knew very little about. I've always said that the purpose of reading is acquiring new knowledge & I did!"

D. West, from an Amazon review of *A Maverick New Zealand Way,* 22 May 2019

'An Interesting Travel Memoir'

From a review of *A Maverick Himalayan Way,* new edition, by 'Piaras', Amazon Vine Voice reviewer, 24 May 2019

… and a further testimonial

"Hey. We met for 9 years in Russia. You told me about your travels, and then I had not yet visited other countries. Now, thanks to you, I have visited 27 countries. Thanks."

Matvei Ogulov, Russian musician, in a recent Facebook message (2020).

***See all Mary Jane's books and blog on* a-maverick.com**

Mary Jane Walker has travelled the world and written 14 books so far, including the award finalist *A Maverick New Zealand Way.*

Finding herself in New Zealand during Covid has made Mary Jane get out and explore even more of her own country, and to look more deeply into its history and indigenous culture.

In *The Sensational South Island,* Mary Jane explores the larger but less populated of New Zealand's two main islands, by way of eight road tours. A ninth section looks at the offshore islands of the South Island, including the remote Chathams group.

The Sensational South Island is a companion to *The Neglected North Island: New Zealand's other half,* judged 'Best Antipodean Cultural Travel Book 2021' by *Lux Life* magazine (lux-review.com).

Email: maryjanewalker@a-maverick.com
Facebook: facebook.com/amavericktraveller
Instagram: @a_maverick_traveller
Linkedin: Mary Jane Walker
Pinterest: amavericktraveller
Twitter: @Mavericktravel0

a-maverick.com

First published 2021 by Mary Jane Walker
A Maverick Traveller Ltd.
PO Box 44 146, Point Chevalier, Auckland 1246
NEW ZEALAND

a-maverick.com

ISBN-13: 978-0-473-53244-4 (paperback), 978-0-473-53246-8 (Kindle), 978-0-473-53245-1 (other epubs)

Disclaimer

This book is a travel memoir, not an outdoors guide. Although the author and publisher have made every effort to ensure that the information in this book was correct at the time of publication, the author and publisher do not assume and hereby disclaim any liability to any party for any loss, damage, or disruption caused by errors or omissions, whether such errors or omissions result from negligence, accident, or any other cause. Some names have also been changed to disguise and protect certain individuals.

Notes on Image Sources

All maps and aerial views are credited with the original source. Abbreviations which may be used in image credits or otherwise are as follows:

DOC: New Zealand Department of Conservation

LINZ: Land Information New Zealand

NZDF: New Zealand Defence Forces

Contents

The South Island in relation to the other main islands of New Zealand. *The map shown is based on NASA Earth Observatory image 2010/099.*

The South Island of New Zealand, with Rakiura/Stewart Island.
Source: detail from the NASA Earth Observatory image 2010/099.
Insert: Southern Rātā, a cooler-climate cousin of the Pōhutukawa, widespread in the South Island and much of the North Island as well. Also symbolic of Christmas and summer.

A Note on Maps and Images

If you have a copy of this book in which the images are printed in black and white, or if you have a Kindle with a black-and-white screen, you can see all of the images in this book that were originally in colour in full colour, and all of the images including chapter-specific maps generally at higher resolution, by going to the blog posts linked at the end of each chapter.

In fact, these blog posts will generally contain more images than appear in the book.

The maps that appear in this book have been drawn from a variety of sources, including two key government agencies, the New Zealand Department of Conservation (DOC) and Land Information New Zealand (LINZ).

Unless noted or indicated otherwise, all maps, aerial photos and satellite images are shown with north at the top.

Readers are in every case urged to make use of original maps (often zoomable if online) and guides when in the outdoors; the maps and aerial/satellite images shown in this book are purely for illustration.

For a literally more all-round perspective, you might also wish to look at some of localities I describe in the 3D view on Google Earth.

Introduction

AMONG all the wonders of the world, it's the business of coming home and tramping (hiking) in New Zealand, a land known more poetically as Aotearoa, that I have most wanted to write about.

This book is a brief, road-trip introduction to New Zealand's South Island, the island that is more often visited by tourists. I've tried to pack as much firsthand, useful experience as I can into a comparatively short book.

An island known by other names

In Māori, the South Island is also known as Te Waipounamu and also as Te-Waka-a-Māui, the canoe of Māui, by which the demigod Māui, and his brothers, fished the North Island (Te-Ika-a-Māui, Māui's fish) out of the great ocean.

Te Waipounamu is the most common of the two Māori names, as it refers to the island's significance as a source of pounamu, or New Zealand jade, also known locally as greenstone: a substance that lies at the centre of Māori culture.

The northern end of the South Island is also called Te Tau Ihu o te Waka-a-Māui, the Prow of Maui's canoe. This name has been adopted by a useful local-history website called the Prow:

theprow.org.nz

A Varied Landscape

The landscape of the South Island, or Te Waipounamu, is divided into several distinct zones, which you can see in a satellite photograph.

The South Island. *NASA World Wind public domain image, via: commons.wikimedia.org/wiki/File:Turbid_Waters_Surround_New_Zealand_-_crop.jpg*

The largest and snowiest peaks of the high mountains reflect light from permanent glaciers. Indeed, New Zealand has more than 3,000 named glaciers, nearly all of which are found in the mountains of the South Island. They are remnants of the formerly much more colossal glaciers that used to cover a quarter of the South Island in the Ice Ages, leaving scooped-out valleys and fiords, knife-edge peaks, vertical rock walls and waterfalls that plunge huge distances.

No Kiwi tourist film is complete, it seems, without the view from a helicopter speeding along Lake Quill, located in the mountains near Piopiotahi / Milford Sound, then over the edge as the waters of the lake unexpectedly plunge to the floor of a flat-bottomed valley down which the Arthur River now meanders.

West of the still-glaciated peaks there is a belt of green mountains (snowy in winter) that extends almost to the sea. Valleys hardly any wider than some of the larger rivers elsewhere are farmed in these parts, which only support a very small population save in the north. Practically nobody at all lives in the far southwest, a land of fiords and UNESCO World Heritage conservation wilderness called Te Wāhipounamu – South West New Zealand World Heritage Area.

The highest peak in the north-east area, Tapuae-o-Uenuku, meaning footsteps of the rainbow god, is 2,885 metres or 9,465 feet high and easily visible, across the water, from the southernmost parts of the North Island.

Visible to the south of the South Island is Rakiura or Stewart Island, the country's largest offshore island, mostly a wilderness as well.

'We don't know how lucky we are'

Since Covid, many Kiwis and the world are now starting to realise how lucky we are and how we should appreciate our own country more.

So, I just started hiking, walking and biking. Tramping clubs seemed overly organised to me and rather stuffy, and I eventually decided my own company was better than belonging with a group, but have Personal Locator Beacon, if you chose to go down that track.

The luckiest New Zealanders of all are those who live in the South Island. For, most of New Zealand's national parks and other nature parks are in the South Island or on nearby Rakiura/Stewart Island.

National Parks in New Zealand

1. Tongariro
2. Egmont
3. Whanganui
4. Kahurangi
5. Abel Tasman
6. Nelson Lakes
7. Paparoa
8. Arthur's Pass
9. Westland / Tai Poutini
10. Aoraki / Mt Cook
11. Mt Aspiring
12. Fiordland
13. Rakiura

Map graphic sourced from the DOC website on 12 December 2016.

From Great Walks to Day Walks

And what are the places that you would like to visit in the South Island, and the walks you might like to do?

The Great Walks are New Zealand's premier tramping tracks. In the South Island, from north to south, the Great Walks are:

- the Abel Tasman Coast Track
- the Heaphy Track
- the Paparoa Track
- the Routeburn Track
- the Kepler Track
- the Milford Track, and, coming in 2022,
- the Tūātapere Hump Ridge Track

On Rakiura/Stewart Island there is also the Rakiura Track.

A much longer list of short walks is provided in DOC's list of 'Family Friendly' walks. This is so extensive that it's best to go online to access the special interactive website, which has a clickable map giving a list of walks for each district:

doc.govt.nz/parks-and-recreation/things-to-do/walking-and-tramping/family-friendly-walks-and-tramps

Many of these, including all the Great Walks, are described first-hand in the present book, along with other tracks and destinations that don't make the DOC shortlists.

I have a list of my own favourite walks and tramps for getting off the beaten track. It follows this introduction as the first chapter of the book.

Nine Tours

In keeping with this informal, do it yourself spirit, the book is organised into eight road tours from which you can step out of the car to go hiking, plus an additional section on the South Island's offshore islands. The road tours include visits to cities.

TOUR 1: The Prow

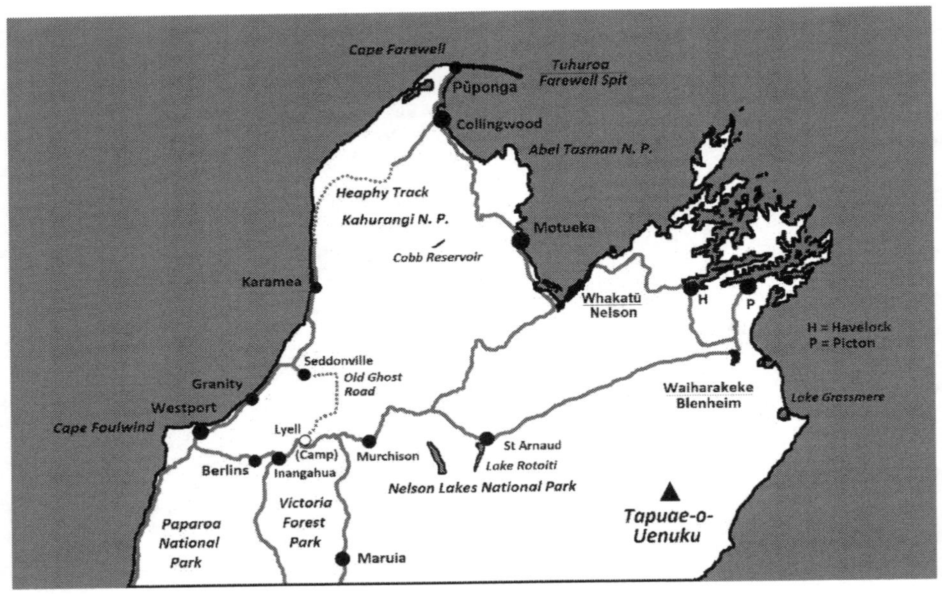

TOUR 2: The Wild West Coast

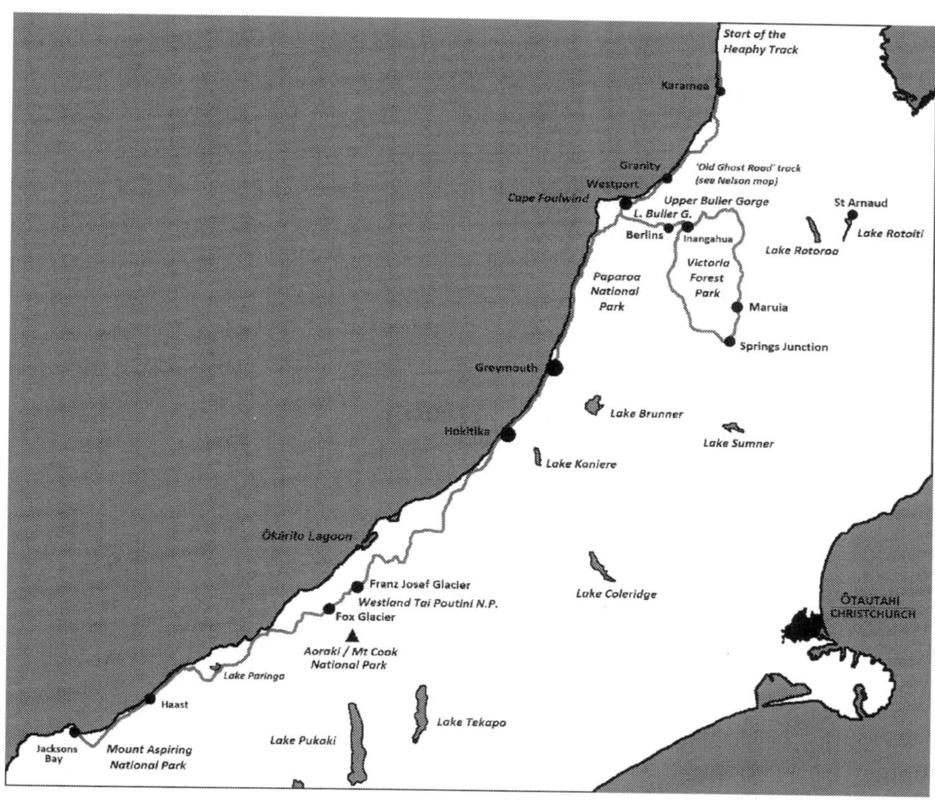

TOUR 3: Arthur's and Lewis Passes

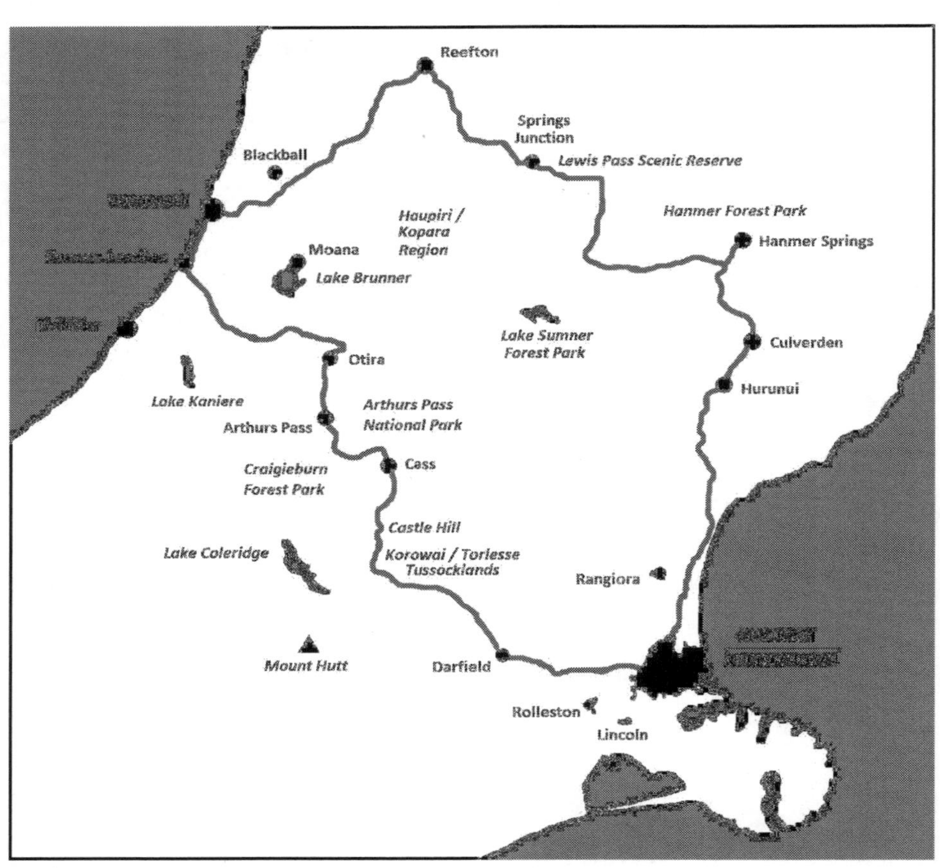

TOUR 4: The Urbane East Coast

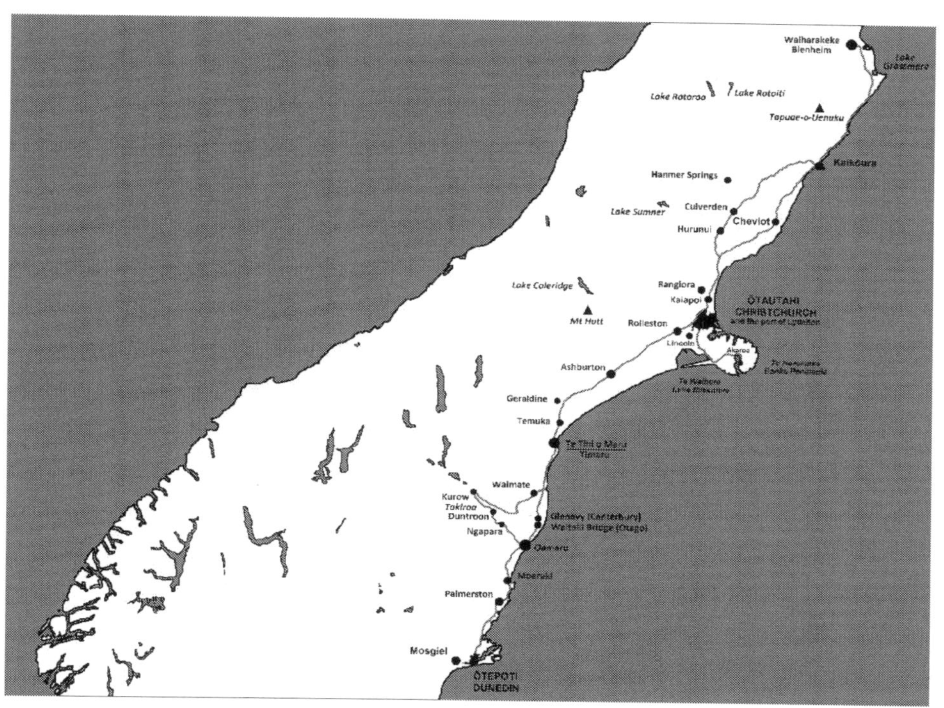

TOUR 5: Aoraki and the Canterbury Lakes

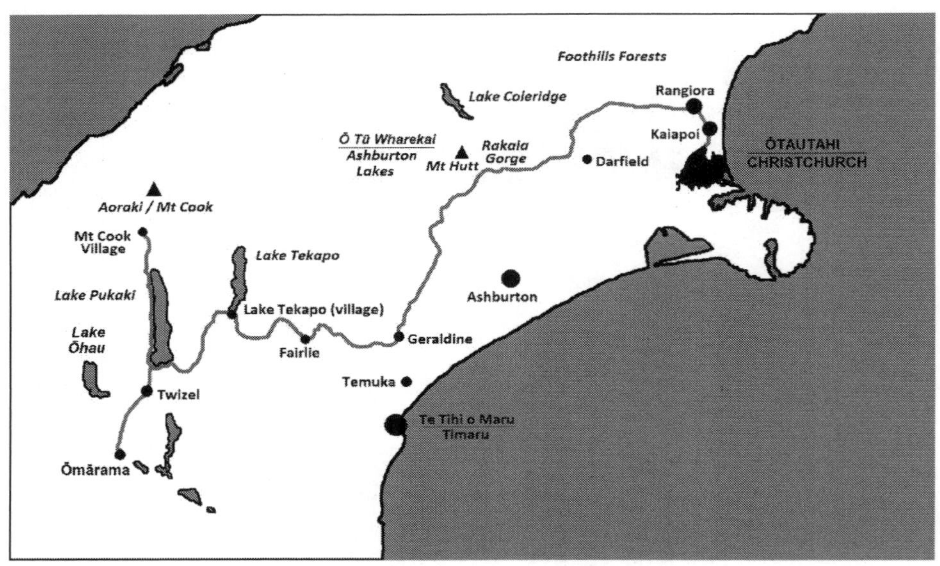

TOUR 6: Queenstown, Wānaka and the Waitaki Valley

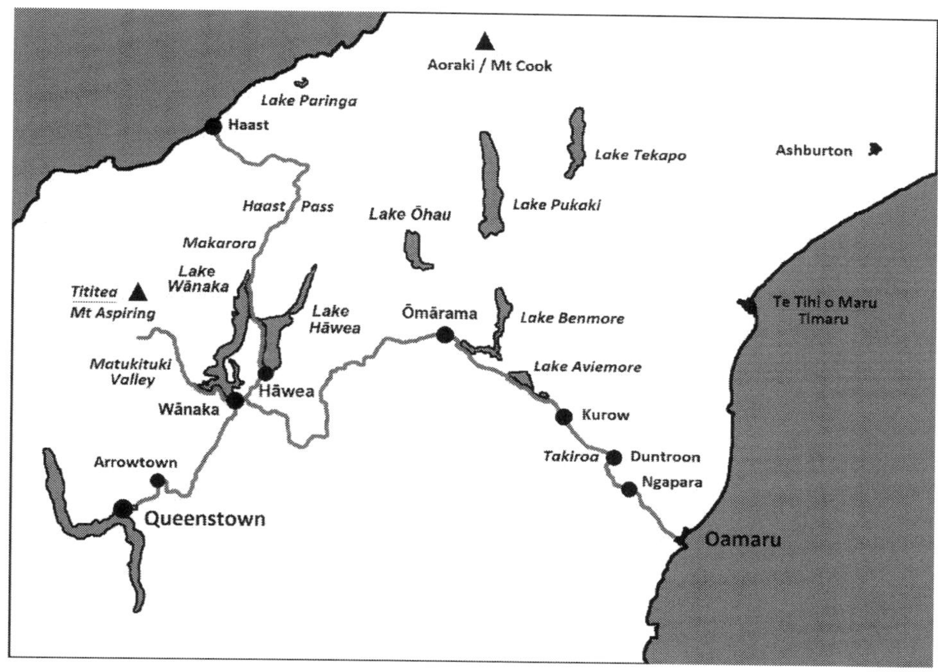

TOUR 7: Otago's Dry Interior

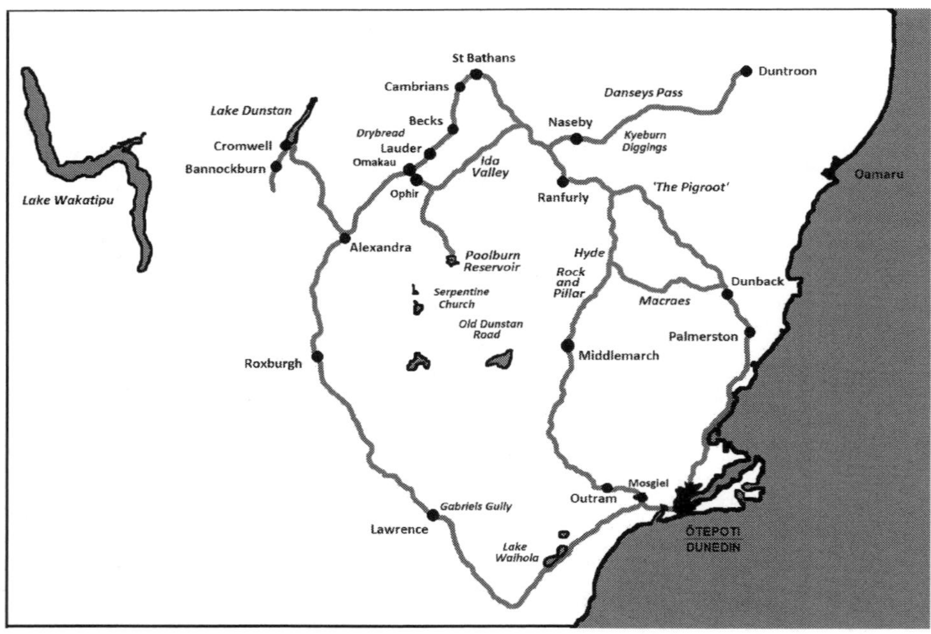

TOUR 8: The Southern Scenic Realm

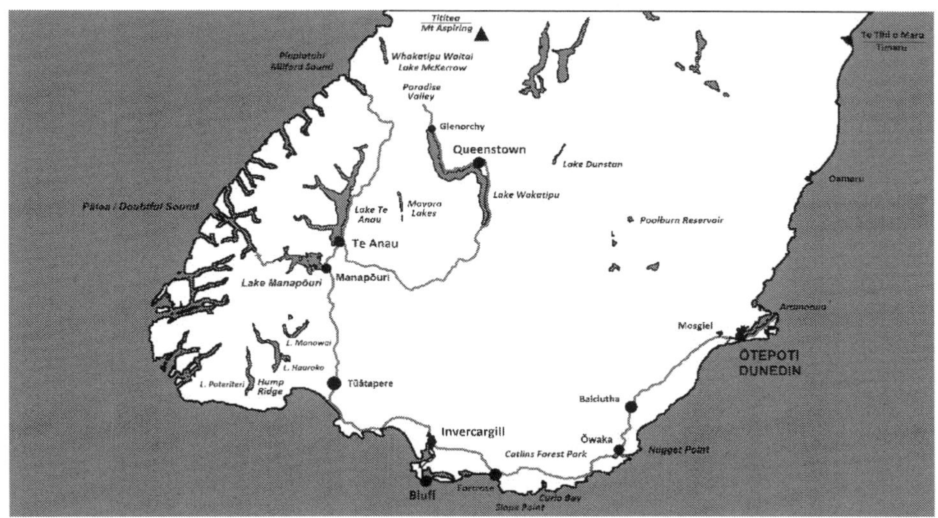

TOUR 9: The South Island's Other Islands

The ninth tour visits Rakiura/Stewart Island and two of its offshore islands, and the Chathams.

Our Heritage is Yours

The next chapter will describe some of my favourite spots and things to do in the South Island.

After that, my Travel Tips chapter will also help guide you for your adventure.

And then I get into the tours.

But you should bear in mind that while I have tried to pack as much as I can into this brief book, it's not an encyclopaedia and there will always be more than I can describe.

CHAPTER ONE

Some of my South Island Faves

WHAT are some of my favourite walks, hikes and places to visit in the South Island?

Well, I've just done the romantically named Moonlight Track, which runs from the beautiful Moke, pronounced Mokeh, Lake to Arthurs Point in the hills behind Queenstown. The track's named after a prospector called George Fairweather Moonlight: but I like to think it would be fun to do it under a full moon as well!

Short but stiff is the Lake Hauroko Lookout Track, in Fiordland. Described by DOC as "steep and rough, but well worth the effort," you get to it by driving from Tūātapere, west of Invercargill in Southland.

There is a whole host of amazing short walks in the Catlins, the southernmost district of the South Island between Dunedin and Invercargill. You could spend a month there, probably.

Closer to Queenstown, once more, I love to visit the Bannockburn Sluicings, a desolate Wild West landscape created by old time gold miners who sluiced away the earth to get at nuggets. St Bathans in the nearby Ida Valley is similar, but with a lake.

Many of the best multi-day hikes take the form of loop routes in the mountains above some lake, of which several of the best are also located close to New Zealand's informal tourist capital of Queenstown. The Kepler Walk is a good example, but there are plenty of others not formally gazetted as Great Walks.

These include the Wilkin-Young circuit north of Lake Wānaka, which you can combine with a visit to the Blue Pools on the Makarora River, just up the main road toward the Haast Pass. Between the catchments of the Wilkin and the Young Rivers you go through the Gillespie Pass, next to Mount Awful, and down the Siberia Stream. Like a lot of the more adventurous South Island trips, this one's really better done in warm weather!

Just north of the Haast Pass, if you really want to make a week of it in this wild yet accessible area (which has several campgrounds), is the Brewster Track up to the Brewster Hut, below to the Brewster Glacier. This is a straight up and down track, arduous, but very scenic. The Brewster Hut looks down on the pass and into nearby canyons from a superelevation of almost a thousand metres. The glacier-covered shoulders of Mount Brewster range more a thousand metres above the Brewster Hut.

Closer to Queenstown still is the Caples/Greenstone loop through the McKellar Pass. You start from a spot near the head of Lake Wakatipu, a delightful area dominated by the Paradise Valley. It's not nearly as gothic and gloomy as the British drama *Top of the Lake* implies!

Also at the top of the lake is the Rees-Dart loop, which offers a side trip up to some additional glaciers and the option of going over the Cascade Saddle Track into the Matukituki Valley, dominated by the once more glacier-covered Rob Roy Peak and further up the valley, Tititea/Mount Aspiring, 'the Matterhorn of the South'.

The Milford Track, our best-known Great Walk, itself mostly fairly easy apart from the bit that leads over Mackinnon Pass, goes past the epically high Sutherland Falls.

(At 750 metres or two and a half thousand feet, the nearby Terror Falls, which drain an un-named lake near Terror Peak, are even taller than the Sutherland Falls. But they aren't as easy to get to. I love some of those names by the way: Terror Peak's not far, itself, from Mount Danger—and so on!)

No doubt the most famous glacial landscape in New Zealand is Milford Sound/Piopiotahi: a fiord to which the Milford Track leads and into which the Arthur River feeds. It is ruled, itself, by Mitre Peak, which rises for a mile out of the waters of the fiord.

Further north on the West Coast, the Fox Glacier and Franz Josef Glacier descend almost to sea level. Among the three thousand glaciers of New Zealand these two are special, as the last two remaining examples of the great glaciers of the Ice Ages: glaciers that didn't hide in the mountains but descended to lower levels to create fiords and big valleys.

At any rate, these two survivors used to come down that far, in historical times. They have retreated due to global warming and changes in snowfall. Still, the sight of two glaciers grinding through green rainforest *almost* to the sea is remarkable, even now.

Some way to the south of the Fox Glacier and the town that bears the same name, a track leads up another glacial valley of the now-empty sort to Welcome Flat. Wonderful natural hot pools are located there. The valley continues up and over the Copland Pass to New Zealand's highest mountain, Aoraki/Mount Cook, and is very scenic. Before Copland Pass it is also a fairly easy tramp, as these flat-bottomed but scenic valleys often are.

Further north still, there are many terrific walks around Arthurs Pass township and, also, in the Lewis Pass area.

Near the township of Kumara on the West Coast, itself not far from the bigger town of Hokitika, there's the Goldsborough Campsite. Reviewers think this is one of the best places to camp in New Zealand, lovely and secluded with lots of scenic walks nearby. It's an old gold mining area and you might still find a few specks in the local streams with the panning gear that New Zealand's Department of Conservation provides for anyone to use, if you're eagle-eyed enough.

I'll have more to say about all these in the forthcoming chapters of this book, and the following blog post also expands on the current chapter, with even more of my favourite things:

For a longer version of this chapter that includes the cities, see:

a-maverick.com/blog/some-of-my-south-island-faves

CHAPTER TWO

The Land and its Peoples

IT'S something of a cliché, locally, that Christchurch is 'English' and Dunedin 'Scottish'. Indeed, for a long time, the different national origins of early settler communities, including a significant number of Chinese gold miners, entirely overshadowed the fact that Māori also inhabited the South Island for some seven or eight hundred years and were the first colonisers, having navigated their way there from the tropical Pacific.

Māori culture was seen as something associated with the North Island and the boiling mud pools of Rotorua, not the South Island: where, indeed, colonial poets wrote about an empty land, untouched by humans until they came along.

It was true that the frost-sensitive crops the Māori brought down from the tropics could only be grown in the North Island and the Prow of the South Island by and large; and, indeed, only with a certain amount of encouragement as well.

But even the chillier parts of the South Island of 700 to 800 years ago were capable of supporting a large population of hunter-gatherers. For in the days when the island really was untouched by human hand it was full of plump, easily-caught flightless birds, of which the emu-like moa are simply the best known. On top of that, there was also an abundance of seals, penguins, ocean fish and fresh-water eels. A number of native plants could be eaten as well.

Regrettably, this abundance did not endure. The moa and some other flightless species became extinct or, as with the takahē, nearly so. Fires were lit to flush out the game or prepare the ground for whatever crops might grow. Australian aborigines have long used the same method, with care. But the early Māori, who came from islands with a different climate and mix of vegetation, seem to have been unaware of the ease with which fires could get out of control in New Zealand: the South Island, in particular.

The Great Fires of Tamātea, as Māori lore records them, resulted in the permanent deforestation of many of the drier parts of the South Island.

(Later British colonists would perpetrate the same mistake in both main islands of New Zealand. Striving to clear small areas of 'bush' they would inadvertently set fire to large, valuable forests.)

A Different Culture

In the meantime, as the South Islanders were accidentally denuding the land and running out of game, the more settled and agricultural Māori of the North Island were becoming more numerous. Before long, the centre of gravity of Māori population passed, overwhelmingly to the North Island.

According to the recent book of maps called *We Are Here: An Atlas of Aotearoa,* compiled by Chris McDowall and Tim Denee, archaeologists have recorded seven thousand pā, or defended Māori village, sites northward of Whanganui in the North Island, but only 321 pā south of that line, of which there are only 144 in the South Island. These totals do not include kāinga or undefended villages, nor the many seasonal campsites known to have existed in the South Island. They do, however, give a very rough indication of the greater long-term density of Māori population northward of Whanganui, including the competition for resources that led villages to become fortified, usually on top of a hill.

But to say that the centre of gravity passed to the North is not to say that South Island Māori faded away completely. Instead, a distinctive culture known as that of the Waitaha people came into being, one of its products being a form of art that looks quite different to the 'classic' Māori art of the North Island.

Here's an example, overleaf, from one of the caves near Timaru, where most of the surviving Waitaha rock art is to be found, in the form of a 1960s stamp. There have been more recent stamp series featuring Waitaha rock art, as well.

1960s postage stamp showing Waitaha rock art. *Crown copyright reserved.*

Then in the 1700s, by the Western calendar, an iwi or tribe that was to become the dominant one in the South Island, Ngāi Tahu, began to immigrate from their original North Island home. Ngāi Tahu tradition holds that their people's colonisation of the South Island was not so much a matter of conquest as of intermarriage and adoption of Waitaha ways.

Ngāi Tahu did fight a rival North Island iwi, Ngāti Mamoe, that was busy doing the same thing. Rangitāne, an Iwi from the district that would later come to be known as Wellington, moved into the Prow. Ngāi Tahu also fragmented, splitting off the Poutini Ngāi Tahu in Westland.

The best-known peculiarity of the South Island dialects is that 'ng' often becomes 'k'. So Ngāi Tahu are just as often called Kāi Tahu and their rivals Kāti Mamoe.

A hard 'g' also crops up in place of 'k' in a number of South Island place names and plant names, like Otago (Ōtākou) and matagouri, a fierce thornbush known elsewhere as tūmatakuru or matakoura or, less flatteringly, wild Irishman, though that name is neither Māori nor official.

Otago was written Otakou in the earliest survey maps, which followed northern usage. Today the same word, meaning the place where red earth abounds, would be spelt Ōtākou. But it was pronounced Otago by the Māori who lived on and around the site of the future Dunedin. And it seems that the local colonists preferred that spelling as well, for in deference to their wishes, on the 26th of December 1848, Sir George Grey, the Governor of New Zealand, proclaimed that the district in which the town of Dunedin had just been founded was to be marked on all future maps as "Otago instead of Otakou."

Here and there the 'r' in Māori words is also replaced with 'l', whence the rather Hawai'ian-sounding name of Otago's Lake Waihola for example.

The Musket Invasions

In the early nineteenth century, the South Island tribes were decimated, or worse—for decimation literally means the killing of one in ten—in a series of raids carried out by North Island Māori from 1828 onwards. These new invaders from the North

Island were armed with muskets, which one of their chiefs had even sailed all the way to England to purchase and bring back.

From Purchase to Pauperdom

Only a decade or so later, at the beginning of the 1840s, British government purchase agents arrived, and soon acquired almost the whole of the South Island very cheaply from locals who were by now in no position to resist anyone.

Ostensibly, reserves that were still quite large were to be left by the British for the indigenous inhabitants. These reserves were known as 'tenths', because the idea was that the British would only take nine acres out of every ten they'd formally purchased, and leave a tenth behind for the original inhabitant. The exact boundaries of the tenths would be decided after the purchase, because the island hadn't yet been surveyed by modern methods. However, as you might expect, this never really happened, and so the South Island Māori have been engaged in a long quest for redress.

In June 1877, a South Island Māori leader named Hipa Te Maihāroa led 150 of his people on a hikoi, meaning protest march or pilgrimage, to Te Ao Mārama, an inland locality on the Waitaki River now known as the town of Ōmārama. The protestors were seeking to reclaim land that they regarded as rightfully theirs.

In August 1879 Te Maihāroa's people were evicted by armed constables from Oamaru and local reinforcements and forced to walk 170 kilometres down the river to the coast, where they established a new settlement just south of the river mouth. It was the middle of winter, and perhaps the closest incident to the episode known in America as 'the Trail of Tears'. Indeed, the parallel is reinforced by the coincidence that Waitaki means water, or river, of tears.

On the facing page, there's a photo of a signboard at Lake Pūkaki in the South Island interior, showing a 1920s gathering of survivors and descendants of those who camped at Ōmārama from 1877 until 1879, with an explanatory caption.

Here and on the next page you can see the caption on the left, and the photo on the right, respectively.

'THE HOLE IN THE MIDDLE'

Lake Pūkaki and the surrounding land are part of what is known by Ngāi Tahu as 'the Hole in the Middle'. The name reflects the iwi's opinion that the high country of Te Waipounamu (the South Island) was never sold.

In 1848 the New Zealand government purchased 14 million acres (5.7 million hectares) of land from Ngāi Tahu in Canterbury and Otago. Ngāi Tahu believed that the foothills formed the inland boundary of the purchase area and that everything beyond there would remain in tribal ownership.

However, the government assumed control of all of the land between the foothills and the Southern Alps. Many Ngāi Tahu became landless and were rendered trespassers when visiting their traditional food-gathering sites, including the rich hunting grounds of Te Manahuna.

Dismayed by the government's lack of progress to resolve the Ngāi Tahu land grievances, the prophet Hipa Te Maiharoa led over 100 people in 1877 to camp peacefully for almost two years near the present-day township of Ōmārama. Following their eviction from Ōmārama, Te Maiharoa led his followers to settle at the old Korotuaheka kāinga near the mouth of the Waitaki River.

This photograph was taken in the early 1900s and includes many of those who peacefully camped for almost two years at Ōmārama. Bill Dacker Collection, Toitū Otago Settlers Museum.

The photograph is credited to the Bill Dacker Collection at the Toitū Otago Settlers Museum, which is well worth visiting. I mention this museum again in my Dunedin chapter.

Not until 1998, in the 150th anniversary year of Mantell's most significant purchases, would there be an agreed settlement of the claims of the largest South Island iwi, Ngāi Tahu, and even then, I wonder if it was a matter of settling for what Ngāi Tahu could get in practice, the horse having bolted so long ago. The amount settled for was NZ $170 million, with a relativity clause for top-ups if other iwi later gained much more per head. The money was invested on behalf of the whole Ngāi Tahu population, about 55,000 today.

According to Te Ara, the online encyclopaedia of New Zealand, Ngāi Tahu have undergone a significant revival since the settlement. As of the time of writing, Te Ara records that:

"One aspect of the cultural resurgence of Ngāi Tahu was the revival of the traditional marae. At Takahanga in Kaikōura and at Bluff new buildings have been constructed. Ōnuku, near Akaroa, acquired a new carved house. In Christchurch, the sub-tribe Ngāi Tūahuriri have assumed the mana of an urban marae, Rēhua. At Waihao, Arowhenua, Taumutu, Kokorarata, Tuahiwi and Mangamaunu existing buildings have been improved or extended. The Puketeraki people of Otago have replaced their original meeting house."

Sheep, Gold and Cities

In the meantime, the South Island's colonists had become quite prosperous, erecting beautiful cities paid for by sheep and gold, which were to be the foundations of South Island prosperity for a century and more, along with engineering industries built up by the more mechanically minded settlers.

The three most historically important and stately of the South Island's colonial cities were Nelson at the top end of the South Island, Christchurch in the middle and Dunedin in the south. Runners-up include Invercargill, the most southerly city of the old-time British Empire. And the amazing 1870s boomtown of Oamaru, with its streets of Victorian limestone architecture.

But even among the settlers themselves, conflict soon broke out between those who'd got in on the ground floor at the time the Māori lost their land, and those who now had to pay top dollar for a farm or a place to live in the city.

Some of the leading social activists of twentieth-century New Zealand came from the South Island. And indeed, even, in the persons of the three architects of New Zealand's 1938 Social Security Act jointly known as the 'Three Wise Men of Kurow', from the very Waitaki Valley itself: as though a torch had somehow been passed down from Te Maihāroa's day.

Language Notes

In the spelling of Māori, the tohutō or macron over certain vowels indicates a lengthening of the vowel. The presence or absence of this lengthening can change the meaning of words that are otherwise spelt the same way, and so the tohutō is more than just a guide to pronunciation. Used occasionally in earlier times, but not very often, it was made official in 1988.

Another point worth noting is that many localities in New Zealand now have two official names, one in English and one in Māori. Depending on the context, both names may be spelled out in full and separated by a stroke: an example is Rakiura/Stewart Island.

For the full version of this introduction to the South Island and its peoples, see the blog post on

a-maverick.com/blog/south-island-peoples-maori-settler

Further Web Resources

Māori Land Loss in the South Island:

teara.govt.nz/en/interactive/36363/maori-land-loss-south-island

The Ngāi Tahu Iwi guide to places and history:

kahurumanu.co.nz

List of iwi (Māori tribes) on Wikipedia:

en.wikipedia.org/wiki/List_of_iwi

One thousand Māori place names explained:

nzhistory.govt.nz/culture/maori-language-week/1000-maori-place-names

New Zealand Herald Māori place names interactive:

insights.nzherald.co.nz/article/our-place-names

Report of the 1881 Smith-Nairn Commission into the alienation of South Island Māori lands:

ngaitahu.iwi.nz/wp-content/uploads/2018/04/AJHR_1881_I_G-06-Smith-Nairn.pdf

'Three Wise Men of Kurow', talk by artist Bob Kerr:

youtube.com/watch?v=MtLTyzyWKXI

CHAPTER THREE

Travel Tips

AT the end of this chapter, I'll link to a blog post of mine that has more travel tips than I could fit in here!

Visitor Centres, i-Sites and Topo Maps

First, to get reliable and up-to-date information about the outdoors in New Zealand, the first place to go, either physically or online, is the New Zealand Department of Conservation (DOC), which has many Visitor Centres around the country plus a website, **doc.govt.nz.**

Many of New Zealand's outdoor destinations are described in a page on the DOC website or in a PDF brochure you can download from it, or both. You can pick up the brochures in paper form from DOC or from other distributors such as the i-Sites (below). And all DOC information is free.

For other tourist destinations, including the cities, an equivalent one-stop wealth of information is provided by the national i-Site system, the 'i-' standing for 'information'. The i-Sites are run by a government agency called Tourism New Zealand, and their website is **isite.nz.**

Camping Information

If you are a camper or a person in a van, it's vital to know where you can camp: knowledge that also helps with planning undisturbed rest breaks.

There's a website that addresses the issue. It's called Camping in New Zealand and its website address is **freedomcamping.org**. The website links to two apps, the CampingNZ app and the CamperMate app.

Tramping, Tracks and Trails

Many New Zealand tracks and trails are on **alltrails.com**.and also on **trailjourneys.co.nz**, which offers bike hire and backup. Local trails for cycling adventures such as the famous Otago Central Rail Trail will also be mentioned in context, below.

In today's outdoor New Zealand, the word 'trail' has a sort of semi-domesticated significance, implying a route that it is possible to ride mountain bikes on.

For instance, as in the expression 'rail trail', meaning an old railway line that's now become a route for cyclists on mountain bikes. Or something even gentler, such as wine trail or a heritage trail.

You may wish to look up some guided walks as well, such as from this provider.

ultimatehikes.co.nz/multi-day-guided-walks/the-classic/itinerary

Be Weather Wise and Avalanche Alert!

Many South Island tracks, walks and trails are very hazardous in cold weather. Avalanches are often a danger, as are ice and blizzards.

Avalanches can happen at any time of year (though commonest in spring and early summer) and can cross well-known walks, tracks and trails. New Zealand's Department of Conservation (DOC) provides online guidance on how best to watch out for avalanche hazards in New Zealand.

doc.govt.nz/parks-and-recreation/know-before-you-go/be-avalanche-alert/

DOC also advises that those going into the back country should always check the Mountain Weather forecasts on Metservice (below). Apart from anything else, this also makes it less likely that you will be caught out by a raging river, which might prevent your safe return from the hills.

Cellphone coverage

Cellphone coverage is poor even in some urban areas such as Queenstown, and in these areas, Spark gives the best coverage.

It Pays to Book

Like many other countries, New Zealand is finding today's tourism numbers increasingly hard to accommodate, in normal times at least.

Remember your sunscreen and insect repellent

Last but not least, when its sunny you might get sunburnt, while in wetter areas of the island, the West Coast in particular, "As soon as the sandflies retire at dark, the mosquitos advance upon their victims" (*Otago Witness,* 4 January 1873, p. 16).

Some other useful web resources and apps

100% Pure New Zealand (website **newzealand.com**). It doesn't get more high-level than that! The New Zealand Government's window on the world. Hit the Travel button if your interest is travel, as opposed to Invest, Study, or Live&Work. Within travel, you can look up travel itineraries to plan your trip.

NZ Places. nzplaces.nz. This describes places in New Zealand, for reference.

MetService (website **metservice.com**, and app). Your go-to site and app for New Zealand official weather updates, including the mountain forecasts.

Star Chart (app). The constellations in the Southern Hemisphere are completely different to the ones in the North, the Milky Way is more impressive down here, and on top of that, New Zealand has many areas with really dark skies. Two out of the world's thirteen International Dark Sky Sanctuaries, the officially darkest of the dark places on land, are in New Zealand. One is on Aotea/Great Barrier Island. The other is on Rakiura/Stewart Island.

A longer version of this chapter, with more information, appears on my website as the following blog post:

a-maverick.com/blog/new-zealand-travel-tips

TOUR 1: The Prow

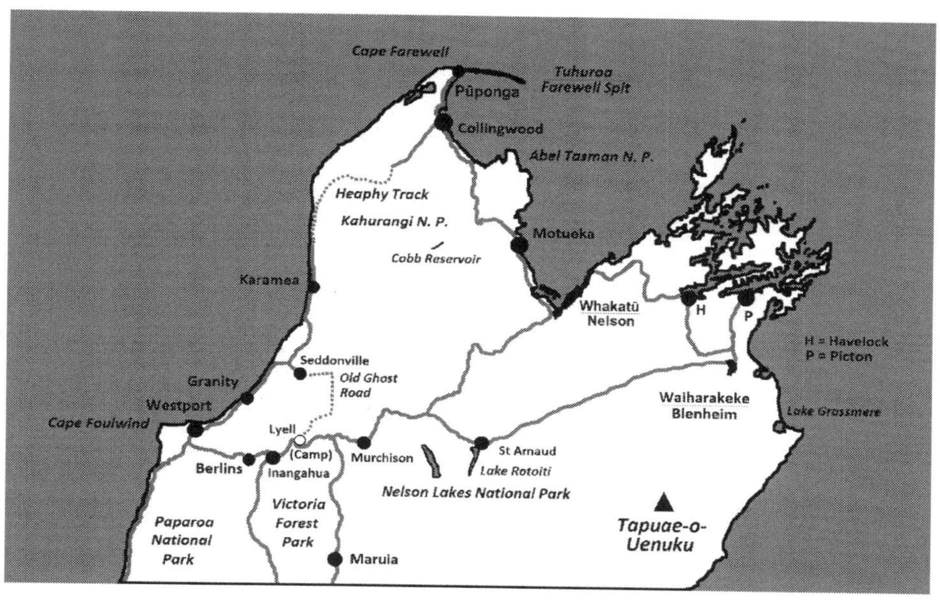

CHAPTER FOUR

Nelson: Town of history and trees

NELSON is a lovely, leafy city at the top end of the South Island. It has a sunny climate, lots of old buildings both in wood and stone, and a frankly amazing abundance of hiking trails in the hills that overlook the town.

Nelson: An old historical precinct downtown

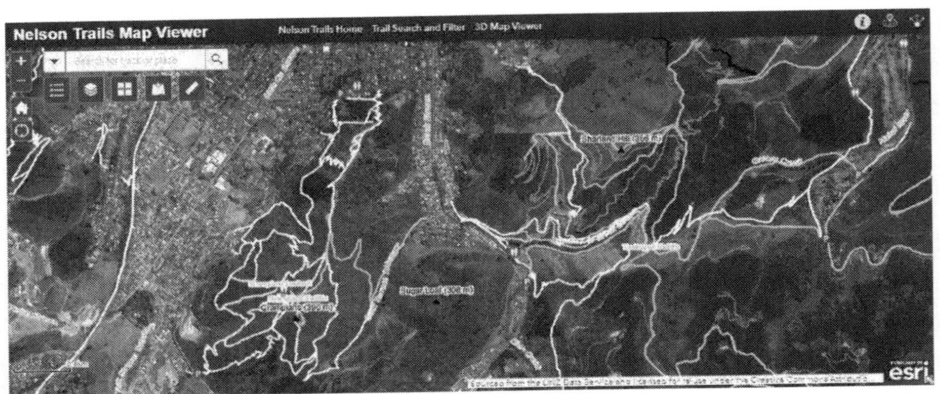

A screenshot of the Nelson Trails Map Viewer, *filtered and rendered in black and white for clarity (2021). The urban area is to the left, an abundance of trails on hills overlooking the city is to the right.*

Nelson was the first New Zealand settlement to be designated a city, as far back as 1859. At that time, it had just gained New Zealand's first would-be Anglican cathedral, called Christ Church, on a small hill down which a terrace of formal steps soon cascaded to the street.

'Nelson Cathedral', *Nelson Provincial Museum, Bett Collection, photo reference no. 314710.*

The hill on which the intended cathedral was built was called Piki Mai meaning 'come hither'. It had formerly been the site of a pā, or fortified village, where worked pieces of a flinty, obsidian-like local mineral called pakohe in Māori and argillite in English, from which tools were made for trade all over pre-European New Zealand, were gathered together for safe-keeping.

In colonial times, hill-forts and stone implements (other than those of pounamu) both became things of the past, and Piki Mai came to be known as Church Hill.

By tradition, the site of a cathedral had to be a city. And so, Nelson became a city by order of Queen Victoria. In truth, the settlement was still little more than a village in those days. But today's Nelson really is a proper city, complete with outdoor cafés and all the rest.

The old wooden cathedral was destroyed by an earthquake and a subsequent fire in the early twentieth century and was replaced by a new marble one, gothic in style but with a distinctive modern bell tower. The terrace is a bit more flash these days, too, as you can see from the photo on the facing page.

The same spot in 2021

One thing you notice in this part of the country is that there are a lot of large, stately-looking trees even in areas that are not actually parkland. Trees that were deliberately planted a long time ago (if introduced), or that generations of otherwise axe-wielding colonists refrained from chopping down (if native), do now lend the Prow region a special charm, both in town and in farming districts alike.

An Auckland newspaper of the 1850s famously complained of how "some goth of a settler" had just chopped down the very last of a grove sacred to the Māori on Maungakiekie, a prominence that had come to be known to the English-speaking majority in Auckland as One Tree Hill: though as of that moment it was no-tree hill. Anyhow, I get the impression that the Nelson colonists did a better job of thinking ahead.

The locality on which Nelson was established is known in Māori as Wakatu or Whakatū: names that look and sound similar but don't mean the same thing.

All the same, Wakatu or Whakatū is routinely used as the Māori name for the modern city of Nelson. Lots of buildings and institutions in Nelson bear the name Wakatu, or Whakatū.

I could go on about the charming and quirky city of Nelson or Wakatu/Whakatū at greater length than space here permits, and indeed I do in a related blog post:

a-maverick.com/blog/nelson-town-history-trees

See also The Nelson App by **nelsonapp.co.nz**

CHAPTER FIVE

The Coast North-West of Nelson

Varied terrain and kayaking

ONE of the classic New Zealand holidays simply involves heading along the coast north-west of Nelson.

The former post office in Wakefield (1909)

You journey south-west to begin with, through Stoke and Richmond, which are now suburbs of Nelson, through Hope and Brightwater, as far as the historic town of Wakefield, which has the South Island's oldest church, St Johns, dating back to the 1840s.

Split Apple Rock, between Kaiteriteri and Marahau

From Wakefield you double back and head on up the coast northwestward through Mapua and Motueka on the main road, and then on minor coast roads to Kaiteriteri and Marahau and the beginning of Abel Tasman National Park. This is a really beautiful stretch of rocky coast, sheltered beaches and tidal sandflats, with famous sights to see and things to do such as the

Split Apple Rock, the Abel Tasman monument and the Abel Tasman Coastal Track.

Even though you are still in the South Island, this area is so warm and sheltered that it seems quite subtropical.

Abel Tasman National Park, tidal sandflats

The coastal roads peter out at Marahau. After that you have to leg it on the tracks of Abel Tasman National Park or take to a coastal canoe. It is indeed perhaps best appreciated by canoe, and that's what a lot of people do.

Back on the main road just south of Kaiteriteri, you go over the Tākaka Hill: a great mass of dark-coloured limestone outcrops with incredible views to the south, the east, and into the Tākaka Valley, which is where you are now headed.

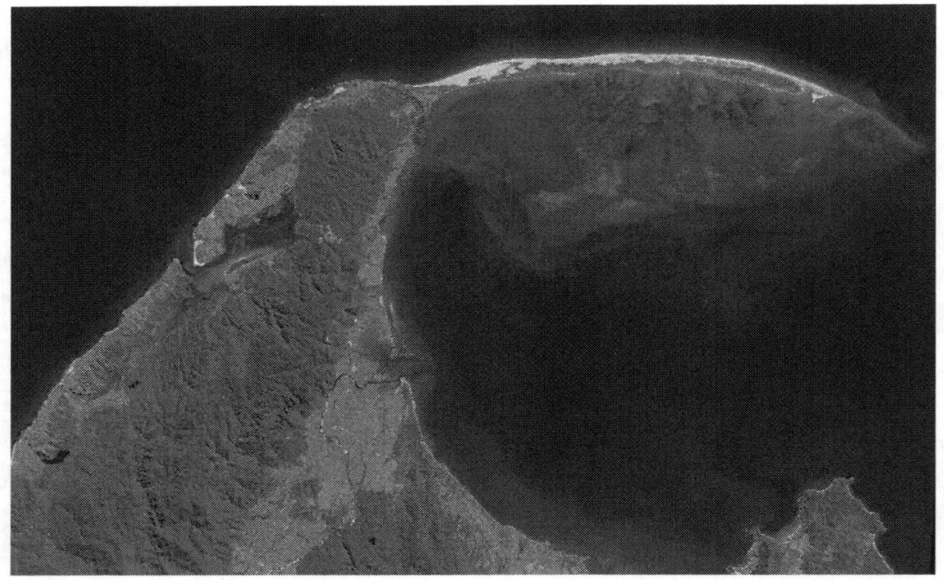

Golden Bay/Mohua, showing Farewell Spit/Tohuroa and the Aorere Valley at centre left. *(Nasa Earth Observatory image 2001044, captured by the ASTER satellite on 13 February 2001). Public domain image, credit to NASA/METI/AIST/Japan Space Systems and U.S./Japan ASTER Science Team.*

The main town here is Tākaka, probably the most isolated spot in New Zealand that still has a supermarket. Further up the coast is Collingwood, named after one of Nelson's colleagues, Cuthbert Collingwood: an apparently exemplary character with no skeletons in his closet, unlike Nelson.

Collingwood stands at the entrance to the Aorere Valley, the gateway to the Heaphy Track, about which I have more to say in another chapter. As for the sea, this area, between Abel Tasman

National Park and Farewell Spit/Tohuroa, is known as Golden Bay, or Mohua in Māori. It is even more sheltered than Tasman Bay/Te Tai o Aorere to its east.

***Engraving of Golden Bay/Mohua by Tasman's artist, Isaack Gilsemans,** depicting a battle between Māori waka taua or war-canoes and Tasman's two ships Zeehaen and Heemskerck. Public domain image via Wikimedia Commons.*

Tasman is a name continually encountered in this area. It refers to the Dutch explorer Abel Tasman, the first commander of any European expedition known to have reached Australia and New Zealand, who anchored for several days in Golden Bay/Mohua in 1642. Tasman named the bay Murderers' Bay, after a misunderstanding that soon developed between the locals and his party, who had after all shown up uninvited. But these days, naturally enough, Golden Bay is preferred.

You are getting pretty close to the end of the line here for ordinary private cars. Driving past the foot of Farewell Spit/Tuhuroa along by-now dusty roads you come to a car park outside a place called the Archway Café: and that's it.

From there, on foot, you walk to the amazing Wharariki Beach and Archway Islands on the north coast.

The Archway Islands

You can also trek to Cape Farewell, the northernmost tip of the South Island, which at 40.5 degrees south is north of Wellington, Levin and Masterton in the North Island. Cape

Farewell. has a sea-arch at the end and thus looks like a bit like an elephant with a trunk.

To go along Farewell Spit/Tuhuroa you can either embark on a long hot walk, which is only allowed for the first four kilometres of its 26 km permanently dry length in any case. Or you can catch a special eco-tourism bus from Collingwood.

You can also drive to the Whanganui Inlet at the northernmost extremity of the West Coast, but the road then terminates there as well. The only way to drive further along the West Coast is to go all the way back to Wakefield and continue along State Highway 6 inland. In between, of course, lies the wild Kahurangi National Park and the Heaphy Track.

On the way back, through Tākaka, you have to take a detour to see Te Waikoropūpū Springs, the largest cold-water springs in the Southern Hemisphere, which also contain some of the clearest natural water anywhere. You can see all the way down into their rather considerable depths and go bushwalking in the vicinity as well.

The author in front of Te Waikoropūpū Springs

Another Tākaka attraction is the Labyrinth Rocks Park, in which you walk on three kilometres of trails between rock walls.

There are also lots of caves all over this limestone country, both little ones that ordinary people can visit and also more epic ones such as Harwood's Hole, into which experienced cavers descend 183 metres, or 600 feet, on a line.

Entrance Pit of Harwoods Hole. *Photo by Dave Bunnell (2005), CC-BY-SA 3.0 via Wikimedia Commons.*

Harwoods Hole is in an area called the Canaan Downs in the back country of the Abel Tasman National Park. It's at the end of a 45-minute walk called Harwoods Hole Track, through spectacular limestone country, from the carpark at the end of the Canaan Road, itself off the main road through the Tākaka Hill. As you can imagine the brochures about the hole, and the track, are hedged about with warnings.

For more on this amazing area, you might want to click on the following blog posts:

a-maverick.com/blog/nelson-abel-tasman-farewell-spit-tohuroa

a-maverick.com/blog/luminate-festival-2017-new-zealand

CHAPTER SIX

Kahurangi National Park

The Cobb Valley, Mount Arthur and the Nelson Tablelands

KAHURANGI National Park is the second largest national park in New Zealand after Fiordland. With over five hundred and seventy kilometres of tracks, including the famous seventy-eight-kilometre Heaphy Track, Kahurangi is tramping heaven. With its coastal palm forests, marble mountains, rare birds like the rock wren and the spotted kiwi, and tussock high country, it's an incredible place to be.

In Māori Kahurangi means treasured possession, which is exactly what this park is. For hundreds of years the Māori used tracks through this region to find pounamu, used mainly to make prized jewellery passed down from one generation to the next.

Part of the Kahurangi National Park, the Cobb Valley can be accessed from the Upper Tākaka district, at the base of the Tākaka Hill along thirty-eight kilometres of unsealed road. Mount Arthur, the principal mountain in the area, can be reached via the Graham Valley Road, thirty-five kilometres from Motueka.

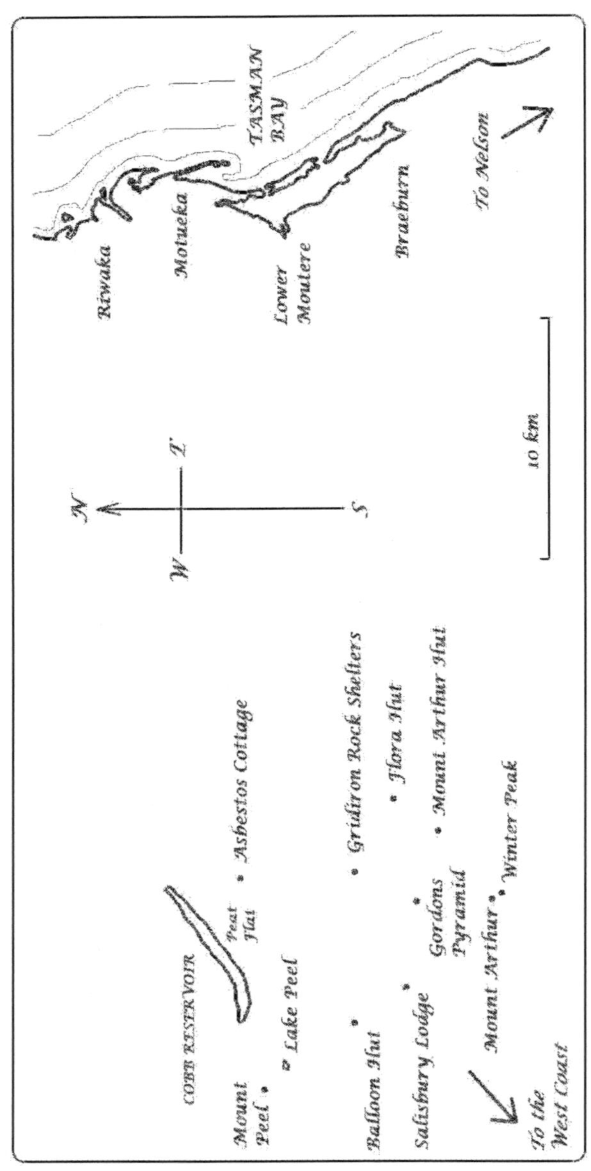

Points of interest on and around the Nelson Tablelands, inland from Motueka

Access to the Nelson Tablelands, a high plateau, can be gained on foot via each of these two routes, and the west coast of the South Island can be reached from the Leslie-Karamea Track.

The diverse terrain I covered included a series of unique geological features. Mt Arthur is made of hard, crystalline marble: below the ground are some of the deepest shafts and most intricate cave systems in the world. Cavers have currently joined two cave systems in the area and made a massive thirty-six kilometres long, twelve hundred metres deep underground labyrinth. Nettlebed is now the deepest cave in the Southern Hemisphere of which the depth is known.

Cobb Reservoir, nominally 819 metres above sea level on the surface.
The tops above the reservoir are as high up again, and it is at that point that the Nelson Tablelands are reached.

The picturesque Lower Gridiron Shelter

I've got much more information and photos in the following blog posts:

a-maverick.com/blog/kahurangi-national-park-cobb-valley-mt-arthur-nelson-tablelands

a-maverick.com/blog/volunteering-kahurangi-national-park-what-could-go-wrong

CHAPTER SEVEN

The Heaphy Track and the Old Ghost Road

Two lengthy trails in the far northwest

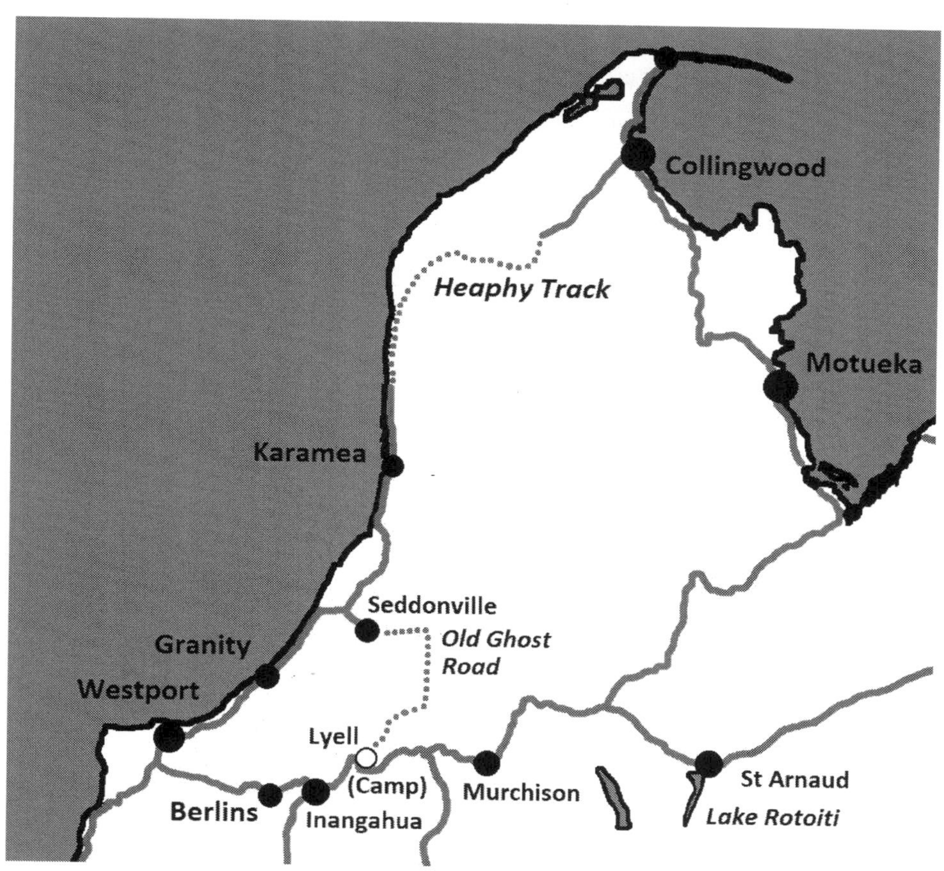

THIS chapter is about two lengthy trails suitable for trampers and mountain-bikers alike, the Heaphy Track and the Old Ghost Road. The Heaphy Track follows the approximate route at one time used by old-time Māori from Golden Bay, the great bay around what's now the town of Collingwood, to get to the West Coast and prospect for pounamu; though by the nineteenth century the route had been abandoned and left to become overgrown. Then, from about 1860 onwards, the track, which would later be named after the New Zealand back-country explorer Charles Heaphy but was simply known then as 'the route over the Gouland Downs', was re-developed as a pack track for prospectors seeking gold in the region.

The pack track was then abandoned and was left to become overgrown for a second time, only to be cleared again after the establishment of the North-West Nelson Forest Park in 1965, forerunner of today's Kahurangi National Park.

In the 1970s there was even a plan to put a road for vehicles through on the same route but, fortunately, that never happened. These days, the Heaphy Track is one of New Zealand's Great Walks. So, I would say that the chances of it being abandoned for a third time, or becoming a motorway, are both now equally slim!

As for the Old Ghost Road, this follows the course of a partly-built nineteenth-century miners' road that was never completed because the terrain in the middle turned out to be just too difficult, and no doubt because the mines ran out as well. There are several ghost towns in the area, including Lyell, the Old Ghost Road's southern terminus.

After well over a century of abandonment paralleling that of the ghost towns, the Old Ghost Road was finished off as a recreational trail for cyclists and trampers. It was officially opened for that purpose on 12 December 2015.

The Heaphy Track

I have tramped the Heaphy Track, one of New Zealand's Great Walks, twice.

The walk stretches through the Kahurangi National Park at the top of the South Island, west of the famous Abel Tasman Track, and winds its way through native bush and tussock downs to the wild Pacific Ocean on the West Coast. The track can be walked in either direction, beginning at the eastern end at Brown Hut, or starting in Karamea on the West Coast by driving fifteen kilometres north to the Kohaihai River campsite.

Bring a tent on a busy walk like the Heaphy: you will have more privacy!

The Heaphy Track comes out at the Heaphy River and continues south along the coast to the Kohaihai Shelter and Campsite, where the West Coast's road system begins (yay).

The Kohahai Campsite has palm trees sprouting from white sand and looks quite tropical: an appearance that's typical of the northern part of the West Coast. The angle of the South Island means that it's not just Nelson that's sheltered from Antarctic winds, but much of the West Coast as well.

See **doc.govt.nz/heaphytrack**

The Old Ghost Road

Carrying on south, you get to the towns of Karamea, Granity and Westport. From Westport, you can go inland by road toward the Buller Gorge until you get to Lyell, and then hike or bike the Old Ghost Road, at 85 km in length New Zealand's longest single track, up to the town of Seddonville.

The Old Ghost Road is quite a bit gnarlier than the Heaphy Track and is in fact the most difficult cycle trail in the official New Zealand Cycle Trail (NZCT) system. It's recommended that every rider cycle it from Lyell north and not the other way, as there is a section that's nearly impossible from north to south, and the trail also contains New Zealand's longest section of 'single track', a very narrow section on an exposed hillside.

The terrain and the views in the middle are, apparently, completely epic and I would love to do it one day.

Check out **oldghostroad.org.nz** and also DOC's page on the Old Ghost Road.

I've got a blog post with more information and photos, on:

a-maverick.com/blog/heaphy-track-old-ghost-road

CHAPTER EIGHT

Between Blenheim and Nelson

From coastal strolls with the birds to hard hill country

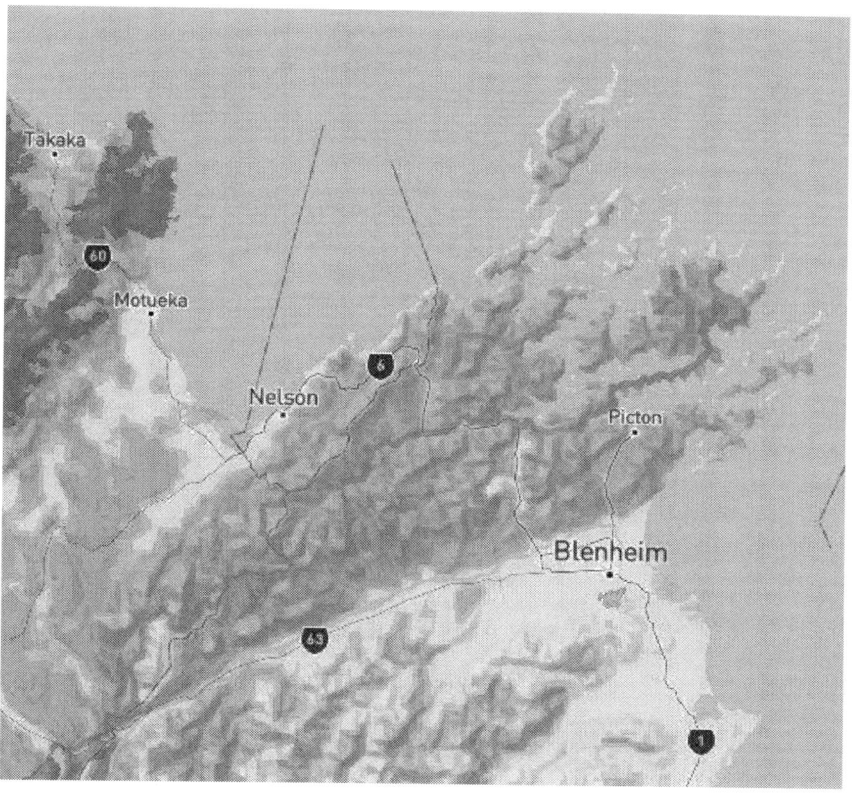

The Marlborough Sounds and the Richmond Range both lie between Blenheim and Nelson. *Image screenshot from* ***walkingaccess.govt.nz****, 4 January 2021. Crown copyright reserved.*

BETWEEN Blenheim and Nelson, there is a ruggedly beautiful area that extends from the Marlborough Sounds in the north east to Nelson Lakes National Park, in the southwest, via the Richmond Range. To the west, and south, of this great triangular block of mountains there are river flats and plains, of Nelson and, on the Blenheim side, the Wairau valley.

Ironically, though Nelson and Blenheim are not far apart, the Richmond Range is a formidable barrier, as is its seaward continuation in the form of the Marlborough Sounds, a collection of drowned river valleys to the north of Picton. The Marlborough Sounds were once above sea level in their entirety but were invaded by the sea at the end of the last ice-age, with.the result that a series of sharp ridges and sharp-edged islands now poke up above the water.

Marked out on the map, on the preceding page, is a section of Te Araroa, the great New Zealand trail, which includes, from top right to bottom left, the Queen Charlotte Track, Anakiwa to Pelorus Bridge, the Pelorus Track, the Richmond Alpine Track and the start of the Waiau Pass Track.

For more on the walks and other recreational opportunities in the area, see:

doc.govt.nz/parks-and-recreation/places-to-go/marlborough

The Pelorus River Scenic Reserve, *a popular holiday spot beside the main road from Nelson to Blenheim*

A place where Māori first began

One of the most special places you might wish to visit, on the coast near Blenheim, is the Wairau Bar, also known as the boulder bank or Pokohiwi, an 11 kilometre-long spit with a long history of human habitation.

There have been extensive archaeological diggings at the Wairau Bar, at the mouth of the Wairau River near Blenheim, ever since ancient remains were first unearthed in 1939. Over time, it has become clear that the area is one of the first to have been occupied by the immediate Polynesian ancestors of the Māori.

According to the website of Blenheim's Marlborough Museum, as of the time of writing, "At least four graves on the Bar belong to the first generation of Polynesian settlers. The latest scientific work has proven that these people were once children in East Polynesia." These settlers lived on the Bar about 700 to 730 years ago.

See **marlboroughmuseum.org.nz/exhibitions/wairau-bar**

Those discoveries were announced in 2012. In 2016, the scientists working with ancient DNA from the site revealed, further, that a number of members of the Rangitāne iwi, which is strong in Wellington and the Prow region, could trace their ancestry to two of the East Polynesia-born individuals unearthed at the Wairau Bar. These two include a woman whose remains were first unearthed in 1939, nicknamed 'Aunty' by Rangitāne kaumātua (elders) even before she was proven to be an ancestor to local Māori, and whose facial appearance has been reconstructed as well.

stuff.co.nz/marlborough-express/news/7880500/Aunty-revealed-after-700-years

The next step in this genetic odyssey is to try and work out which specific islands in East Polynesia the people of the Wairau Bar came from.

Ancient, excavated waka (canoes) in the Marlborough Museum

Along with its general fertility and fishing resources, the Prow contained minerals that were just as important to Māori as the pounamu of the West Coast, if less prestigious. These included coloured oxides that were important for making dyestuffs and a form of rock called called pakohe in Māori and argillite in English, a rock with glassy qualities which fractures like obsidian or flint and holds a sharp edge, and was therefore good for making every-day tools. There is evidence of very extensive pakohe / argillite workings on Rangitoto ki te Tonga (D'Urville Island), the largest island in the Marlborough sounds.

Interlopers who might have sought to seize these resources were, perhaps, put off by local tales of a flesh-eating monster called Kaiwhakaruaki, which had an insatiable desire for human flesh. Anyone whom Kaiwhakaruaki saw was doomed. According to the historian Jock Phillips, this story, too, is a link to island Polynesia, as are several associated placenames:

"It is a local version of the legend of the Polynesian monster 'Aifa'arua'i, the scourge of voyagers between the Pacific islands of Parapara, Ta'a'a, Motue'a and Ara'ura. The tale transplants these island names, which are still in use today – Parapara, Takaka, Motueka and Arahura on the West Coast."

Here's the link:

teara.govt.nz/en/photograph/539/the-story-of-kaiwhakaruaki

On the topic of monsters, Kupe, the semi-legendary navigator who discovered New Zealand for the Māori, is supposed to have killed a giant octopus or squid called Te Wheke-a-Muturangi in the section of water known as Kura Te Au or Tory Channel. This well-known tale accounts for the local placename Whekenui (big octopus) Bay.

Kupe's feat has lately been repeated. So maybe that fishy tale was for real, unlike the more dubious one about the monster with an insatiable appetite for trespassers.

stuff.co.nz/science/119577707/kiwi-scientists-stunned-after-catching-giant-squid-in-nz-waters

According to the census of 2013, some 8,800 people in the Nelson and Marlborough districts claimed descent from the eight iwi that are counted as tribes that have a traditional claim on the land of the Prow. These include Rangitāne, but not Ngāi Tahu, which is strong in the rest of the South Island.

The Queen Charlotte Track: An Introduction to Te Araroa in the South Island

I tramped the Queen Charlotte Track one summer. This is a track that follows the length of Queen Charlotte Sound, officially Queen Charlotte Sound/Tōtaranui. As the map above shows, it is the first stage of Te Araroa, the great New Zealand trail, in the South Island if you are starting from the north.

There's no road to the beginning of the track at Meretoto / Ship Cove, so all trampers must be dropped off here by boat from Picton and can choose to hike with their gear or have it transported by one of the many water taxi companies in the area.

The three to five-day hike along the coast is a comfortable walk and can be a great alternative to the often-overcrowded Abel Tasman Track in Abel Tasman National Park.

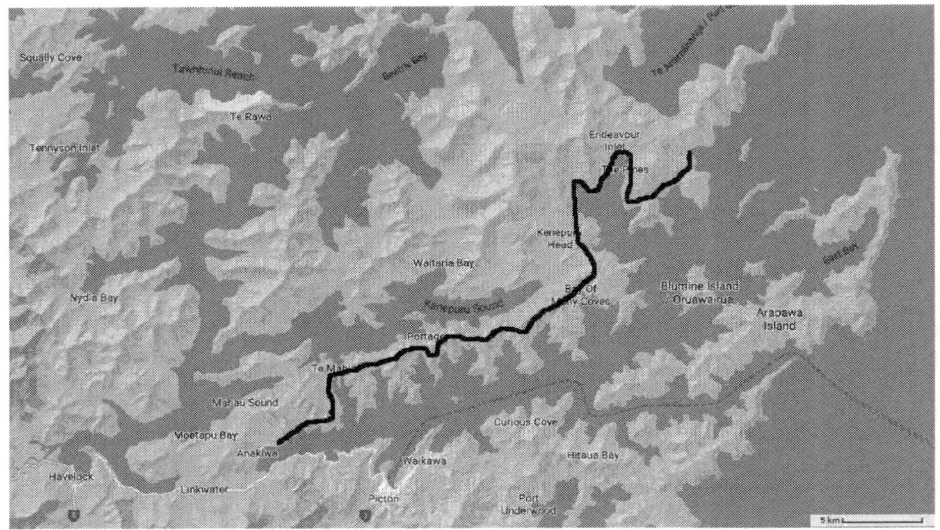

The Queen Charlotte Track, in black, *at the north-eastern end of the South Island. Background Map data ©2021 Google*

Queen Charlotte Sound is one of the main inlets in the Marlborough Sounds. The area was first settled by Māori around 800 years ago, and they built villages and made canoe voyages through the sound.

I was dropped off by the ferry at Meretoto, at the easternmost end of the track, and after stopping to admire the memorial to Captain Cook, I began by hiking north and west through forested ridges to get around Endeavour Inlet and reach Kenepuru Saddle Campsite. I stayed at the Kenepuru Saddle where the dawn chorus of birds was the best I've heard in the country.

Other parts of the track were open grass plains and I found them quite difficult in the hot summer weather. It was hard going in my thick, leather tramping boots and merino socks and I do remember getting blisters here.

After the steep climb to Eatwell's Lookout, where the long south-westward leg of the track begins, I followed the ridges to Torea Saddle with views of Queen Charlotte Sound and Kenepuru Sound.

The next day I followed the track through to the picturesque Lochmara Bay, and from there to Anakiwa. I was amazed by this small, coastal village hiding at the edge of the Queen Charlotte Sound – it was beautiful. I stayed with a friend who lived there, and then hitchhiked to the larger port town of Havelock, about eighteen kilometres away; from which you can do tours of the sounds on the Mail Boat, as it's called, since it also delivers the mail.

The very colonial Havelock i-Site

The Mail Boat (themailboat.co.nz)

There are a number of detours and side-tracks along the Queen Charlotte Track, including Eatwell's Lookout and one that ascends a peak overlooking Lochmara Bay.

The official website of the Queen Charlotte Track is **qctrack.co.nz**

More of Yesterday's Men

Regarding the colonial names of towns in this area, it's much the same as in the Nelson area further west. The Marlborough Sounds are named after John Churchill, an ancestor of Winston Churchill who lived in the late 1600s and early 1700s, and who is better known as the Duke of Marlborough. The town of Blenheim is named after the Duke's most famous military victory, in 1704.

Havelock is named after a general who died in the so-called Indian Mutiny of 1857, and Picton is named after Thomas Picton, the highest-ranking officer to fall at the Battle of Waterloo.

As we know, some of these empire builders' reputations are getting a second look these days. Picton is perhaps the latest to go under the microscope. For, people are starting to remember that nine years before Waterloo, Picton was put on trial for the torture, over two days, of a girl who worked in a café to try and get her to confess the whereabouts of some property that had, supposedly, gone missing.

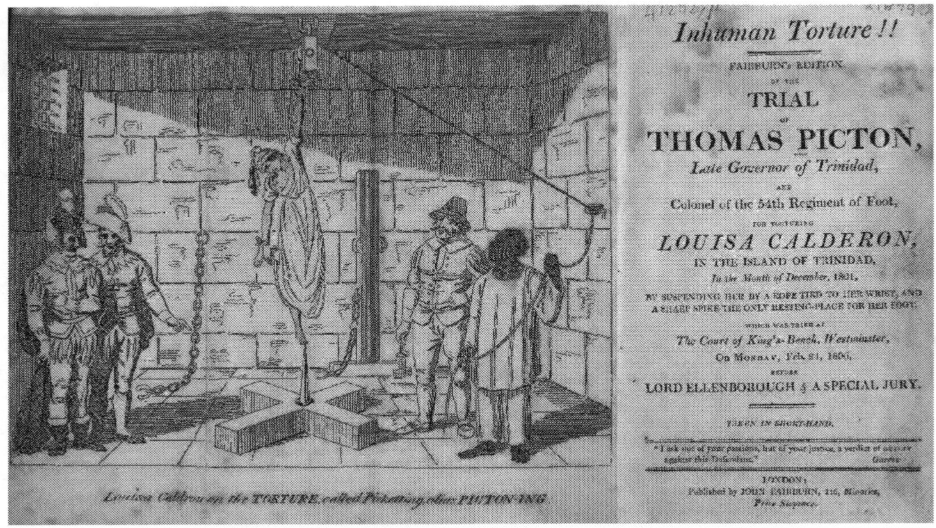
Inhuman Torture!!

FAIRBURN's EDITION

OF THE

TRIAL

OF

THOMAS PICTON,

Late Governor of Trinidad,

AND

Colonel of the 54th Regiment of Foot,

FOR TORTURING

LOUISA CALDERON,

IN THE ISLAND OF TRINIDAD,

In the Month of December, 1801,

BY SUSPENDING HER BY A ROPE TIED TO HER WRIST, AND A SHARP SPIKE THE ONLY RESTING-PLACE FOR HER FOOT.

WHICH WAS TRIED AT

The Court of King's-Bench, Westminster,

On MONDAY, Feb. 24, 1806,

BEFORE

LORD ELLENBOROUGH & A SPECIAL JURY.

TAKEN IN SHORT-HAND.

LONDON:

Published by JOHN FAIRBURN, 146, Minories,

Price Sixpence.

Perhaps it's as well that some of the towns in this area also have well-established Māori names. Picton was Waitohi for a long time before it was Picton. Just saying.

I've got more information in a blog post, which also describes a lovely scenic reserve on the Pelorus River and the attractions of the town of Havelock, among other additions:

a-maverick.com/blog/between-blenheim-nelson

See, also, the Marlborough App

CHAPTER NINE

The Nelson Lakes and the Travers-Sabine Circuit

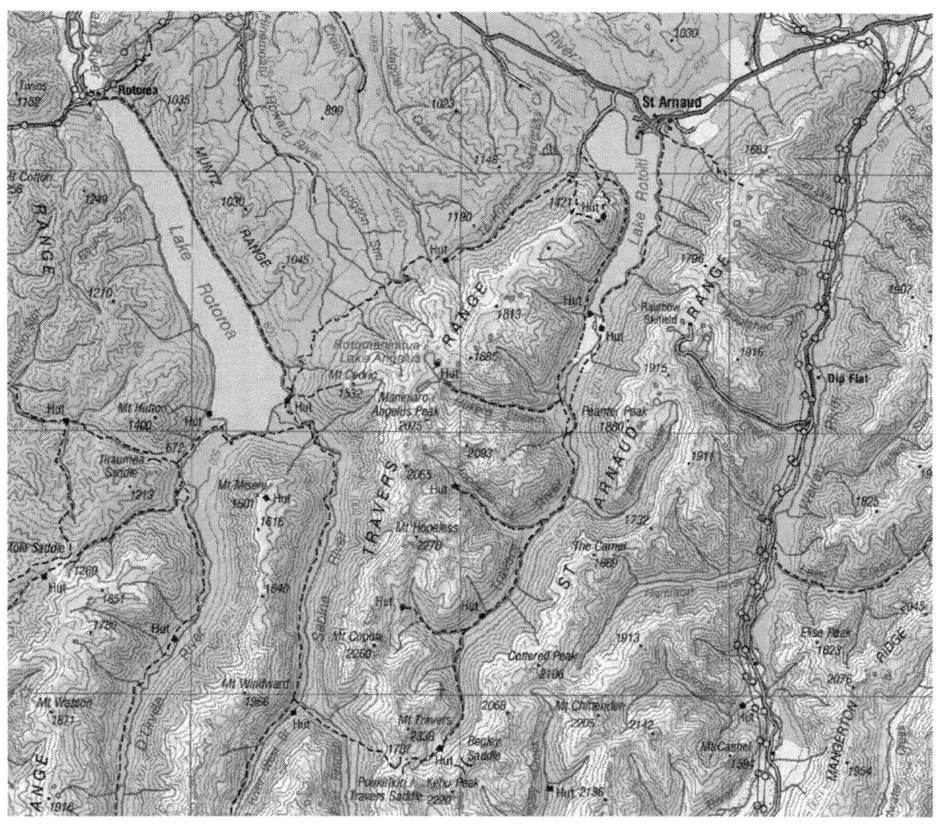

The Nelson Lakes, Travers Range, and the Travers River-Sabine River Circuit. *Imagery from LINZ via NZ Topo Map (topomap.co.nz), 2021.*

THE Nelson Lakes, Rotoroa and Rotoiti, and the associated Travers-Sabine Circuit are really one of the gems of the

New Zealand outdoors. The scenery is magnificent, there are plenty of huts to stay in and good tracks.

The lakes are very historic, as Lake Rotoiti has a large population of eels, which Māori travelling overland to the sources of pounamu on the West Coast used to dry and smoke for sustenance on the way.

Reaching in behind the lakes, the Travers-Sabine Circuit is about eighty kilometres (fifty miles) long. It reaches deep into the mountainous country behind Lakes Rotoiti and Rotoroa and involves one significant alpine saddle, the Poukiriri or Travers Saddle which has its summit at 1,787 metres or nearly 6,000 feet above sea level and can be icy even in summer.

The usual route passes around the Travers Range, of which the northern half is called the Robert Ridge. Having said that it's possible to follow an alternative route up Robert Ridge, which is very scenic in fine weather and has the added advantage of bringing you to Rotomaninitua ('isolated pleasant lake') or Lake Angelus, a small alpine lake at an altitude of 1,650 metres in the middle of the Travers Range.

The poled route eventually climbs to a maximum elevation of 1,794 metres at the Julius Summit.

The route then descends slightly to the Angelus Hut and Campsite, beside the lake of the same name.

The last time I did the Travers-Sabine we took the Robert Ridge Route. Rotomaninitua / Lake Angelus was mesmerising: its shiny waters were surrounded by snow. By the way we were tramping in summer, in December to be precise. That's what I mean about totally alpine.

You have to pre-book the hut there in order to be sure of a place as, in spite of its remoteness, altitude and difficulty of access, this little beauty spot is quite popular.

Rotomaninitua/Lake Angelus in the summertime, with a glimpse of the hut railing at bottom left. *This place would probably be packed out, with a hotel and a gondola, if was in the European Alps or anywhere like that.*

To continue the Circuit, you go down the Cascade Track to the Travers River and spend a night at the John Tait Hut. There are a couple of side trips you can do along this stretch into scenic chasms beside the track: one of them to the Hopeless Hut at the end of the Hopeless Track (what wonderful names!), and another up the Cupola Track to Cupola Hut.

But if you continue along the main route, you proceed over the Poukirikiri/Travers Saddle and down to West Sabine Hut, which is 1,107 m below the saddle.

Poukiriri/Travers Saddle

From West Sabine Hut I made it to Rotomairewhenua / Blue Lake, a small lake with incredibly pristine waters at an elevation of 1,200 m above sea level. This requires heading southward along the Blue Lake Track, off the topographical map above, and then back-tracking to the West Sabine Hut before carrying on. But it's worth the detour, as you can see!

Rotomairewhenua/Blue Lake

It's a further five-hour walk or so through the valley following the river to the Sabine Hut and its wide views of Lake Rotoroa, and then another five hours up towards Speargrass Hut through a series of small valleys and wetlands.

For more on my adventures on the circuit, see the following blog post:

a-maverick.com/blog/nelson-lakes-travers-sabine-circuit

TOUR 2: The Wild West Coast

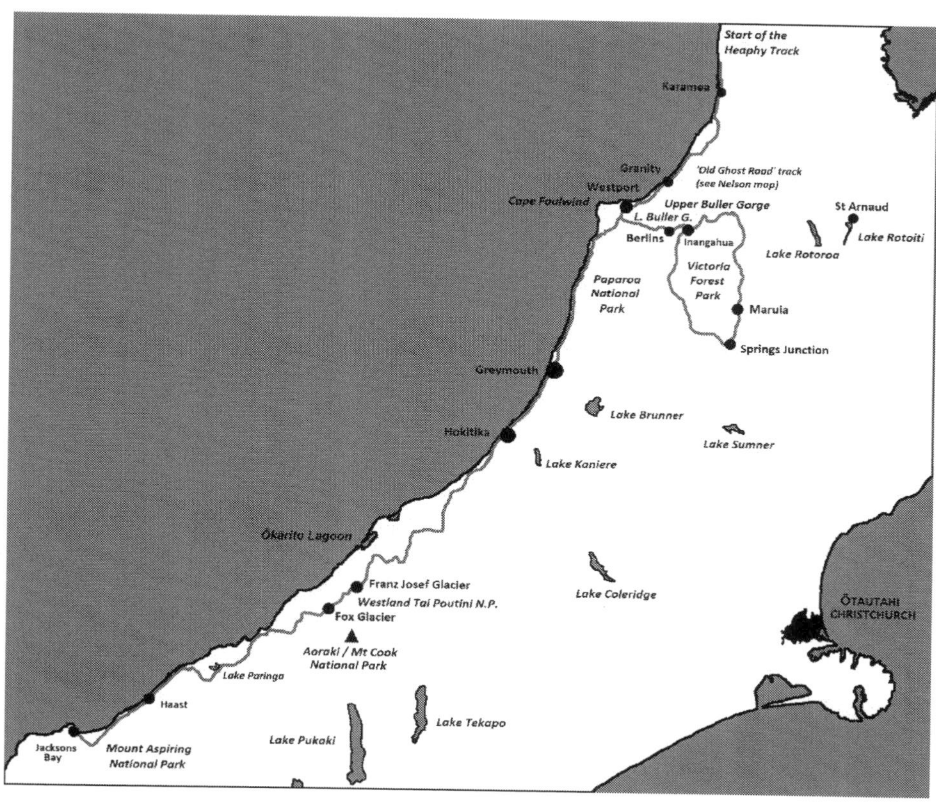

CHAPTER TEN

The Waters of Jade

Down the South Island's beautiful West Coast

THE West Coast of the South Island stretches for about 800 kilometres (500 miles) from Cape Farewell in the far north of the island to Puysegur Point in Fiordland; though by convention the 'Coast' ends at Jackson Head just south of Haast Pass, everything south of that being Fiordland.

From the north, the West Coast begins with the Whanganui Inlet west of Cape Farewell, followed by a stretch of trackless coast north of the Heaphy River.

South of the Heaphy Track, in the vicinity of Karamea, there are the caves and arches of the Ōpārara River, in lush, tropical-looking forest (for more on this, see my blog post linked at the end!).

From Westport, you can drive toward the Buller Gorge and further inland to drive around the Brunner and Victoria Ranges, including Victoria Forest Park, in a loop via Springs Junction, Reefton and Inangahua. This is a really scenic inland region with lots of places to go tramping and a strong mining history.

Heading back to Westport you might want to visit Cape Foulwind, obviously not named by a real estate agent, but actually by Captain Cook after his ship *Endeavour* was blown offshore in this area in 1770.

Cape Foulwind is a bracing short walk, which can indeed be very windy, with cliffs and seals: DOC has a web page on the Cape Foulwind Walkway and PDF brochure on Walks in the Westport area which includes other walks.

South of Westport, on the coast road, is the epic Paparoa National Park, which includes the Paparoa Track (Great Walk) over the tops, the low-altitude Inland Pack Track which follows on from it with incredibly lush ferny bush, and the must-see coastal locality of Punakaiki. The Pike29 Memorial Track, in honour of twenty-nine miners killed in the unsafe Pike River coal mine in 2010, is due to open in 2021.

See the DOC webpage on Paparoa National Park

Punakaiki

The pancake rocks at Punakaiki

The pancake rocks are not the only attraction at Punakaiki, a beautiful place with nīkau palms, cafés, and dramatic standing rocks on the beach.

The local Punakaiki tourism website is **punakaiki.co.nz**

The next sizable town, heading southward along the coast, is Greymouth. This is the biggest town on the West Coast, with a population of a bit over eight thousand.

You can see the South Island's great, long mountain range, commonly known as the Southern Alps, quite well from Greymouth, as indeed, from much of the central part of the West Coast.

The Southern Alps are known in Māori as Kā Tiritiri o te Moana, which literally means that which is cultivated by the sea but has a more poetical significance, I believe.

Not far south of Greymouth is the still rather frontier-like town of Hokitika (population just under three thousand) where some of the action in the 1999 New Zealand period drama *Greenstone* and the more recent BBC drama *The Luminaries* is set.

Hokitika hasn't changed a heck of a lot since the days of the *The Luminaries,* except that the boats have now got motors and the roads are tarsealed.

Between Greymouth and Hokitika, and going inland, are several other interesting places to visit. These include Lakes Kaniere, Brunner/Moana and Mahinapua, the last of which is small but scenic.

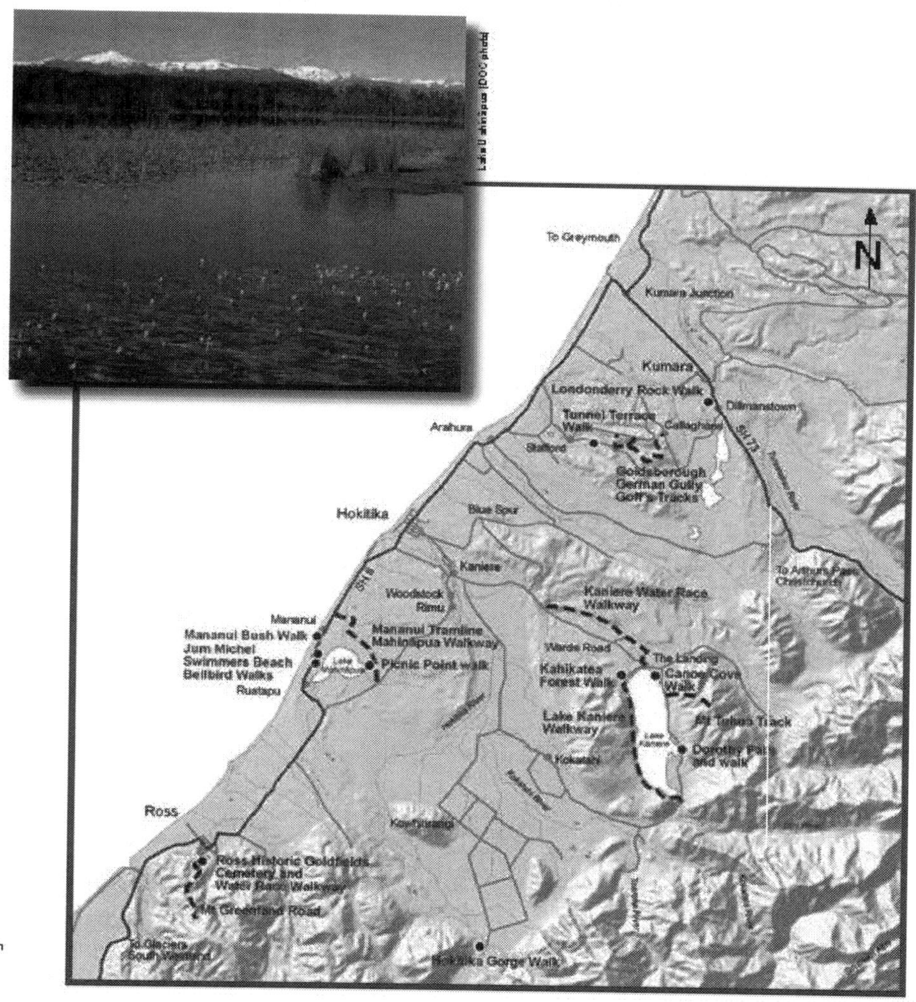

***From* Walks in the Hokitika area from Kumara to Ross,** *New Zealand Department of Conservation, 2008, extracted 30 December 2020, CC-BY-SA 4.0*

See the DOC pamphlet *Walks in the Hokitika area from Kumara to Ross,* which includes the Ross Historic Goldfields to the south of Hokitika; also the DOC webpage on the Lake Brunner area.

I've included a map and inset photograph from the pamphlet, above, on the previous page.

It's in this area that you can also do the West Coast Wilderness Trail on foot or on a bike: **westcoastwildernesstrail.co.nz**.

You can do it freelance, and there are also operators who will provide accommodation and bikes.

On the facing page, I've included a rough map screenshot from the West Coast Wilderness Trail website, which also has an app you can download as well as a more sophisticated downloadable map.

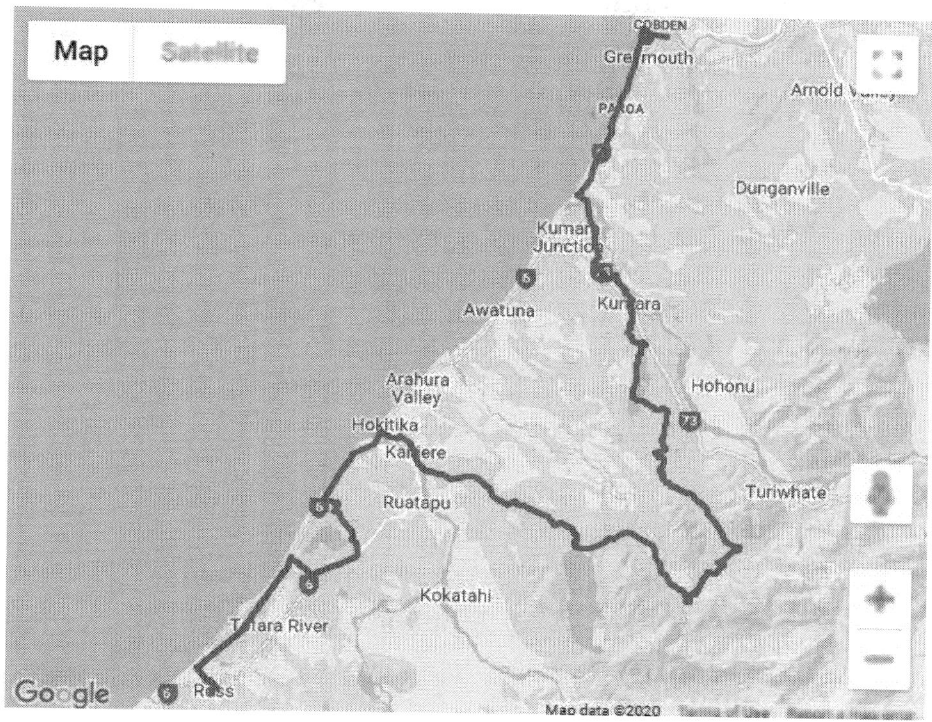

***The West Coast Wilderness Trail.** Google maps control icons blurred out for this book, as they are not active in the screenshot. Background map data ©2020 Google.*

One thing the Wilderness Trail doesn't take in, but that is mentioned in the DOC pamphlet, is the Hokitika Gorge with its blue pools, 33 km southeast of Hokitika via Kokatahi. These blue pools are sometimes milky, and sometimes clear.

South of Ross, the West Coast gets a lot wilder still. Before going on to talk about the area that's also known as South Westland, I'll describe the West Coast's historical importance to Māori as the source of pounamu, also known as greenstone or New Zealand jade.

Te Wai Pounamu

The West Coast of the South Island is known in Māori as Te Tai Poutini, the coast of Poutini, a tāniwha or water-monster that swam up and down the coast.

But this coast is also known in whole or part as Te Wai Pounamu, or the waters of greenstone. Indeed, the West Coast bestows this name on the whole of the South Island as well.

For the Māori have long extracted the semi-precious substance known as pounamu, also known in Australia and New Zealand as greenstone, from the mountain torrents of the West Coast.

Scientifically speaking, pounamu can be either of two minerals, nephrite or bowenite. Nephrite is one of the minerals that is classified, outside of New Zealand, as jade. Most pounamu objects are made from nephrite, and thus from jade. In New Zealand, nephrite mostly occurs in the form of heavy boulders that accumulate in mountain streams, above all on the west coast of the South Island.

In either case, pounamu is generally green and translucent and capable of being carved into beautiful ornaments.

The following page displays a portrait of one celebrated nineteenth century rangatira, or chief, holding his ceremonial mere (pronounced mereh) of office, a flattened club which is quite sharp at the broad end, like an axe-head. Around his neck the rangatira wears a hei tiki, or humanoid pendant. Both artifacts are made of pounamu.

Wahanui Reihana Te Huatare, by Gottfried Lindauer. *Public domain image via Wikimedia Commons.*

By law, the extraction, carving and sale of pounamu is controlled by Māori; specifically, the Ngāi Tahu iwi of Te Wai Pounamu, the South Island. There are, nevertheless, certain defined areas of the island where the public may fossick for small amounts. All the details are set out in a living document called the Pounamu Management Plan.

Here is a useful summary on *Te Ara,* the online Encyclopaedia of New Zealand: **teara.govt.nz/en/pounamu-jade-or-greenstone**

World Heritage: The South of the West

South of Ross, we are now starting to get into a part of the country where the hand of European colonisation and even the presence of the Māori, save for gathering pounamu, has only been lightly felt. In fact, all the National Parks from Aoraki/Mount Cook National Park southward are included in a larger conservation area called Te Wāhipounamu/South-West New Zealand World Heritage Area. Te Wāhipounamu means 'the place of pounamu'. The national parks are Westland Tai Poutini, Aoraki/Mount Cook, Mount Aspiring and Fiordland; and land in this part of the country is more likely to be in a national park than not.

The coast road now heads inland, as the true coast is now wild and swampy, with lowland forest and lagoons. There will be no more seaports to compare with Westport, Greymouth or even

Hokitika; only the small fishing settlement of Jackson Bay just north of the roadless wilderness of Fiordland.

The most significant place that a traveller comes to, south of Hari Hari, is the road that turns down to the tiny coastal settlement of Ōkārito and the huge, ecologically significant lagoon of the same name.

There is a campground at Ōkārito, and it's not a bad place to stay, in part because the region's extreme average rainfall drops mainly in the hills and on the mountains.

South of Ōkārito we come to Lake Mapourika which reflects the local scenery, and the townships of Franz Josef Glacier and Fox Glacier on the now-inland road. Both towns are named after their namesake glaciers, which descend, famously, through rain forest to a surprisingly low altitude.

At Fox Glacier, you can turn off down the Cook River toward Gillespies Beach. Part-way to the beach there is a side road to Lake Matheson, a small but famous scenic lake which has a walking track around it and a café, and a great view of the mountains and tall rain forest nearby when it isn't cloudy or misty or raining. When it is, the tops of the trees loom impressively out of the mist. The track around the lake also branches off to the more elevated Lake Gault. At Gillespies Beach there is a campsite, and it seems like a great place to get away from it all.

See DOC's page on the Lake Matheson / Te Ara Kairaumati Walk

South of Fox Glacier we come to the Karangarua River and the Copland Track, which leads to Welcome Flat and its hot pools and then on to the Copland Pass, which leads in turn to Aoraki/Mount Cook. The track, the pass and the tributary of the Karangarua River that bears the same name are pronounced Copeland, not cop-land as in the American film *Copland.*

(I talk about a hike to the Welcome Flat hot pools in the next chapter.)

After the Karangarua River, the main road (State Highway 6) briefly veers back to the actual coastline at Bruce Bay, and then inland once again past Lake Paringa where there's a salmon farm and salmon farm café. If you're lucky you might get to see the rare white heron or kotuku, which is seldom seen in other parts of New Zealand—Māori legend had it that you saw the kotuku only once in a lifetime—but which is drawn to the salmon farm. I wonder why? I talk about an incident in which a kotuku dropped in to see me at Paringa, one time, in the next chapter but one.

South of Paringa, the road rejoins the coastline at Knights Point, where there is a great lookout over wild cliffs, and then, not long after that, you get to Haast, the turnoff to the Haast Pass, the route to Wānaka and Queenstown.

At Haast, you can take in the Ship Creek Walk and Monro Beach, which lead through rare low-lying kahikatea swamp forest to the beach. Between July and December, you might see Fiordland crested penguins, and you might see Hector's dolphins too. A second half-hour walk leads to a dune lake, through stunted coastal forest. There are viewing platforms from which to take photographs over Lake Mataketake to the sweeping coastline to Jackson Head.

See the DOC pages on 'Walks north of Haast township' and 'Ship Creek area', of which the latter has a sweeping aerial photo by the celebrated landscape photographer Andris Apse as its hero image, as well as the page on Ship Creek and Monro Beach on **westcoast.co.nz**.

You can then continue along the coast road to the fishing settlement of Jackson Bay and a four-wheel drive road up the Jackson River, which leads via the Martyr Saddle (wonderful names!) to a track down the Cascade River. And that's basically the end of the line.

If you take the Haast Pass road inland, which is the main road of course, it turns out that there are several tracks which lead off this road even before you get to the pass, also known as Tioripatea, itself. Perhaps the biggest walk that comes off the Haast Pass/Tioripatea Highway west of the pass is the walk that leads up the Landsborough Valley, a really big valley like something out of some Western and a typical product of glacier country. And finally, if you are coming this way, check out the blue pools at Makarora, though that's past the Haast Pass summit and so I talk about them in Tour 6, in the context of Wānaka.

I have more to say about the West Coast, with more images in particular, in the following blog post:

a-maverick.com/blog/waters-jade-pounamu

See, also,

westcoast.co.nz

CHAPTER ELEVEN

Welcome Flat

The best hot pools

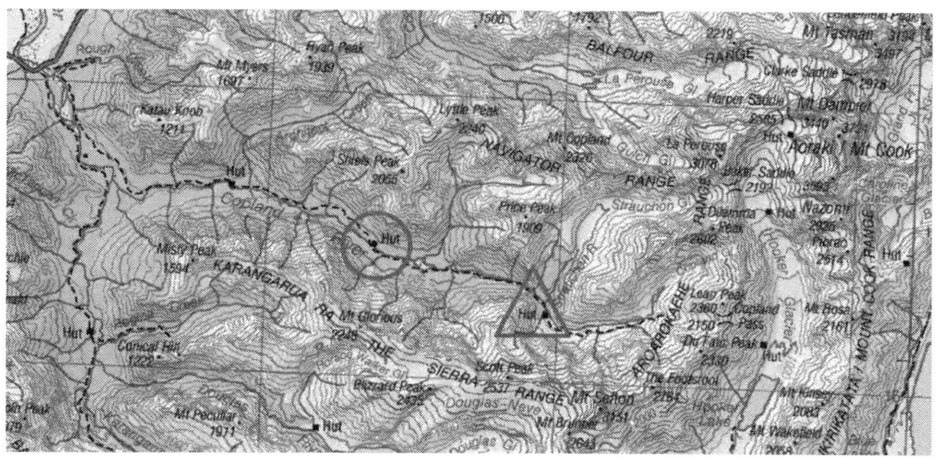

The Route to Welcome Flat *from State Highway 6 south of Fox Glacier Welcome Flat Hut is indicated by a circle, Douglas Rock Hut by a triangle. Background map by LINZ via NZ Topo Map, 2020.*

MY favourite tramping-track hot pools are at Welcome Flat on the Copland River.

The Copland is a tributary of the Karangarua, River which runs from the Southern Alps down to the Tasman Sea at a location south of Fox Glacier. Welcome Flat is on the lower part of the Copland River, at an altitude of about 430 metres, with a very flash hut.

Further east you come to the much more mundane Douglas Rock Hut, surrounded by giant mountains. Douglas Rock Hut gives people a taste of being in the Southern Alps without having to do serious climbing. But it is serious thereafter. The track terminates at an altitude of 2,150 metres at the Copland Pass, by which stage you are halfway up Aoraki/Mount Cook.

Welcome Flat Hot Pools, Sierra Range in background

Kea playing

For more, see my blog post:

a-maverick.com/blog/welcome-flat-best-hot-pools

CHAPTER TWELVE

A Visitation at Paringa

TALKING of wild and endangered species which can sometimes become tame and come in from the wilderness such as the kea, I recall how I once visited the South Westland Salmon Farm & Café near Lake Paringa, close to the Haast Pass in remote South Westland. At the café, we could drink coffee and look out on ponds full of the farm's stock splashing about.

***New Zealand two-dollar coin** showing the locally-rare Kōtuku or White Heron*

Earlier, I had caught a glimpse of the highly conspicuous yet seldom-seen white heron or kōtuku, which appears on the New

Zealand two-dollar coin and is a by-word in Māori culture for all that is rare and special.

So rare is the kōtuku that it is thought that only 100 to 120 of them live in New Zealand at the present time, so that it is even more rare than the kākāpō. Thankfully the kōtuku (*Ardea alba modesta*) is not confined to New Zealand, and also lives in flocks of thousands in Australia and Asia, where it is known in English as the eastern great egret.

But in New Zealand, by Māori tradition, you only see one in a lifetime. I had thought that glimpse was, indeed, my lot.

Well, imagine my surprise when a kōtuku actually dropped in and landed on our table, hoping for salmon scraps!

For more, see my blog post:

a-maverick.com/blog/visitation-paringa-egret-heron

TOUR 3: Arthur's and Lewis Passes

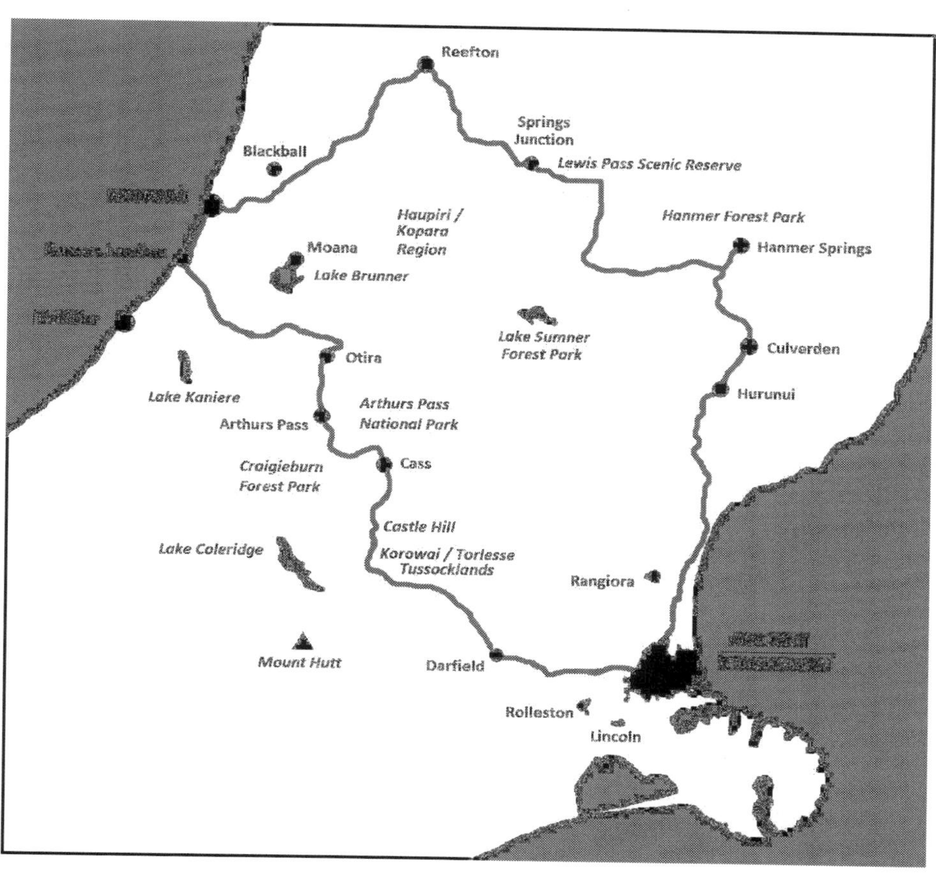

CHAPTER THIRTEEN

St James Walkway and the Lewis Pass Tops

Mountains, rivers and old huts

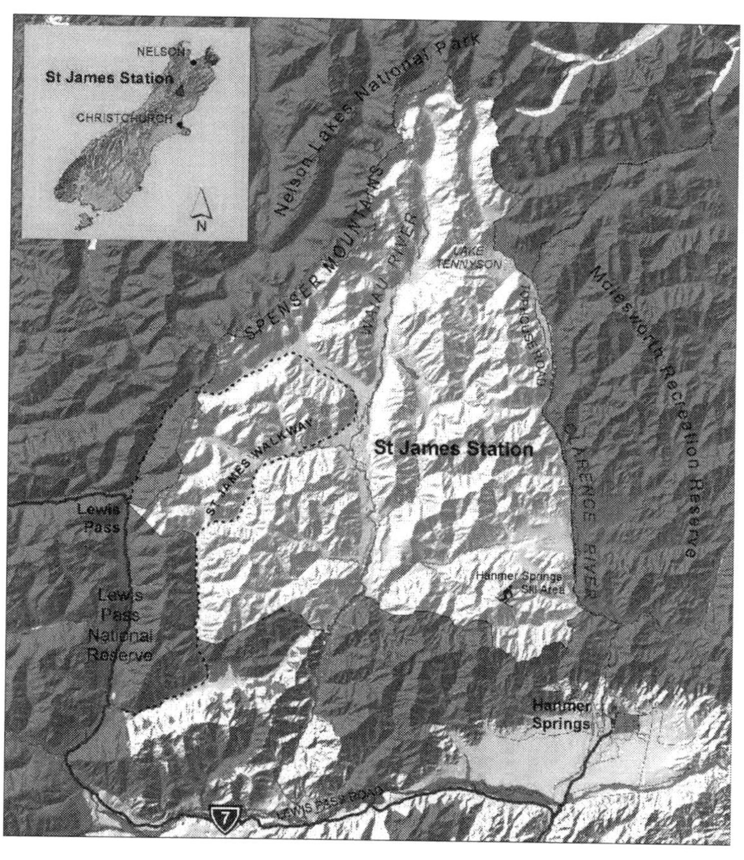

St James Station, after which the St James Walkway was named, *was acquired by the New Zealand Government in 2008 and incorporated into a wider St James Conservation Area. The Lewis Pass Tops are just on the other side of State Highway 7, in Lewis Pass National Reserve. (DOC graphics, from press release 'St James Station', 8 October 2008.)*

THE St James Walkway is named after the former St James Station upon which most of the walkway's sixty-six kilometres is located.

By New Zealand standards the St James Walkway is a comparatively easy tramp, though there is a lot of exposure to Alpine weather. Most of the distance is tramped on river flats, but nowhere is below five hundred metres of elevation and the highest point, the Anne Saddle, is over eleven hundred metres up. There are eight huts along the way.

The St James is in one of my favourite parts of New Zealand, the Lewis Pass / Muruia Valley area in the middle of the northern half of the Southern Alps.

You get there by means of State Highway 7, which zigzags through the area. There are numerous other tramps off to the side of State Highway 7 in the Lewis Pass / Maruia Valley area, such as the Lake Daniell (formerly lake Daniells) tramp, Lake Christabel, the Lewis Tops Track, and others.

The Maruia Valley is also famous as the place where a key document of the modern conservation era, the Maruia Declaration, was first signed in 1975. Circulated as an ultimately successful petition against the logging of native forests, it gained 340,000 signatures by 1977, which at the time meant that over one New Zealander in ten signed it and a still higher proportion of adults.

I talk about all this, and my hikes in the area, in more detail in the following blog post:

a-maverick.com/blog/st-james-walkway-and-the-lewis-pass-tops

CHAPTER FOURTEEN

Arthur's Pass

ARTHUR'S PASS is the second great pass in the Canterbury region and the most commercially important. It's certainly the only one with a regular train service, stopping at a rather Swiss-style mountain station at the Pass. The A-frame design has paintings on the ceiling inside.

Arthur's Pass Train Station. *Photo by 'Francis Vallance (Heritage Warrior)', 22 June 2015, CC-BY-2.0 via Wikimedia Commons.*

The train service is a scenic excursion train called the TranzAlpine. In the South Island north of Christchurch, the Coastal Pacific and the TranzAlpine normally run daily services, year-round in the case of the TranzAlpine but not in winter in the case of the Coastal Pacific.

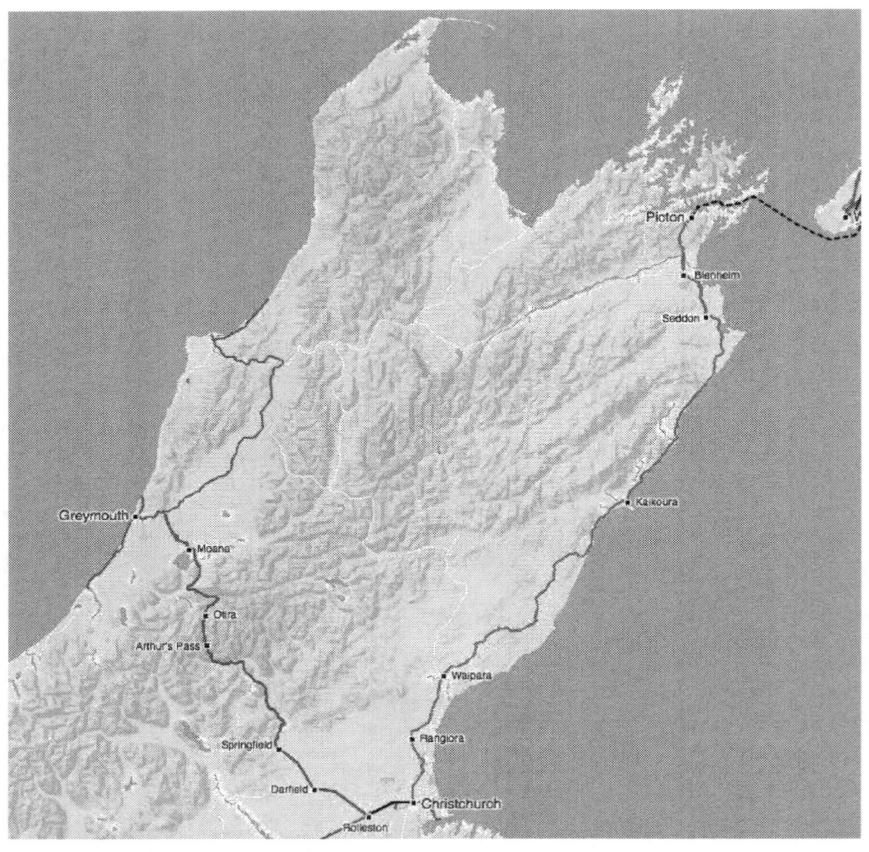

The TranzAlpine (Christchurch–Greymouth) and Coastal Pacific (Christchurch–Picton). *Map by Jkan997, CC-BY-SA 3.0 via Wikimedia Commons. Both services terminate in Christchurch,*

This is the link to the TranzAlpine:
greatjourneysofnz.co.nz/tranzalpine

Once you get there, by car or via the TranzAlpine scenic excursion train service, you will find that are lots of tramps and other things that can be done in the pass.

Overleaf, I've included a map from an excellent DOC brochure called *Discover Arthur's Pass* which I've rendered in monochrome via filters in such a way as to make the tracks stand out.

There are also lots of things to do, and heritage trails, in the town itself, and they are described elsewhere in the brochure.

You can download the full brochure from **arthurspass.com/pdf/arthurs-pass-brochure.pdf** and also from DOC's web page on Arthur's Pass. The local website **arthurspass.com** is also informative in more general terms.

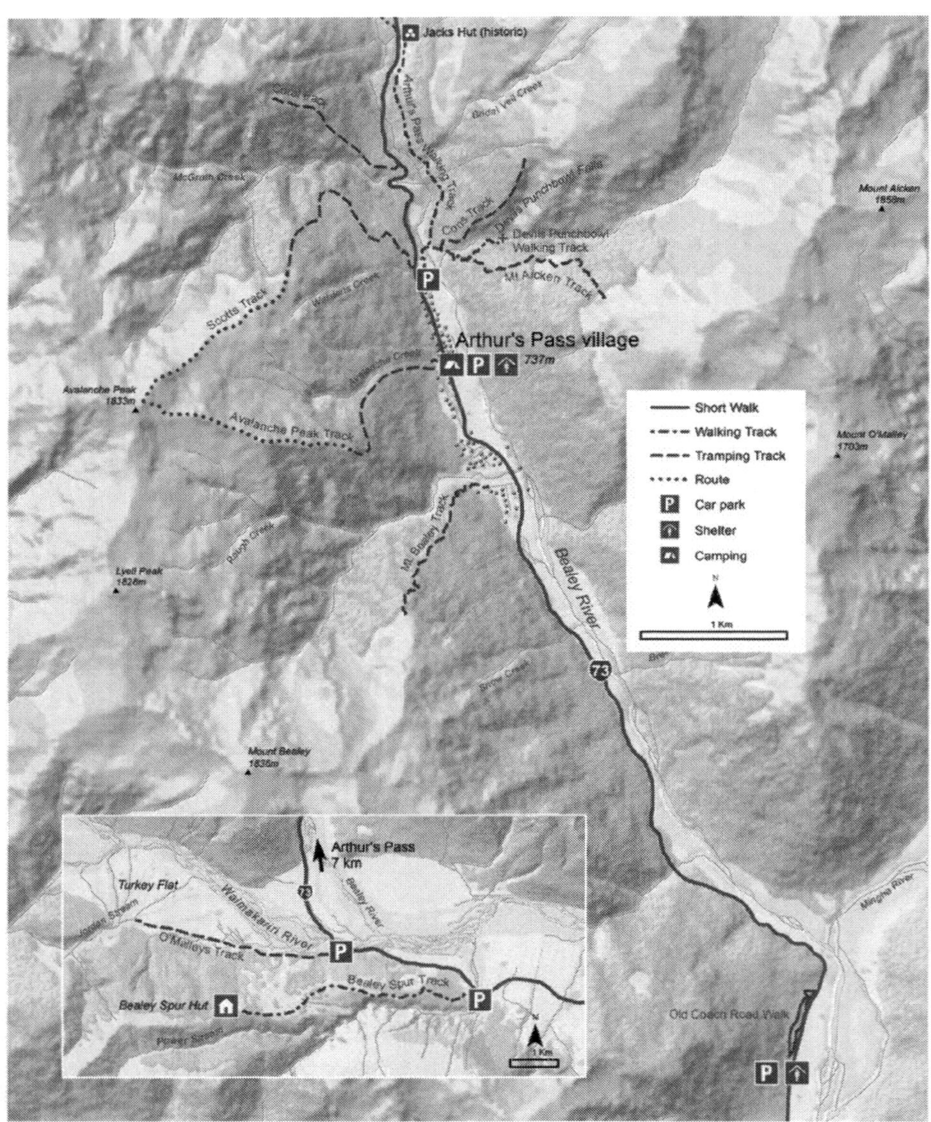

Trail map from* Discover Arthur's Pass *(brochure), *New Zealand Department of Conservation, 2019. Rendered monochrome via filter.*

Craigieburn and Kura Tāwhiti (Castle Hill)

Before you get to Arthur's Pass, travelling westward from Christchurch, you go through Porters Pass, which is 920 metres or just over three thousand feet above sea level. That's higher than the township of Arthur's Pass, which sits at 739 metres or 2,425 feet, and coincidentally the same height as the Arthur's Pass summit, also 920 metres. Between the two passes, you drive through an upland landscape of lakes and river flats – cold, bleak and bracing.

There are four skifields in this part of Canterbury: Porters Ski Area, Mount Cheeseman, Broken River and Craigieburn. There is also the Craigieburn Forest Park with its many tramping tracks.

Check out DOC's web page on Craigieburn Forest Park

But probably the most *culturally* important thing that you will come to, between the two passes, is Kura Tāwhiti, also known as Castle Hill, beside the main road to Arthurs Pass.

I hesitate to call Kura Tāwhiti Castle Hill: not only because it is very sacred to Māori and should therefore have its proper name, but also because there are Castle Hills everywhere in New Zealand and even another in the very same area, so it gets confusing!

Kura Tāwhiti means 'treasure from afar' and refers to the cultivation of kūmara or sweet potatoes in this area, unusually far south for kūmara cultivation but very sunny and sheltered between the rocks. The area was long used for shelter from the biting local winds by humans as well and has traces of 500-year-old charcoal drawings done by the Waitaha people.

Kura Tāwhiti/Castle Hill. *Note the tiny human figures on the trail and beside it.*

The Kura Tāwhiti Access Track does a loop behind the stones of Kura Tāwhiti, a loop which goes close to the top of Castle Hill (also 920 metres). Kura Tāwhiti is quite close to Craigieburn Forest Park and very close to a locality called Castle Hill Village, from which a number of other tracks go up into the hills including the local Leith Hill Loop Track and the Hogs Back Track that leads to Mount Cheeseman, Broken River and Craigieburn skifields, and to Craigieburn Forest Park more generally.

Here's a story on Kura Tāwhiti, from the pages of New Zealand Geographic: **nzgeo.com/stories/the-rocks-of-castle-hill.** You can also look up DOC's webpage on the Kura Tāwhiti Conservation Area, as the site is officially known.

By the way, you have to go by road to get to Kura Tāwhiti, as the TranzAlpine's line takes another route through these parts, through a district called Avoca, which has an interesting history of its own to do with now-defunct coal mines.

A Difficult Pass to Keep Open

The name Arthur's Pass refers to Arthur Dobson, the explorer who supposedly discovered it: though it goes without saying that the Māori generally knew of all the larger features of the interior, including its useful mountain passes.

In the case of the pass that would be called Arthur's, Dobson and his party were told where to go (in a friendly manner) by a rangatira named Tarapuhi.

Though it formed part of a traditional trail, the pass presented engineering difficulties for anyone who proposed to build a road or a railway. Indeed, its advocates were lampooned by those who favoured other routes, such as Browning Pass.

The difficulties and expense were so great that there was no railway until 1923, when a rail tunnel through the summit of the pass between Arthur's Pass township on the Canterbury side and Ōtira on the West Coast side was completed. At more than 8.5 km (5.3 miles), the Ōtira tunnel was one of the longest in the world at the time. People on one side of the mountains would peer down the tunnel to get an idea of weather conditions on the other side!

An 1865 cartoon representing supporters of the Arthur's Pass route as deluded and drunk, *from* Punch in Canterbury. *Alexander Turnbull Library, natlib.govt.nz/records/23091108, via Te Ara, the online Encyclopaedia of New Zealand*

As for the road, though it was built earlier, it clung to the side of the mountains over the same stretch and was regularly wiped out by landslides. Indeed, the skeptics had the last laugh in a way, when, after about 130 years the government gave up on trying to repair the worst section and replaced it with the 440-metre long Ōtira Viaduct.

Ōtira Viaduct, *photo by 'Mattinbign', 30 November 2011, CC-BY-3.0 via Wikimedia Commons*

I've got more to say about the pass in the following blog post:

a-maverick.com/blog/arthurs-pass

TOUR 4: The Urbane East Coast

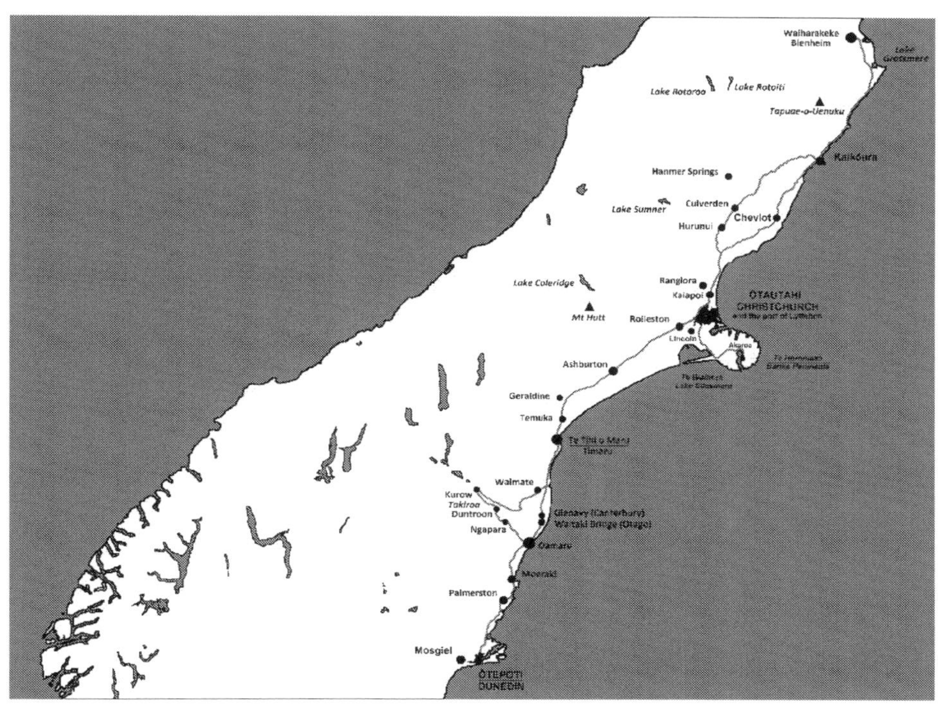

CHAPTER FIFTEEN

Kaikōura: Eating crayfish and watching whales

KAIKŌURA is the most important holiday destination on the east coast between Blenheim and Christchurch. The town sits just to the landward side of a deep submarine trench, whose chilly uplifting waters nourish large populations of crayfish, the namesakes of Kaikōura, which means 'eat crayfish' in Māori.

The town is also just to the seaward side of two ranges of lofty coastal mountains shooting all the way up to the 2,885 m or 9,465-feet Tapuae-o-Uenuku, a very prominent and Himalayan-looking peak that's easily visible from Wellington.

But there's a lot more than just crayfish living in the waters off Kaikōura. Their cousins, the shrimp-like krill that feed the greatest whales, also thrive in these waters, which plunge rapidly to great depths just offshore, as quickly as the mountains rise onshore. These great, cold depths create upwellings that fertilise the sea and nourish the krill. This brings whales that feed on krill, sucking in entire shoals and then filtering out the water through a comb-like structure in their mouths made of a substance called baleen.

Tapuae-o-Uenuku from the Clarence River side. *Photo in* New Zealand Tramper *by lewshaw, added 8 October 2012,*

Another quite different kind of large whale that is often seen at Kaikōura is the sperm whale. Sperm whales can dive up to two thousand metres down or more than a mile, in fact: going down for about 45 minutes at a time and then catching their breath for about fifteen minutes on the surface.

Toothed and predatory in nature, sperm whales actively hunt the giant squid and the even larger colossal squid, the latter as long as the sperm whale at fifteen metres (50 feet) or so, that both dwell in the inky depths. Sperm whales are also believed to prey on the large but inoffensive megamouth shark, a filter feeder which dwells at a similar depth to the huge squid.

Such deep-water prey is sought by the sperm whale, because it needs to eat about a ton of food each day. On the surface the sperm whale is easily seen, in time for any surface creature big enough to be of interest as a meal to get out of its way. So, instead, the sperm whale dives into the sunless depths and seeks out its prey down there. A greater depth of water also offers a greater volume in which to find large prey, which are of course rarer than the small fish that dolphins chase on the surface.

That difference apart, the sperm whale is otherwise a lot like a giant dolphin. For instance, it uses a system of sonar clicks, very similar to that of dolphins, to first find and then stun the creatures it wishes to eat.

Kaikōura is one of the very few places where sperm whales can be seen close to land, as coastal waters are normally too shallow for their style of hunting.

Predators themselves, the giant and colossal squids are almost certainly the kernel of truth behind the tales of horrible sea-monsters that you find in every oceangoing culture from the English to the Māori. Including, in this connection, the tale of Kupe and Te Wheke-a-Muturangi, a struggle that did not take place all that far from Kaikōura after all.

In the words of the nineteenth century French novelist Victor Hugo,

> "These animals are indeed phantoms as much as monsters. They are proved and yet improbable."

If you go online, you can see all sorts of lurid images of sperm whales doing battle with the krakens of the deep. Images that draw their inspiration from actual injuries and scars borne by many sperm whales.

Display of sperm whale and giant squid, Museum of Natural History, New York. *Photo by Mike Goren (2005), CC BY 2.0 via Wikimedia Commons.*

And yet, just as Hugo wrote of the "proved and yet improbable" nature of the largest squids, no such fight to the finish has yet been witnessed by humans even today. If anybody does eventually get photographic proof that these battles royal of the deep really do take place, it may well be obtained off Kaikōura.

"Both jaws, like enormous shears, bit the craft completely in twain."

—*Page 510.*

Vintage Illustration from Moby-Dick

The sperm whale is also the type of whale that features in Herman Melville's *Moby-Dick:* the maddened bull of the seas which, after a day spent fighting tentacled monsters, takes no nonsense from puny human beings either.

You occasionally see photos of people swimming with whales. That's not encouraged at Kaikōura, not only for reasons of sensitivity but also because sperm whales do bite, and also have a powerful sonar that they use to stun their prey even without getting close.

All these whales were, of course, hunted by humans from New Zealand's shores at one time. But today, Kaikōura is a major whale-watching venue. We went for a ride in a plane to try and see some, but we didn't see any whales on this flight, only dolphins (it's a bit of a lottery).

The next day, I paid for another ride in a boat, encouraged by the fact that the boat operators offered an 80% refund if I still didn't see any whales. But fortunately, I did see a couple in the end, and filmed one diving with its flukes in the air.

Sperm Whale diving and blowing at Kaikōura *(video stills)*

As you can see in the photo from the whale-watching plane above – there are several operators by the way, this isn't the only one – the town of Kaikōura is on a rocky peninsula that juts out into the sea. It's a former island with plains to its west now joining it to the mainland, and curving beaches north and south.

There's a lookout on the peninsula where you can look west to both beaches, the plains and the mountains.

The Kaikōura Lookout, looking northward

One thing you can see from there is the oddly terraced nature of the beaches, the result of a 2016 earthquake that raised the whole area by several metres.

Beach on the north side of Kaikōura *(January 2021, a bit over four years since the local 2016 earthquake)*

We stayed at two campgrounds, the Kaikōura Top 10 Holiday Park, which had all the facilities you can think of and is billed as Kaikōura's only 5-star holiday accommodation, and the Kaikōura Peketa Beach Holiday Park, billed as Kaikōura's only beachfront holiday camp. The Peketa camp was more basic and further from town but it was cheaper and, indeed, right on the beach.

My father also had a great fish chowder at the Why Not Café, in the middle of town. That's another recommendation from experience.

A further thing to take in if you are based at Kaikōura, if the weather is good and if you are feeling fit and adventurous, is the relatively easy climb of Mount Fyffe (1,602 metres or 5,256 feet). The summit of Mount Fyffe is only about ten kilometres inland from Kaikōura as the crow flies and there is a four-wheel-drive road all the way to the hut at approximately 1,000 metres, though the gate is normally locked, and you have to gain authorisation to use the road. There are also a number of shorter trails and hikes on the mountain.

Coastal walks in the area are excellent as well. The Kaikōura Peninsula Walkway is public, and there is also a two-day private walk called the Kaikōura Coast Track, which takes in normally inaccessible sections of coast and gullies on private farmland.

Here is the website for the Kaikōura Coast Track, which includes all the details and an impressive photo gallery:
kaikouratrack.co.nz

The Conway Flat Road, which leads to the Kaikōura Coast Track

I did this track, run by local farming families, which includes ravines filled with native bush, over a two-day period. The organisers weren't very good at confirming receipt of my earlier payment and thought I hadn't paid at first. But on the other hand, the families have done wonders for conservation and have transferred some of their land into the Queen Elizabeth II National Trust for conservation and reafforestation purposes. As a casual adult I paid NZ $220 plus $80 for breakfast and cut lunch for two days. I should have paid another $100 for two laid-on evening meals as well – don't be stingy like me!

If you are lucky enough to be in Kaikōura at the right time of year, as we were, you might even see an abundance of kekeno or New Zealand fur seals raising their little pups, which stumble about like adorable kittens, constantly mewing for their mothers.

These rookeries tend to be in secluded spots where people don't go. There is a publicly advertised seal colony at the tip of the Kaikōura Peninsula, which you have to walk to, but at least it is known. On the other hand, we got this last photo, and some videos I shot and put online, entirely by accident. We were driving along an uninhabited stretch of coast near Kaikōura and stopped to take a photo of some rocks with seals on them, a common enough sight on remoter stretches of the New Zealand coast, when we were surprised to see the seals actually nesting under the road-embankment.

It's great to see the population of these colonies coming back: as they, too, were nearly hunted to extinction back in the old days. Today's visitor, not intent on harm, would of course be unwise to get close. For that would not only spook the babies but also incur the ire of the large, bear-like males that guard the colony.

And finally, there are also crags on which seabirds roost, such as Otumatu Rock.

Otumatu Rock

Altogether, the Kaikōura area really is a special and abounding place. You can read more, and see more images, on:

a-maverick.com/blog/kaikoura-eating-crayfish-watching-whales

Other Resources:

The Coastal Pacific railway excursion train runs through Kaikōura. The link is on this website: **greatjourneysofnz.co.nz**.

On the Inland Kaikōura Road, you might also wish to visit the Mount Lyford Lodge and lakes: **mtlyfordlodge.co.nz.**

And you can drive the Alpine Pacific Triangle Route, which includes the Inland Kaikōura Road and a trip further inland to the thermal baths of Hanmer Springs: **newzealand.com/nz/feature/alpine-pacific-triangle.**

CHAPTER SIXTEEN

Christchurch: Gateway to Antarctica, rich in heritage, recovering from crises

WITH an abundance of gothic stone architecture and a large pedestrianised area downtown, Christchurch is more like a quaint old city in Europe than a brash colonial metropolis.

The Christchurch Botanic Gardens, where I'm standing in the photograph above, are next to the Canterbury Museum, founded in 1870, and also on the edge of the vast, downtown, Hagley Park.

The green-banked Avon River that snakes through the middle of town adds further charms to Christchurch. The river isn't named after the Avon in Stratford, England, but after another River Avon in Scotland.

The Avon also bears the Māori name of Ōtākaro, meaning 'of games', because children always traditionally played alongside it while adults gathered food such as flounder, eels, ducks, whitebait and freshwater fish from the river, its swampy surroundings and its estuary, which it shares with another small river called the Ōpāwaho, or Heathcote.

Today's city has the Māori name of Ōtautahi, meaning 'of Tautahi', a rangatira whose pā was on the ground of Banks Peninsula, the rocky quasi-island then known to the Māori as Horomaka or Te Pātaka [storehouse] o Rakaihautū.

Before the days of Tautahi, there was a Waitaha pā on the Ōtākaro called Puari, but in later years it seems that the site of the future Christchurch was abandoned as a permanent habitation, as opposed to a place where one went to gather food.

All in all, the place that Cook named Gore's Bay was a most unpromising place to build a future city.

And yet there is one now. Indeed, I never get sick of visiting the thriving metropolis of Christchurch, or Ōtautahi, which is in fact now the largest city in the South Island, its current population about 420,000 overall.

The city was founded in 1851 by the so-called Canterbury Pilgrims, settlers backed by the Church of England, who decided to build their city on the site the Waitaha had abandoned, investing the more materialistic side of their faith in modern drains.

> **The World Monuments Fund has an online flier with** colour images of the pre-quake Canterbury Provincial Council Buildings and their Great Hall, including its stained-glass windows: wmf.org/sites/default/files/interpretation_panels_-_canterbury_provincial_government_buildings.pdf

The more you think about it the more improbable the very existence of Christchurch, and then the way it turned out, all seem!

It's there now, so enjoy it!

Well, first on my list would be the Christchurch Botanic Gardens and Hagley Park, against which I'm photographed at the start. You could spend hours here, even without visiting the adjacent Canterbury Museum. The small and attractive Robert McDougall Art Gallery, behind, was also an attraction once upon a time; but it closed in 2002 in favour of a new and larger Christchurch Art Gallery Te Puna o Waiwhetū, which opened in 2003 on a different spot.

To continue, Christchurch has strong Antarctic traditions. The New Zealand, American and Italian Antarctic programmes are all based in Christchurch. The unique working museum known as the International Antarctic Centre, beside Christchurch International Airport, is definitely worth a visit.

See the website of the Christchurch Antarctic Office: **christchurchnz.com/christchurch-antarctic-office**.

Here's a picture of me walking through Cathedral Square in autumn with a statue of an early founder, John Robert Godley, in the background.

The city used to be famous for cycling in the 1950s, till they were driven off the roads by automobile traffic. But today, cycling has come back into vogue. There's now an extensive network of cycleways in Christchurch, including Te Ara Ōtākaro Avon River Trail.

Since the earthquakes, the city centre has also started to be encompassed by a ring of parkland called the Frame, built on demolition sites. This should make the downtown area even more pleasant.

For many years there has also been a tourist tramway, which snakes right through some of the buildings downtown and trundles up and down a number of the downtown's quieter streets.

The tramway passes by the Art Deco-style Bridge of Remembrance on Cashel Street

The Bridge of Remembrance, Cashel Street, Christchurch. *Photo by Krzysztof Golik, 15 November 2017, CC-BY-SA 4.0 via Wikimedia Commons.*

Another Christchurch must-see is the still-damaged Christchurch (Anglican) Cathedral in the middle of Cathedral Square. There also used to be an equally impressive Catholic basilica a short distance from the Anglican one, but unfortunately it could not be saved.

On the other hand, there is now a 'Cardboard Cathedral', a temporary but innovative structure designed by the architect Shigeru Ban and made, as the name suggests, of cardboard. Which is apparently quite strong if it's laminated enough times.

Officially called the Transitional Cathedral, this is on the corner of Hereford and Madras Streets.

The banks of the Avon/Ōtākaro are especially attractive to wander along as well. You can even go punting! Punts are held in candy-striped wooden buildings that date back to Victorian times, the Antigua Boat Sheds, which have been used for their original purpose and in their original form since 1882.

Some of the old wooden buildings and archways in Christchurch are just as interesting as the ones made of stone.

It was near the Avon or Ōtākaro, on the west side of Hagley Park, that the tragic mosque shootings of 2019 took place.

Messages on a fence near the Al-Noor Mosque

On a more positive note, another must-visit part of Christchurch is the Arts Centre precinct of old gothic buildings just east of Hagley Park. The tourist tramway goes here as well.

Finally, for the seaside, locally, you can go to New Brighton and Sumner Beaches. New Brighton Beach has a pier that sticks out from an 18-km long beach that extends from the Waimakariri River to the tip of Te Karoro Karoro, the Brighton Spit, which guards the estuary of the rivers, while Sumner Beach has big rocks and is also easier to get to from most parts of town, with a broad promenade.

You can see a longer version of this chapter, with more photographs including photos of the Arts Centre, on **a-maverick.com/blog/christchurch-gateway-antarctica-heritage-recovering-crises.**

See, also, this blog post:

a-maverick.com/blog/autumn-impressions-south-island-new-zealand

And there's a Christchurch App!

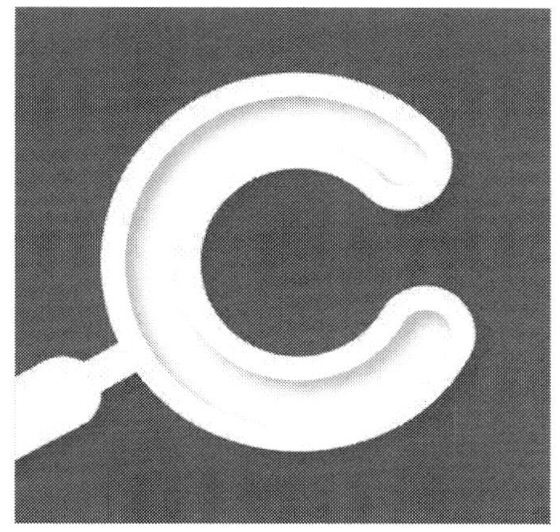

CHAPTER SEVENTEEN

Banks Peninsula and the Port Hills: Hikes, Harbours and more History

Banks Peninsula: *cropped from earthobservatory.nasa.gov/images/3217/christchurch-new-zealand. North near top but not quite at top.*

BANKS Peninsula is an eroded volcano, originally an offshore island, which possesses several natural harbours today. In its topography it resembles one of the Hawai'ian islands, though naturally somewhat colder and bleaker. The biggest harbours on the peninsula are Lyttelton Harbour just south of Christchurch and Akaroa Harbour further east, on the south side.

The peninsula has two Māori names, Horomaka ('foiling of Maka'), a name that refers to events during an ancient punitive raid, and Te Pātaka o Rakaihautū, meaning the storehouse of a famous Māori explorer of the newly occupied land of New Zealand, Rakaihautū.

Legends also have it, variously, that the peninsula was scraped up from a reef, or that the demigod Māui heaped stones over an evil giant or octopus that now sleeps beneath and occasionally cracks the land open when it stirs, a story that's a little too close for comfort in view of the recent Christchurch earthquakes.

Over a long period of time the plains of Canterbury have grown outward toward the peninsula so that it is now no longer an island, just as debris from the mountains has also done at Kaikōura, another former island.

The Port Hills are full of parks and reserves, scenic drives in the form of the Summit Road and Mount Pleasant Road, and rock-climbing cliffs. They yield stunning views of the city and its port of Lyttelton, and there is even a scenic gondola. There are also various windswept hikes that you can do on the tussocky tops. Altogether, like many New Zealand cities, Christchurch is really blessed with nearby nature.

A view from the Christchurch Port Hills, showing Te Karoro Karoro or the Brighton spit, *which guards the estuary of the Avon and Heathcote Rivers and is 'away from it all' even though it's in a city. On the near side of the unbridged estuary, just around the point, is another seaside resort called Sumner. We stayed at the South Brighton Holiday Park, on the spit.*

The hills run down to the sea to form the beaches that lie between the entrance to the Avon/Heathcote estuary and the entrance to Lyttelton Harbour. These beaches include Sumner Beach with its promenade and a smaller one known in Māori as Te Onepoto or 'the short beach' and in English as Taylors

Mistake, after the captain of a little ship who thought he was entering the estuary but wasn't!

A couple of other places to see in this area are:

Āwaroa/Godley Head. The subject of a DOC webpage.

Packhorse Hut. Another attractive short walk is to Packhorse Hut, also the subject of a DOC webpage.

South of the hills, the port town of Lyttelton, with its steep streets and taverns on the corners, reminiscent of some British fishing village, is worth spending time in, itself.

Lyttelton

The other big harbour on the peninsula, Akaroa Harbour, is much quieter. Its main claims to fame predate the foundation of

Christchurch. At the head of the harbour is the site of the Ngāi Tahu pā of Ōnawe on a whale-shaped peninsula that is an island at high tide.

In the summer of 1831-1832 the pā was destroyed, and its inhabitants mostly massacred, by two groups of raiding North Island Māori under the command of the notorious North Island warlord Te Rauparaha.

The 1840 signing of the Treaty of Waitangi was done, locally, in one of the smaller harbours of Banks Peninsula, at a place known as Kawatea or, subsequently, Okains Bay.

The other great pre-Christchurch foundation event on Banks Peninsula was its colonisation by the French, a small-scale event that resulted in the founding of the town of Akaroa and a few other localities with French names such as Duvauchelle and Le Bons Bay.

Akaroa Street Sign showing French street names. *Photo by Egghead06, 17 March 2010, CC-BY-SA 3.0 via Wikimedia Commons.*

The name Akaroa reflects the often non-standard form of South Island Māori dialects (the standard is based on the speech of the more numerous North Island Māori). It's a local variant of Whangaroa, meaning long bay, with k for ng as is common in the south. In addition, the locally rather soft version of the Māori 'wh' sound, common at the beginning of Maori placenames and usually pronounced like a cross between 'wh' in English and an English f, was accidentally omitted by the colonists who first recorded the area's name on paper.

Other such mis-hearings, in other areas, have given rise to placenames that begin with W- or H- alone, in ways that also obscure the original meaning.

There is pressure to restore the 'wh' to all of these non-standard names, which in most cases would require only one more letter and wouldn't alter the name by much. Though, in the case of Akaroa, the Ngāi Tahu spokesperson and tribal leader Tipene O'Regan concedes that any reform that adds two letters to its name may take time to get used to and shouldn't be rushed.

By the time the French got to Akaroa, or Whakaroa as it may yet be known, they found that their rivals had run up the Union Jack at nearby Kawatea (Okains Bay) only a few weeks before. Perhaps if, instead of a village in a remote spot the French had founded a city on the plains where the English would later establish Christchurch, or if they had otherwise just been a big quicker off the mark, France might have had more luck in establishing a South Pacific equivalent of Québec – *c'est la vie.*

'A Walk on the Wildside': The Banks Track

In January 2021, I went for an amazing three-day hike in the hills and down to the coast southeast of Akaroa, at the very extremity of Banks Peninsula. This was the Banks Track, billed as New Zealand's "original private walking track," established by local landowners to bolster their conservation efforts such as the saving of penguins, which it underwrites. I would say that the Banks Track was on a par with one of the Great Walks, and it seems to get nothing but raves on the review sites. I did a blog post all about this track, linked at the end of the present chapter. In the meantime, here is the Banks Track website:

bankstrack.co.nz

All the Peninsula and Port Hills Walks

Including the ones I've mentioned above, there are many walks on Banks Peninsula today. The Rod Donald Banks Peninsula Trust classifies the walks into five groups by area:

- Akaroa Walks
- Diamond Harbour Walks
- Governors Bay Walks
- Lyttelton Walks, and
- Greater Banks Peninsula Walks

The website of the Trust is **bankspeninsulawalks.co.nz.**

Tracks on the Port Hills right next to Christchurch aren't all listed on the Trust website, however. These are listed on a Christchurch City Council website:

ccc.govt.nz/parks-and-gardens/explore-parks/port-hills

These include trails and roadhouses created by the eccentric visionary Harry Ell, whose most imposing legacy is the Sign of the Takahē, a restaurant and conference centre constructed in a style probably best described as Persian gothic.

The Sign of the Takahē. *Photo by Greg O'Beirne, 30 September 2006, CC-BY-SA 3.0 via Wikimedia Commons.*

To see a longer version of this post with more photos, see

a-maverick.com/blog/banks-peninsula-port-hills-christchurch

I also have a separate post on the Banks Track:

a-maverick.com/blog/walk-wildside-new-zealands-banks-track-near-christchurch-yet-remote

Further Resources

Sign of the Kiwi Café and Bar: **signofthekiwi.co.nz**

Sign of the Takahē: **signofthetakahe.co.nz**

DOC.govt.nz Banks Peninsula page:

Akaroa iSite: **visitakaroa.com**

CHAPTER EIGHTEEN

Timaru

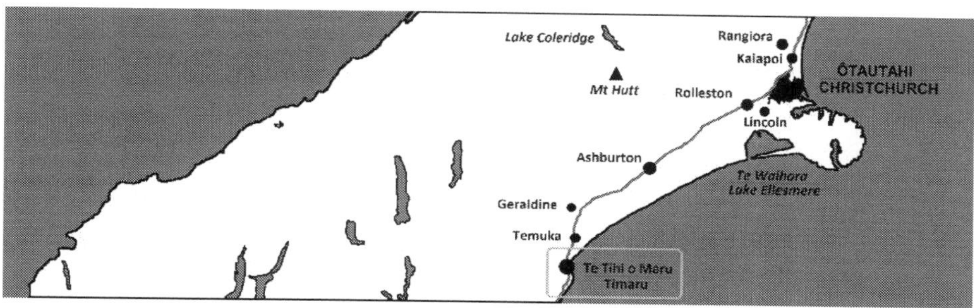

IN Timaru, south of Christchurch, I went to the amazing Te Ana Rock Art Centre, run by the biggest South Island iwi, Ngāi Tahu. Te Ana means 'The Cave'. It displays rock art done by some of the earliest Māori to settle in the region, basically the local equivalent of European ice-age cave-paintings or Aboriginal rock art in Australia. Such 'primitive' art is often amazingly polished and dynamic, as in this museum replica of French cave-paintings of lions, overleaf . . .

Museum replica of a detail from the Chauvet Cave paintings, public domain image via Wikimedia Commons, self-photographed by 'HTO' and taken in the Anthropos museum, Brno, Czech Republic (2009).

. . . and the New Zealand version is no exception. At Te Ana, the local Māori seem to have anticipated Pablo Picasso. As do the Chauvet Cave paintings, come to think of it.

Te Ana is conveniently located in downtown Timaru, in George Street. The museum also runs guided tours into the countryside, to investigate the actual honest-to-goodness caves.

TE ĀNA
NGĀITAHU
Māori Rock Art
Explore the original art
galleries of Aotearoa
Personalised guided tours of our world-class
rock art centre and ancient Māori rock art sites
Open daily: 10am – 3pm
0800 468 3262
www.teana.co.nz

This is what I mean about Picasso:

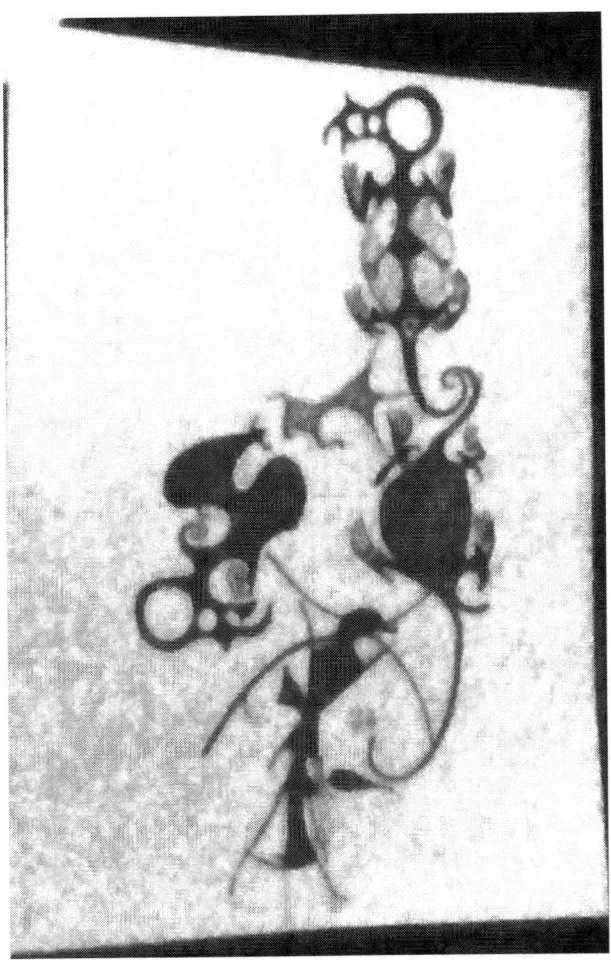

Replica of several cave art motifs at Te Ana

Unfortunately, I wasn't able to get a sharper photo! To make up for it, there's a video of a projected display showing many of the same designs in a blog post that I reference at the end of this chapter.

As you can see from the 1960s example in Chapter 2, Māori rock art has appeared on New Zealand postage stamps. I also noted there that at least one more recent series of Māori rock art-themed stamps has come out: specifically, in 2012.

Many of the rock drawings at Te Ana are a bit different to what most people would think of as traditional Māori art, works such as this, which scholars describe as being in 'classic' style:

Detail from a tāhūhū (ridgepole of a house), Māori, Ngāti Warahoe subtribe of Ngāti Awa, Bay of Plenty, *New Zealand, circa 1840. Believed to represent one of two ancestors: Tūwharetoa or Kahungunu. Auckland Museum, 20 May 2006. Uploaded as a public domain image by 'Kahuroa', via Wikimedia Commons with title information as supplied.*

The differences arise partly because the rock art at Te Ana is a few hundred years older than the 'classic' style. Its origins and significance are also much more obscure. A lot of classic Māori art, like the carving described just above, has a detailed provenance. On other hand, as the first of the following Te Ana displays says, "We don't know exactly who made the rock art."

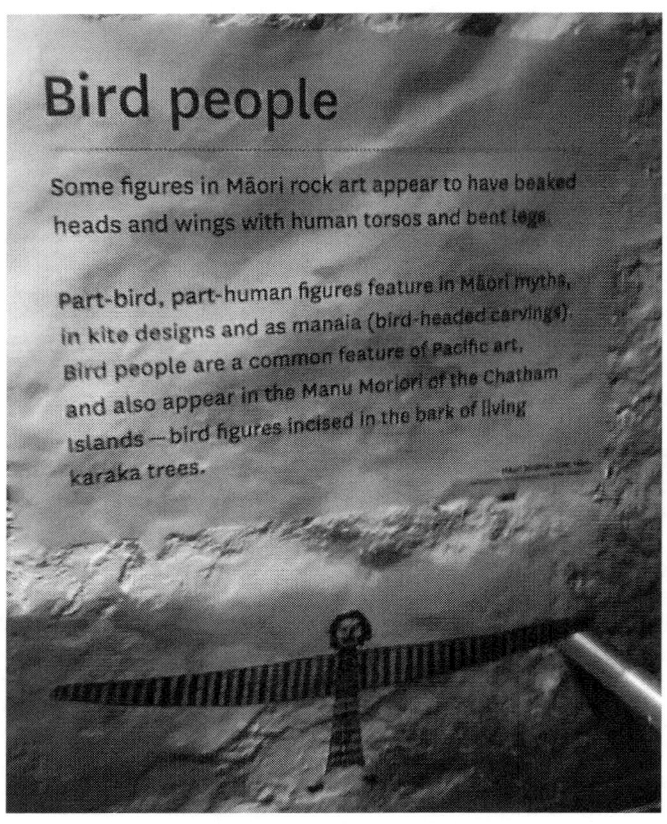

But as I also mentioned in Chapter 2, both the old-time South Island Māori and more recent cultures have in any case developed in ways that are a bit distinct. The person in charge that day, named Wes, filled me in on the local indigenous history as well as some of the differences between the Māori of the South Island and their North Island cousins.

To round off this section, most surviving South Island rock art is found within 70 km of Timaru, and that's why Te Ana is where it is.

Train Time for Timaru

Another thing I noticed when I arrived in Timaru was the not-so-old railway station — now a café.

On the facing page, I've included a map of New Zealand's railway lines at the present time, including the locations of Timaru and Oamaru.

From transport.govt.nz/rail/rail-in-new-zealand, 2020. Crown copyright reserved.

Apparently, tourists turn up all the time at the station café expecting to catch the train. But there ain't none, at least not since 2002.

Passenger trains did run from Christchurch to Dunedin via Timaru and Oamaru until 2002. Oamaru has an older wooden main station dating back to 1900, which had a huge dining room in its day and is still a well-regarded restaurant. In other words, the dining room remains in business even if the passenger trains are not.

In the past, there was also a branch line that went inland from Timaru via Washdyke Flat, Pleasant Point, Cave and Albury to a point just past the touristy inland town of Fairlie, at the foot of the Southern Alps. The Fairlie Branch line followed the approximate course of the modern highway that runs through the same locations.

Here's a map, on the next page, showing the locations of Timaru and the Mount Cook village in yellow boxes in the colour version, and of Pleasant Point and Fairlie in reddish-orange boxes, which look similar in black and white but are a little thinner as drawn.

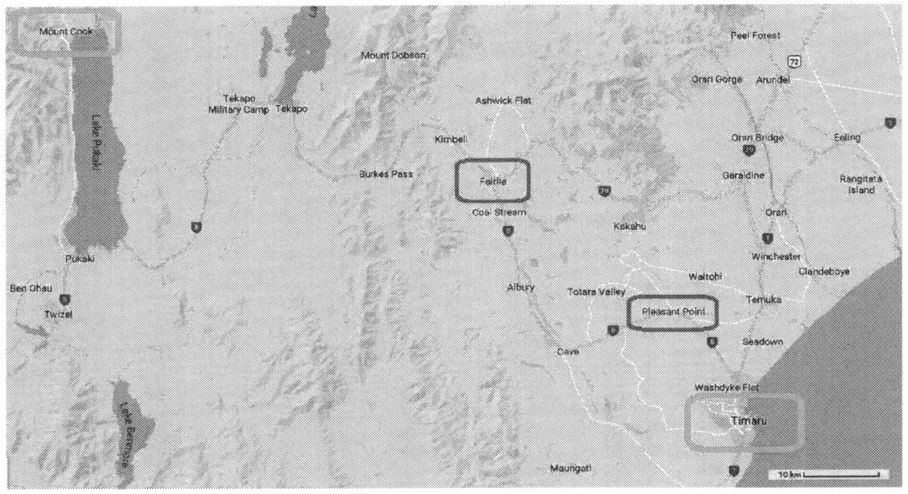

Background map data ©2020 Google

The Fairlie Branch closed in 1968. But before that it took travellers roughly halfway to Aoraki / Mount Cook, with the last part of the journey having to be completed by bus.

Old poster at the Timaru railway station

In those days transport was very strictly regulated in New Zealand, and private buses and trucks weren't allowed to compete head-to-head with the state-owned railways. So, the bus had to wait at Fairlie and couldn't just pick people up at Timaru.

That policy was upheld for many decades on the grounds that if free competition was allowed, the railways would unravel and far too many cars, trucks and buses would end up on the roads.

Just about every town of any size in New Zealand was on a railway line in those days. And each line generally served several towns strung along it like beads on a necklace.

As long as the railways could be kept going — so the politicians of that era maintained — road traffic would be light and accidents infrequent, and the national burden of imported motor vehicles and fuel would also be kept to a minimum. Unlike cars, trucks and buses, trains were built locally from scratch, and powered by local coal and hydro-electricity.

Two and a half kilometres of the Fairlie branch line remain open at Pleasant Point, for excursions.

Freight trains still run through Timaru, servicing its local port.

There are long-distance excursion trains that operate out of Christchurch, and also medium-distance ones that operate out of Dunedin.

But there aren't any excursion trains at Timaru, apart from the Pleasant Point railway.

The mayor of Timaru, and other local worthies, are agitating for Timaru's main-line passenger rail services to be restored.

In a climate-change world, main-line passenger rail may well revive. Indeed, it's perhaps all the more essential that it does in New Zealand, for our tourism numbers are constantly on the up and up, in ways that are leading to more road congestion and road accidents. We drive on the left; most of our tourists come from countries where they drive on the right and, occasionally, they forget what side of the road they are meant to be on or get confused at intersections.

Traffic on State Highway 8, which follows the course of the old Fairlie Branch line and then on to Tekapo, the turnoff to Mount Cook, Ōmārama and points south and inland, is often extremely congested. So, there's a case for reviving not just the Southerner, but also the branch line as well. Perhaps.

At least the roads were congested before Coronavirus. They're quiet now, as of the time of writing. But they will probably keep on becoming more congested after things get back to normal. Recent projections are for 5.1 million overseas tourists a year by 2024, up from 3.7 million in 2017. That is a 37 % increase.

(The title of this section pays homage to John R. Stilgoe's book Train Time: Railroads and the Imminent Reshaping of the United States Landscape.)

The Historic Bluestone Town

As Oamaru (next chapter) is whitestone, so Timaru is bluestone. Which in the local context, refers to a bluish basalt. This is actually fairly common in New Zealand as a source of building-blocks, and not as distinctive as the easily-carved whitestone of Oamaru down the road. Still, it's charming enough.

Some of the bluest bluestone I saw!

Timaru by the Sea, for you and me

I loved the way that Timaru's old buildings clustered around the waterfront and beaches of Caroline Bay. Back in the day, Timaru had a reputation as a sort of Riviera by the sea — like much of New Zealand, in actual fact.

TIMARU
by the Sea
ALL AB

Posters outside the former Timaru Railway Station

Indeed, it pretty much still is like that.

The Otipua Wetland

South of the town, on Saltwater Creek, there is the Otipua Wetland, sixty to seventy hectares or a bit less than two hundred acres of marshy habitat that has been under restoration, by an army of volunteers, for more than twenty years. I got some good photos there too.

The wetland joins up to a coastal track that leads both northward back to the town via Patititi Point, and southward to another prominent coastal point.

For more on Timaru and the neighbouring area, see the following blog posts on my website:

a-maverick.com/blog/from-oamaru-to-timaru

a-maverick.com/blog/train-time-for-timaru

Useful Links

The Te Ana website is linked in the text, but here it is again: **teana.co.nz**

For more on Timaru attractions in general, with an emphasis on things you can do for free, see **wuhootimaru.co.nz**

See also the Timaru App, available on **southcanterbury.org.nz/business-listing/timaru-app**

CHAPTER NINETEEN

I can't believe I haven't stayed here before': The Wonderland of Oamaru

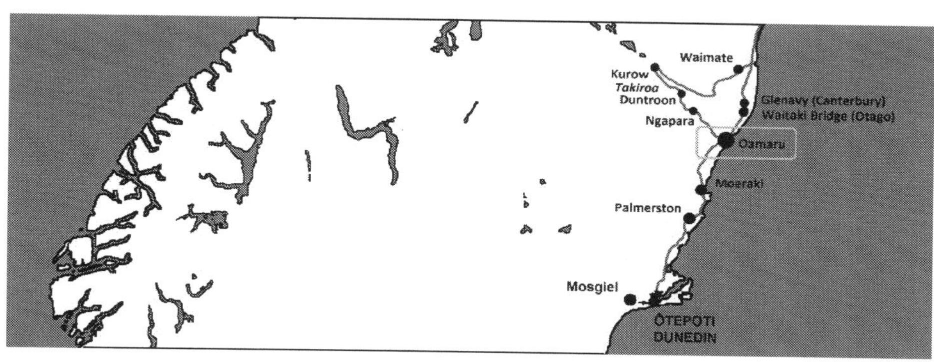

THE archetypal New Zealander is often depicted as some sort of rough and ready type. You might think the towns are, as well. But that's not true of Oamaru, at all, which is very charming and also famous as the home of the writer Janet Frame for the first nineteen or so years of her life.

Information Panel in Eden Street, Oamaru

There's a great early Jane Campion film about Janet Frame called *An Angel at My Table* (1990). These days, Jane Campion's been directing *The Power of the Dog.*

Oamaru is also famous for the grand-looking stone buildings that line its main streets. Public magnificence was a top priority for Oamaru's founders, who exploited nearby outcrops of limestone to craft a town nicknamed 'the Whitestone City', even though it only has a population of fourteen thousand.

You can see some of these outcrops on a scenic road into Oamaru, the road from Duntroon via Ngapara: they're well worth visiting in their own right! Limestone is made from millions of seashells squashed together, and the limestone outcrops occasionally yield larger fossils. There's even a 'Valley of the Whales' similar to Egypt's Wadi El Hitan, of which the latter has received a lot of publicity in print and on the TV from National Geographic and was designated a World Heritage site in 2005. The Valley of the Whales near Oamaru isn't as famous or protected as yet.

Looking toward the south end of Thames Street, Oamaru

Another view along Thames Street

Formal gardens lead, by way of the Oamaru Walkway, to a lookout point from which you can gaze down onto the town.

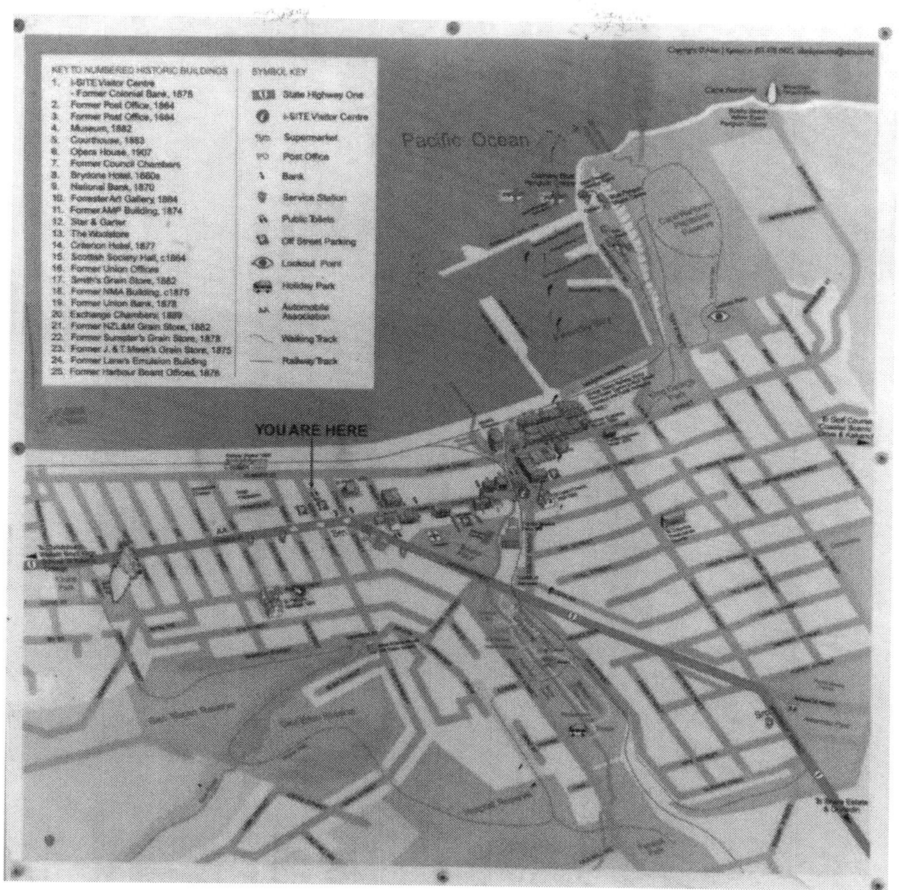

Photograph of a public information sign showing the layout of Oamaru's parklands, *artwork by Allan Kynaston Visual Communications, of Dunedin*

Wharves and penguins

Oamaru used to be quite an important port for the offloading of rural produce from North Otago, which is where all the money came from to build the town in the old days. It's got a sort of industrial foreshore with lots of wharves and warehouses, all fairly disused these days other than as tourist attractions. Hold that thought, for I'll be coming back to it!

There's a lookout at a still-forested place near Oamaru called Bushy Bay where you can hear, and occasionally see, the yellow-eyed penguins that nest there. There are lots of signs up saying not to disturb them, though there doesn't seem to be any actual enforcement as such. There are also seals at Bushy Bay: snoozing females and males that rear up if anyone gets too close. Again, this seems fairly unregulated.

Bushy Bay lookout

You can also go on tours of (less endangered) little blue breeding sites, where seeing the penguins is more or less guaranteed, though it costs NZ$40 and I'd already seen one! In fact, if you hang around this locality for long enough, you're bound to: 'penguins crossing' is not a joke sign, in these parts it's for real.

The Moeraki boulders

Further south, there are the epic Moeraki boulders, weird spherical concretions that have grown like giant pearls around some initial irritant of nature. They seem to have grown in the sand-cliffs above the beach, which are constantly being eroded by the waves. The round boulders pop out and lie on the beach.

A few of the Moeraki boulders

The industrial district

Meanwhile, back in Oamaru town, there's a present-day industrial precinct toward the workaday northern end, where the tourists don't go. Even this has some remarkable Victoriana amid the more recent wonders of the electric age.

Oamaru Railway Station buildings at dusk

The origin of the name Oamaru, and whether it should now be spelt with a tohutō (macron), both seem uncertain at present. It may mean 'place of Maru': a semi-mythological folk-hero to whom the name of Timaru, further up the coast, may also refer.

Oamaru has lately reinvented itself, and its oldest colonial precinct, as New Zealand's capital of Steampunk and Victoriana.

And so, the very oldest part of town has become a sort of walk-through museum of colonial days.

A museum of everything from a rather impressive collection of penny-farthings to paisleyish William Morris wallpaper (and souvenir coffee-mugs in the same style).

The buildings themselves are half the exhibit.

I walked through Atomic Café, one of the biggest cafés in the world it would seem, a whole block wide:

And I visited the community radio station headquarters, where there are a lot of old radios — admittedly not Victorian in origin!

But for me the real highlight was the Steampunk HQ: the steampunk museum, if you can call an exhibition of things totally made-up a museum.

A literally underground railroad locomotive

There's also a great waterfront park area nearby.

The Oamaru waterfront park

I explored the city's Victorian churches, all of them built in the 1860s and 1870s — another source of local magnificence altogether!

For more on Oamaru, including a lot more visual material, see the following post on my website:

a-maverick.com/blog/wonderland-oamaru

CHAPTER TWENTY

The North Coast into Dunedin

THE coast between Moeraki and Dunedin is a really attractive area, with lots of beaches.

Waikouaiti Beach, Karitane Headland and Karitane Beach, looking north from Seacliff

The coast north of Dunedin. *Background imagery ©2019 CNES/Airbus, Landsat/Copernicus, Maxar Technologies, Planet.com. Map data ©2020 Google.*

At the main-road junction town of Palmerston, between Moeraki and Waikouaiti, I stopped to take a picture of the historic St James Presbyterian Church, built all the way back in 1876, and the adjacent Clark Sunday School Hall. This isn't the only 1870s building in Palmerston, either. Pretty impressive for a small town: Otago's like that!

The area is famous for its fishing industry. And so, at Waikouaiti, which also sports a nature reserve, I stopped in at the hamlet's famous Fish Inn for some very nice and reasonably affordable fish and chips.

Waikouaiti is culturally significant to Māori. You can do guided walking tours, conducted by local Māori, of the Huriawa Pā which sits on a spectacular headland, and also explore the river mouth in outrigger and double-hulled waka (canoes): see **karitanemaoritours.com**.

I turned left to go to Matanaka Farm. This is thought to be the oldest surviving commercial farm in New Zealand, dating back to 1838. The buildings, erected soon after the farm was established, are said to be the earliest colonial farm buildings to still stand in their original position in New Zealand.

The farm was founded and settled by a band of Australians led by a Sydney-born whaler named Johnny Jones. The Australians brought everything they needed over from Sydney including the materials for the buildings. The big trees in the photograph below are Australian eucalypts ('gum trees'); a larger grove of eucalypts casts the shadows that you can see.

Matanaka Farm

From Matanaka I slowly continued on, via Seacliff, to the gothically-lettered city limits of Dunedin.

For a continuation of the story, see my blog post:

a-maverick.com/blog/north-coast-into-dunedin

CHAPTER TWENTY-ONE

Dunedin: the 'Edinburgh of the South'

AFTER travelling down the coast, you can go up and over the hills north of Dunedin, past the Orokonui Ecosanctuary and over Mount Cargill via the local road, which is an alternative to the faster but more boring State Highway 1.

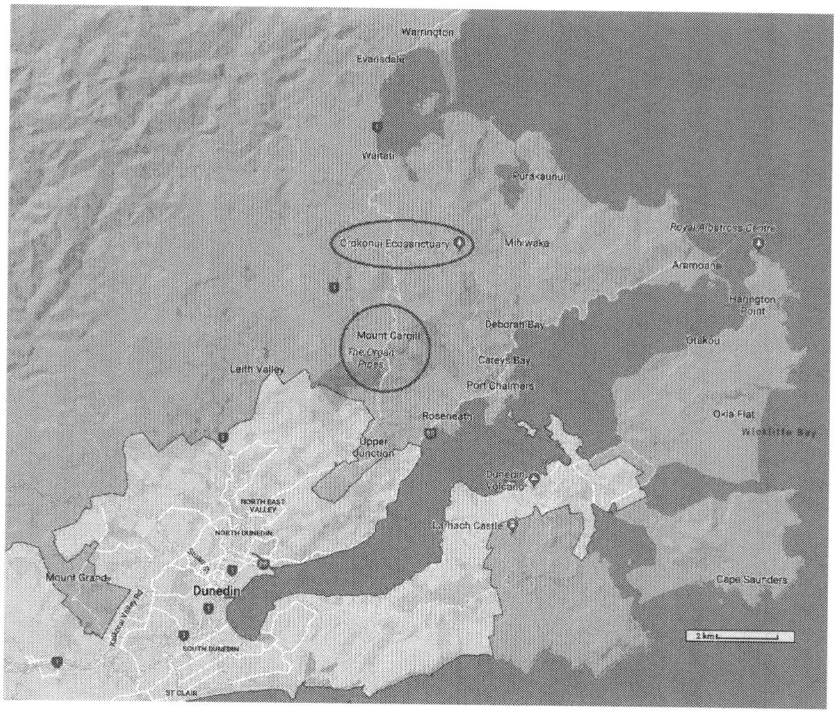

Dunedin and Port Chalmers. *Background map data ©2019 Google. Red circle and ellipse indicating the sites of Mt Cargill and the Orakonui Ecosanctuary added.*

From Mount Cargill, you can see downtown Dunedin and also Port Chalmers. There's also a short but steep track to the Organ Pipes, a natural formation of six-sided basalt columns similar to the ones that can be seen in Holyrood Park, Edinburgh.

The track continues to the top of Mount Cargill, which is also accessible by way of a gravel road called Cowan Road (there's a TV tower on top) and several walking tracks in fact.

But when I entered Dunedin, I took the alternative, quicker route via State Highway One. I would backtrack to Mount Cargill later on.

If you are driving, the best place to park once you make it into Dunedin's built-up area is in the industrial area east of the city's amazing, heritage-listed railway station. You can then walk to the city by way of an overbridge across the railway lines.

On the Dunedin Railway Station Overbridge

A better view of the station and the gardens in front

A signboard showing major downtown attractions

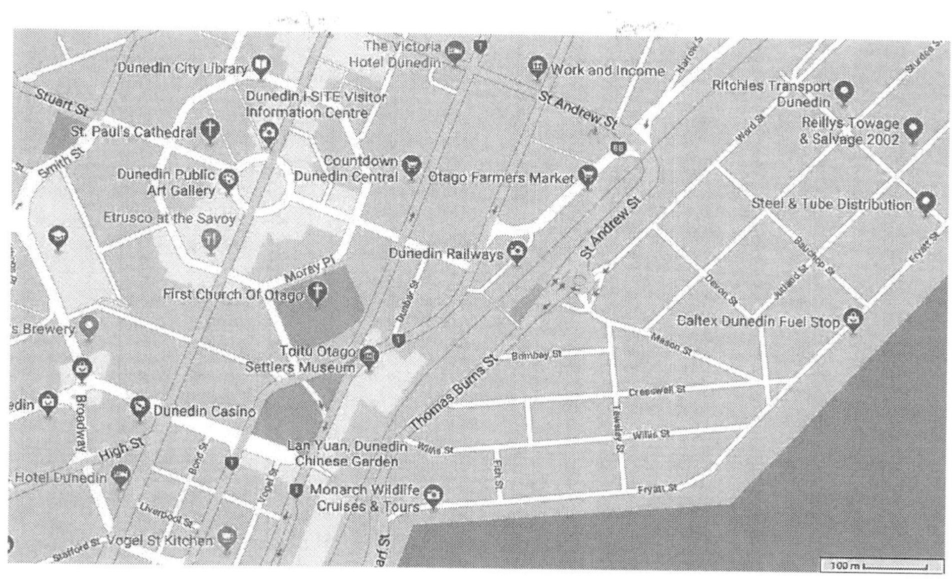

The industrial area east of 'Dunedin Railways', Thomas Burns St and St Andrew St is the best place to park. *Map data ©2020 Google.*

I walked around the middle of the city, which I never get tired of visiting. West of the railway station, the central area is dominated by a plaza called the Octagon, which has a row of bus stops under street trees in the middle.

The Octagon is modelled on Moray Place in the New Town of Edinburgh, with its own Moray Place around the outside of the Octagon. Indeed, Dunedin is sometimes referred to as the Edinburgh of the south. Its very name is based on the Scots Gaelic name for Edinburgh, that is, Dùn Èideann.

Downtown Dunedin and St Clair Beach. *Map data ©2020 Google*

I went to St Clair beach south of Dunedin for a while, and then to the Art Gallery, which I could get into for free. They had an exhibition of the paintings of Frances Hodgkins, a noted New Zealand artist of the early 20th century. Hodgkins was famous for her later cubist works, but I liked her earlier, more naturalistic paintings better.

More exciting, perhaps, was the Warrior Museum. This is full of lifelike and expressive statues of warriors from around the world. I don't know whose idea this was, I suspect it's some kind of spinoff from the whole *Lord of the Rings* thing.

The Dunedin Town Belt is a historic and enlightened bit of Victorian town planning, similar to the Adelaide Parklands in South Australia. In Dunedin, the Town Belt surrounds the inner city almost completely on the landward side, linking up to the Dunedin Botanic Gardens in the north.

You can just see the edge of a sign here saying 'Town Belt'

The inner city is in a sort of a bowl surrounded by a suburban plateau, with some notoriously steep streets leading down to the inner city (steeper than anything in San Francisco).

Steep streets

Parts of the town belt are also on Dunedin's steep terrain. But the town belt doesn't just include steep bits. It also includes more level areas such as Woodhaugh Gardens. I went for a walk with my Airbnb host in these gentler parts.

In the middle of the town belt, there's the historic homestead of Olveston House, built by the Theomin family. The Theomins were friends and supporters of Frances Hodgkins, and also of Truby King, one of Dunedin's many social reformers.

After the Town Belt, I backtracked to Mt Cargill and went for a serious hike there.

Dunedin from Mt Cargill, *with the inner harbour visible as a blue pond, the middle harbour hidden by a hill*

Port Chalmers outer harbour from Mt Cargill

The Orokonui Ecosanctuary is a place I would like to visit next time. Mount Cargill is up high, but nearby Orokonui is actually a low wetland, now being ecologically restored. The same is being done at St Clair Beach south of Dunedin.

There's a lot more in the blog posts that I link to at the end of this chapter. But before I round off with a discussion of the Māori history of the region, I should add that there are also some very worthwhile excursion trains to go on, both up the Taieri Gorge into the interior, now called the Inlander, and also along the northern coast, the subject of the last chapter, as far as Oamaru. That service is called the Seasider.

Here is the the website for Dunedin's excursion trains:

dunedinrailways.co.nz

These days, Ōtepoti is an accepted if unofficial alternative name for Dunedin, and there is also mockup of the old former pā of that name, on the site of what's now the downtown area, in the Toitū Otago Settlers Museum. Which is hugely worth visiting, by the way, along with the Otago Museum. Here are their respective websites:

toituosm.com and **otagomuseum.nz**

But, aside from the terms of the Ngāi Tahu settlement in 1998 and a few others like it, I don't see the former Māori inhabitants of cities like Dunedin recapturing any of the real estate gains that have been made since the official culture of the town was changed from Māori to Scottish and Ōtepoti transformed into the Octagon, any time soon.

Finally, for a visitor, I'd just like to say that this chapter has barely scratched the surface of all that Dunedin/Ōtepoti has to offer, and I you may wish to click onto the blog posts at the end of this chapter as well as the websites I mention, and download the My Little Local Dunedin tourism app:

Visit Dunedin: **dunedinnz.com**. See, in particular, Visit Dunedin's guide to Walking Tracks and Trails, which includes everything from city heritage walks to more adventurous rambles in the great outdoors some distance from town: **dunedinnz.com/visit/see-and-do/outdoor-activities/walking**

VisitaCity: Comes up with 66 recommendations if you enter Dunedin, New Zealand: **visitacity.com**

The Otago Central Rail Trail starts from Middlemarch, at the extreme end of the Inlander's rail excursion line (though the Inlander only runs to Hindon at present), following the remainder of the old railway route into the interior: **otagocentralrailtrail.co.nz**. You can do the trail, or a section of it, either freelance or as a paid package, including transport, provided by local tourism operators. For instance, **trailjourneys.co.nz** offers a one-day package from Dunedin where you cycle from Waipiata to Hyde through a section of the upper Taieri Gorge. There are also plans for a cycle trail along the north coast, from Dunedin to Oamaru!

Local Tourism App

My Little Local Dunedin

Blog Posts with More Images

a-maverick.com/blog/dunedin-and-the-taieri-gorge-railway

a-maverick.com/blog/sounding-out-dunedin

a-maverick.com/blog/dunedins-town-belt-olveston-house-backtrack-mt-cargill

TOUR 5: Aoraki and the Canterbury Lakes

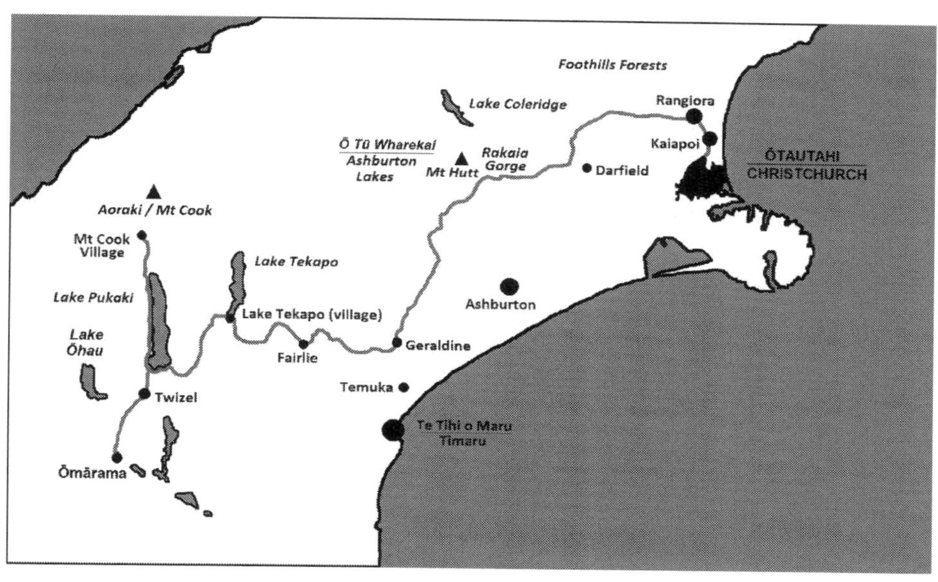

CHAPTER TWENTY-TWO

Canterbury Surprise: The Foothills of the Alps

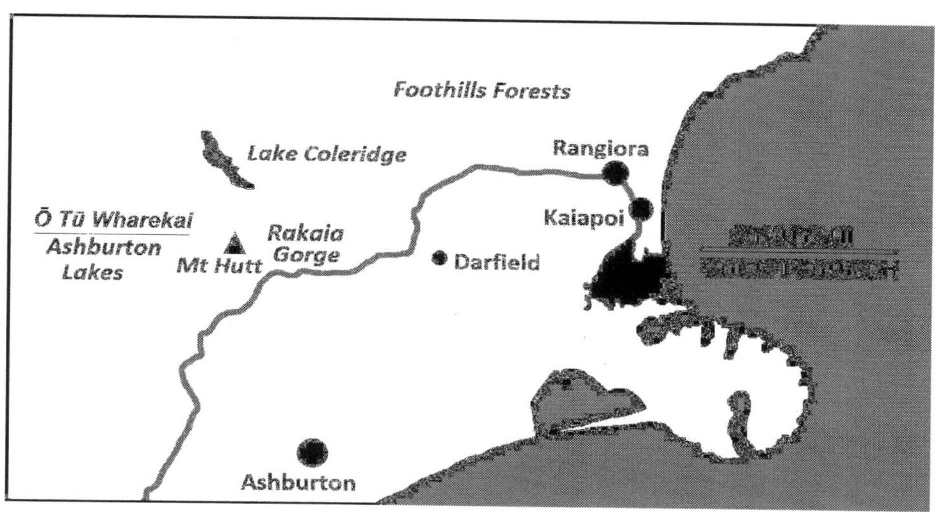

To the West: The Ashburton Lakes (and Mountains)

IN the Ō Tū Wharekai/Ashburton Lakes district southwest of Christchurch, Mount Guy (1,319 m/4,327 feet) and the chilly Lake Clearwater (667 m/2,188 feet) are in the middle of a nexus of tracks and a cluster of other lakes and peaks, foothills of the Southern Alps.

DOC describes the area, with its twelve smallish lakes and the headwaters of the Rangitata River and damp hollows in the ground called kettle-holes, left by melting blocks of ice, as a nationally significant intermontane (between-mountains) wetland system.

Whence the name Ō Tū Wharekai, which builds on the word for banquet hall or dining room (wharekai) and refers to the fact that the wetlands in this area were an important source of food in earlier times. The area is also one through which people used to travel on the way to gather pounamu on the West Coast, stocking up on food as they did so.

Today, you can camp by the lakes, as I did recently, and spend your time doing several day-walks including the Mount Somers Circuit.

The Te Araroa Trail, New Zealand's long trail, runs through this area.

You are also close to Erewhon, the setting of the English writer Samuel Butler's fictional utopia *Erewhon,* but also an actual place.

See the DOC page 'Lake Clearwater tracks'

Driving from Christchurch to Lake Clearwater via the Inland Scenic Route, you can also stop off at:

- **Washpen Falls.** This is a privately-owned locality on a private track through a scenic gorge. It's very highly rated by 'glampers', but basic access only costs NZ $10 for adults, on **washpenfalls.co.nz**. The private website notes that Washpen Falls has featured as a Hollywood filming location.

To the North: The Foothills Forests and their Peaks

To the north and northwest of Christchurch, four joined-together forest parks called the Oxford, Glentui, Mt Thomas and Mt Grey/Maukatere Forest Parks form a ring partway around the city. Within the Foothills Forests, as they are called, several medium-sized mountains, more foothills of the Southern Alps, look directly down on the city and the plains and also into the interior, with summit tracks that range from easy to advanced:

- **Mount Grey/Maukatere.** The 934 m (3,064 feet) Mount Grey or Maukatere is not the highest peak in the area, but has the advantage of being comparatively easy to ascend by way of one of the tracks to the top. See the DOC page on 'Mount Grey/Maukatere tracks'.

- **Mount Oxford.** (1,364 m / 4,475 feet). See the DOC page on 'Mount Oxford tracks'.

- **Mount Thomas.** (1,023 m / 3,356 feet). See the DOC page on 'Mount Thomas tracks'.

- **Mount Richardson.** (1,047 m / 3.435 feet). See the DOC page on 'Mount Richardson tracks'. These include the Glentui Loop Track partway up Mount Richardson, itself the subject of a DOC webpage.

The Foothills Forests also contain:

- **Ryde Falls.** A five-tier waterfall on a lengthy, but easy walking track. See the DOC webpage on 'Ryde Falls tracks'.

In Between: Mount Hutt, Lake Coleridge, and the Rakaia Gorge

On the eastern fringes of the Hakatere Conservation Park you find Mount Hutt, a well-known skifield in winter, also has some tracks that you can explore in summer. Mount Hutt is close to Lake Coleridge, the largest lake in the region, which also has one of New Zealand's earliest hydroelelectric power stations on it; and, to the scenic Rakaia Gorge and its walkway.

Here's a longer version of the current post, with photos and personal stories including my ascent of Mount Somers:

a-maverick.com/blog/the-foothills-of-the-alps

More resources:

backyardtravelfamily.com/washpen-falls-canterbury

DOC: 'Canterbury Foothills Forests Brochure' (PDF)

CHAPTER TWENTY-THREE

Aoraki/Mount Cook: another deadly peak

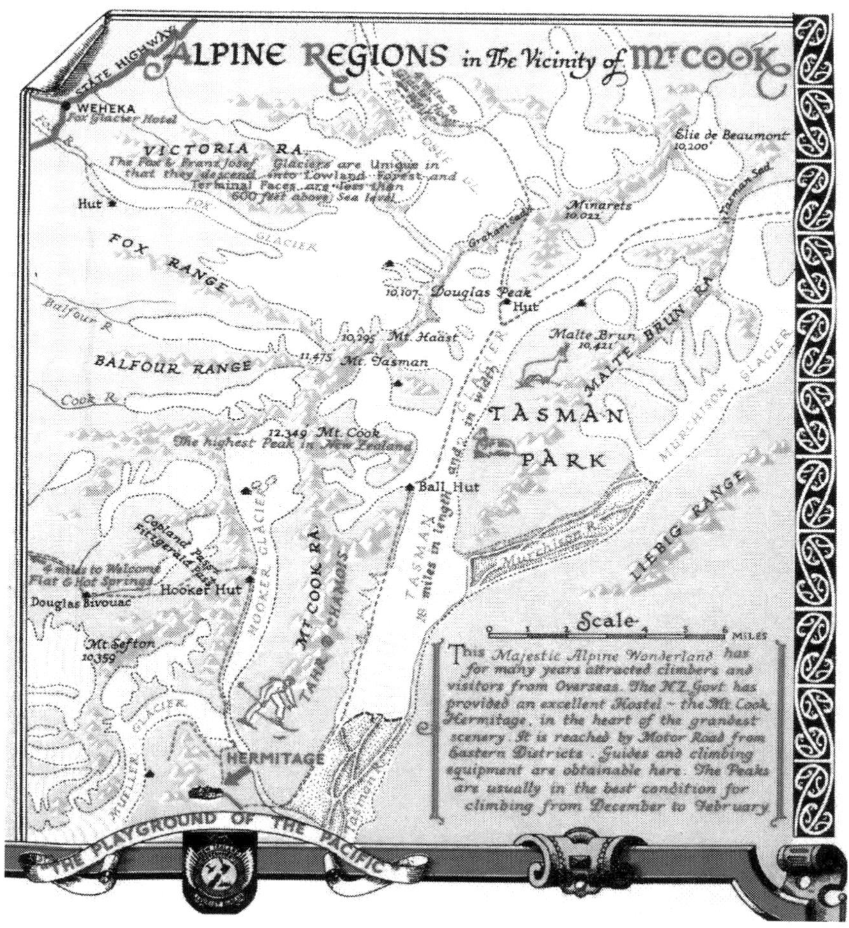

***Map of the Aoraki/Mount Cook Region dated 1946,** a detail from a larger 'Tourist Map of New Zealand' drawn for the NZ Government Tourist Board, on display at the Auckland Public Library in April 2018. Crown copyright reserved.*

NEW Zealand's highest peak, Aoraki/Mount Cook, lies at the heart of a national park that combines dangerous mountaineering opportunities with simple, scenic daywalks and the start of the Alps 2 Ocean cycle trail, which goes all the way down to Oamaru.

Mount Cook Village, at the foot of Aoraki/Mount Cook, is totally accessible by car and bus, and you can use it as a base for activities that are as adventurous as you like.

Walks you can do in the vicinity of Mount Cook Village without getting into actual mountaineering include the Hooker Valley Track, which gets close to the Hooker glacier, and walks along the Tasman Valley that in their turn bring you to the Blue Lakes and the Tasman Glacier.

At the Hooker Glacier, Aoraki/Mount Cook

An old 1930s-type poster at Mount Cook Village

See the webpage **doc.govt.nz/hooker-valley-track**, and also download the brochure *Walking Tracks in Aoraki/Mount Cook National Park* from DOC, which covers the Hooker Valley Track more briefly and also a range of others including the Tasman Valley walks.

For the cycleway from the Hooker Valley to Oamaru, see **alps2ocean.com.** The Alps 2 Ocean cycle trail also has an alternative beginning at nearby Lake Tekapo.

In the remainder of this chapter, I will talk about a gnarly mountaineering skills training adventure I went on, and then reflect on earlier generations of climbers, including women who went up in long dresses and hobnailed boots.

My High Alpine Skills Training adventure

WE started our High Alpine Skills training course near Mt Cook Village, staying at the New Zealand Alpine Club's Unwin Lodge, which was a very eerie place. Every time I had stayed there, I couldn't believe the stories I heard about dreadful accidents from people who'd actually seen them happen. For instance, one time I was sitting in the lounge and a party of four climbers came up and were let in sombrely by the hut warden, as they had lost someone on the mountain. It was the sort of place where death was quite a frequent occurrence.

As with diving, you always climb with a partner too (at the very least, somebody has to hold the other end of the rope!) Before the course started, I remember talking to a woman who told me that she and her climbing partner had pitched their tent half under a flat rock face and half out in the open. An avalanche had come down and completely covered her climbing partner. She had to dig her partner out and said they were lucky to be alive because they both could have died.

I remember thinking, 'Oh, this climbing business is *quite* risky'; for generally I am fairly conservative when it comes to taking risks.

Aoraki/Mt Cook foothills terrain: *Tramping back to the Unwin Lodge*

At 3,724 metres high (12,218 feet), Aoraki/Mt Cook is New Zealand's tallest mountain and one that has long offered a challenge for aspiring climbers. To Ngāi Tahu, the peak also represents a revered ancestor from the days when the forebears of the Māori left island Polynesia for their new home, and is therefore tapu, meaning sacred or forbidden.

All the same, European explorers have come to the area from the time of earliest settlement until now to attempt the climb. These include Sir Edmund Hillary, who learnt his mountain-craft on Mt Cook and its surrounding peaks.

Current New Zealand Government cultural guidelines recommend not standing right at the top, not cooking or eating right at the top, and to bring down all rubbish and toilet waste (which people should do anyway).

The Aoraki/Mt Cook National Park was established in 1953 to protect the mountainous area, even though some of the land in the park is still privately owned.

To start with, we trekked some way up the nearby Sealy Range, and my feet became covered in blisters. We did some training and learnt belaying, and then tramped back down to Unwin Lodge. From Unwin Lodge, we flew by helicopter up and over the charming Sealy Tarns to the Barron Saddle Hut to start our alpine training in earnest.

Once we got there, we found out that an earlier hut at a nearby location, the Three Johns Hut, had been blown over a precipice by the wind in 1977. Three people inside at the time were killed. Huts on Mt Cook have also been taken out by avalanches.

The Barron Saddle Hut was a metal cylinder which looked like it been designed by an engineer to handle extreme natural forces. Even this survival bunker had lately had some of its windows blown in, or sucked out, by the local whirlwinds. Their empty frames were covered over by wood. I got no sleep whatever at first, worrying about all the ways the elements seemed to be conspiring against us.

From the hut, we went via Barron Saddle to stay overnight on Mt Annette on the Sealy Range. There was a beautiful sunset over the Mt Cook/Aoraki mountain range. I'd brought a 'bivvy' on the trip, a weatherproof bag that zips over your sleeping bag for sleeping outdoors. But I had left it behind in Barron Saddle

Hut by mistake, because I was so tired. In the end, I had to borrow an emergency blanket off one of the instructors. I wrapped the survival blanket around my sleeping bag and our group slept outside under the stars that night, huddled together.

It was beautiful, though cold. But I had enough clothes on, about three or four layers, to cope.

The instructors were more than professional, keeping an extra eye on people like me who were relatively inexperienced. After getting nervous initially due to the unnerving Unwin Lodge tales and the history of Barron Saddle and Three Johns, I felt completely safe in the hands of the instructors.

It had been quite an adventure and Mt Cook was stunning, but the whole time I just didn't feel comfortable with my level of alpine skills. I haven't given up on that sort of thing, but I'm going to take a step back and think I'm better off with a guide in such mountainous areas.

I'll probably need to get some better climbing boots too because at the end of the alpine course it took my feet a month to repair from all the blisters I got.

***Top to bottom:** The High Alpine Skills course class photo; learning knots; one of the Sealy Tarns*

Top to bottom: *The Barron Saddle Hut; a closer view of the Barron Saddle Hut with its damaged windows; sleeping out under the stars.*

The ones who began it all

Having done all this training, I am in awe of early climbers who ascended these mountains in hobnailed boots. I was fascinated to learn how the nail-heads poking out of the bottoms of the boots, initially quite blunt, took on more and more pointy forms until one day someone hit on the idea of removable crampons, which could be made pointier still and then taken off when they weren't needed.

Climbers also ascended in long skirts and generally respectable looking attire if they were women in the Victorian era, as surprisingly many were. A more informal look had come in by the 1930s, however.

On the facing page, I've put together a collage of some photographs of well-known early climbers in this area.

'Mountaineering Group' photographed by Joseph James Kinsey, 20 Feb. 1896, at Kea Point near today's Mount Cook Village. From left, rear, Matthias Zurbriggen, unidentified, Jack Clarke. From left, front, 'Signor Borsalino', unidentified, May Kinsey, unidentified. Zurbriggen and Clarke were prominent, pioneering alpinists in New Zealand at this time, and J. J. Kinsey would later be knighted for services to Antarctic exploration.

Ref. PA1-q-137-66-1, Alexander Turnbull Library, Wellington, New Zealand.

Freda du Faur, first woman to climb Aoraki / Mount Cook.

Photograph by George Mannering *circa* 1910, Canterbury Museum, Christchurch, NZ.

'Mount Oates Mountaineering Party at the Mingha River', 15 February 1931. From left, Betsy Blunden, John Dobree Pascoe and Bryan Barrer. Betsy Blunden was the first woman to work as a guide at Mount Cook, from 1928 onward, and the world's first female alpine guide. Pascoe would go on to become a famous photographer. Barrer was also a well-known mountaineer.

Ref. PA1-o-407-089-5, Alexander Turnbull Library.

For more, see my blog post:

a-maverick.com/blog/aoraki-mount-cook

CHAPTER TWENTY-FOUR

An Accessible – not inaccessible – wilderness for solo women travellers!

IN NEW ZEALAND, it is easy for solo women travellers to get into the wilderness, whether you are an adventurer, hiker, mountaineer or photographer, or just an ordinary person.

You can find cheap places to stay everywhere, using campsite phone apps.

Whether you choose to buy a car or rent a car there are so many ways of travelling New Zealand, on good roads.

Here is my latest story.

I parked my car at Christchurch airport, where they charged $7 a day, while I was in Auckland on business.

When I arrived back at Christchurch, I got picked up from the plane by the carpark operators and taken to the carpark, all part of the service.

I drove south to Queenstown with a friend named Diana, through the picturesque towns of Fairlie and Tekapo.

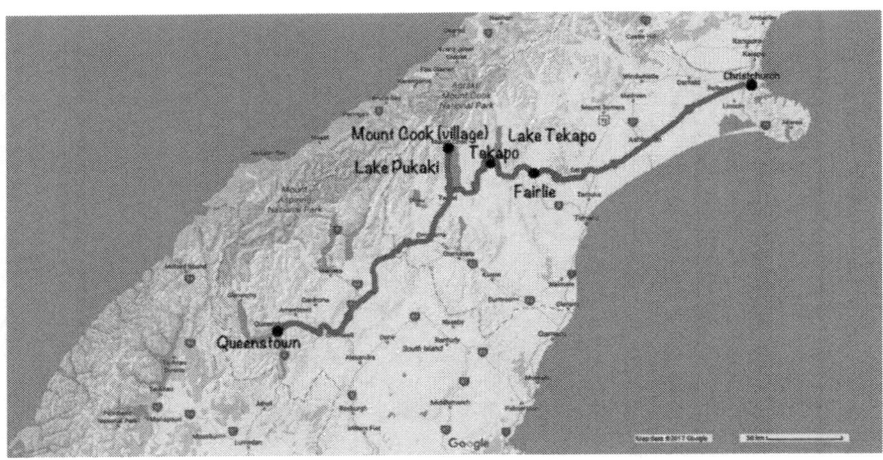

Journey from Christchurch to Queenstown, with places mentioned in the text. *Background map data ©2017 Google. The route taken was added in red. Five places visited were added similarly as black dots, and six place names were added in the Noteworthy font.*

There's a really excellent Youtube video of Tekapo, showing the picturesque Church of the Good Shepherd, which looks very old but was actually built in the 1930s. 'Lake Tekapo—New Zealand' by Mark Gee, 'The Art of Night' (2016) This area is an International Dark Sky Association Dark Sky Reserve, actually the largest in the world and excellent for stargazing.

We detoured west along the shore of Lake Pūkaki and stayed at a backpackers' hostel at Mount Cook Village.

***Lake Pūkaki.** Photo by Krzysztof Golik, 17 November 2017, CC-BY-SA 4.0 via Wikimedia Commons.*

Variable weather made for a more interesting holiday, and more interesting photos, than if the weather had been totally fine!

Here are some of my photos:

Dramatic flaring skies

Dramatic skies on the road

At Aoraki / Mount Cook

For more, see these blog posts:

a-maverick.com/blog/new-zealand-accessible-wilderness-solo-women-travellers

a-maverick.com/blog/autumn-impressions-south-island-new-zealand

TOUR 6: Queenstown, Wānaka and the Waitaki Valley

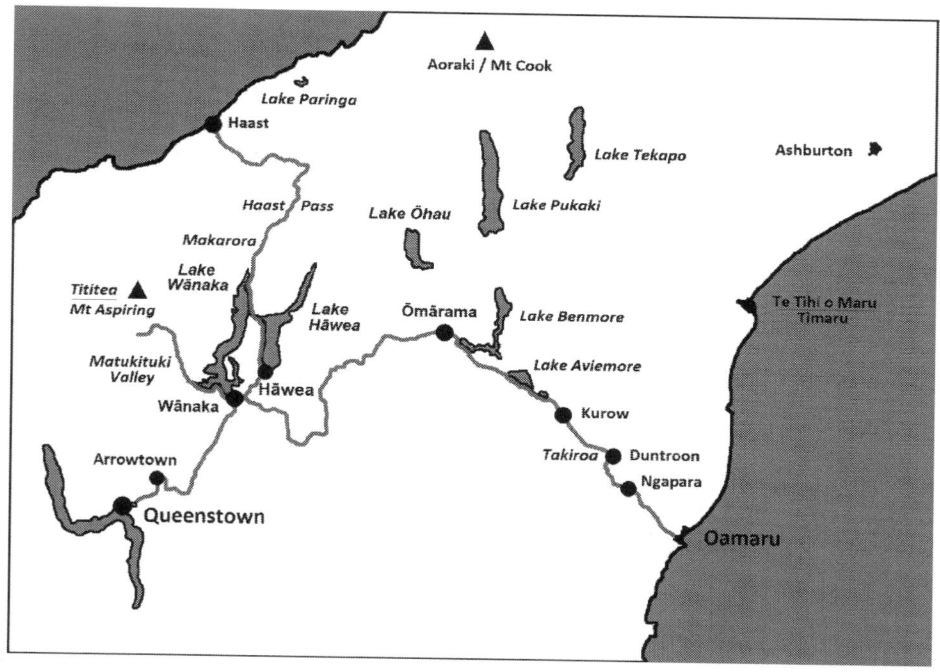

CHAPTER TWENTY-FIVE

From Haast to Wānaka

A scenic highway with lakes and hikes

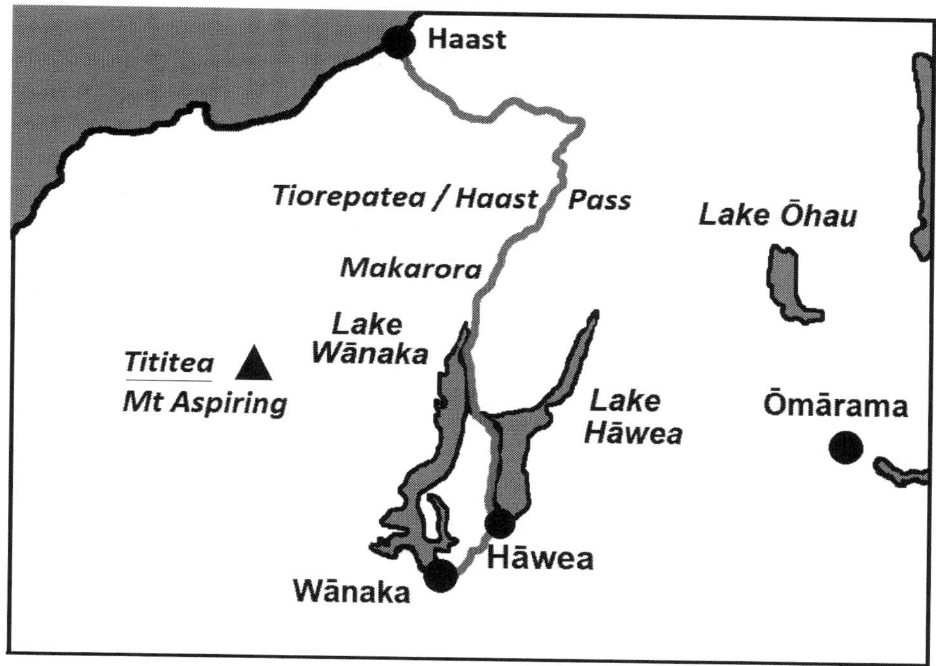

PARTICULARLY SCENIC is the section of highway that leads between Haast and Wānaka via the Haast Pass/Tiorepatea.

Historically, this was an important route for Māori pounamu prospectors, as the top of the pass is only 562 m or 1,844 feet above sea level. This makes it the lowest of the passes traversing the Southern Alps. However, it is girded by mountains, and important tramping tracks branch off to the sides.

On the way inland from the township of Haast the road, the Haast Pass/Tiorepatea Highway, a section of State Highway 6, passes up the Haast River. The pass itself is actually quite a long way inland, after the road has turned south.

After the summit of the pass, the road follows the Makarora River downstream and wends its way toward lakes Wānaka and Hāwea where it takes the form of a lengthy lakeshore drive first down Lake Wānaka and then down Lake Hāwea after crossing over at a spot where the two lakes nearly join called The Neck, which is overlooked by a mountain called Isthmus Peak (1,386 m or 4,547 feet). This is not very high by New Zealand standards but still slightly higher than Ben Nevis in Scotland and possibly with a better view, between two big lakes with interesting shorelines and islands and higher mountains behind them including the serious peak of Mount Aspiring / Tititea, 'The Matterhorn of the South'.

Eventually you arrive at the small lakeshore township of Hāwea and then at the larger one of Wānaka, an important tourist town in its own right and the gateway to the Matukituki Valley, the subject of the next chapter.

There are lots of short walks off the Haast Pass/Tiorepatea Highway from Haast to Wānaka, and a number of longer tramps.

In the longer version of this chapter, posted on my blog, I describe a long tramp around the Gillespie Pass (Wilkins-Young) circuit. Here, I am just going to list the shorter and longer walks:

Short Walks (all but one with times by DOC)

- Roaring Billy Falls (25 mins return)
- Pleasant Flat (5 mins return)
- Thunder Creek Falls (5 mins return)
- Fantail Falls (5 mins return)
- Haast Pass Lookout Track (1 hr return)
- Cameron Lookout Walk (20 mins return)
- Blue Pools Walk (1 hr return)
- Makarora Bush (15 mins return)
- Kidds Bush Nature Walk (30 mins loop)
- Sawyer Burn Track (2hr to the bushline and return, with superb views over Lake Hāwea and into the mountains)
- Bottom Bay Track (on Lake Hāwea, not listed by DOC)

Longer Hikes

As marked on LINZ topographical maps, these are:

- Landsborough Valley Track, from Pleasant Flat (a big valley, like in the Wild West)
- Wills Valley Track, from the Gates of Haast Bridge
- Bridle Track, south from Haast Pass summit (an old route)
- Makarora Track, which starts near a bridge between Kiwi Flat and Davis Flat

- Brewster Track to Brewster Hut, below the Brewster Glacier. Excellent views into the pass and one of my faves.
- Cameron Track, from a short side road near Cameron Flat (Cameron Flat Campsite is further along the road, about 1.5 km).
- Blue Valley Track
- Blue Young Link Track
- Gillespie Pass Circuit Track (with sub-tracks and track and route to Crucible Lake)
- Mt Shrimpton Track
- Boundary Peak Track
- Isthmus Peak Track
- Craig Burn Access Track
- Glen Dene Ridge Track

There are some other tracks that don't seem to have names on the map. But this gives you some idea of the profusion of places to explore just along this section of highway.

As for the town of Wānaka itself – its name not yet officially spelt with a tohutō or macron, unlike the name of the lake – it is a lovely little place famous for the Instagram meme of #ThatWanakaTree, growing all gnarled and Japanese-looking out of the lake.

***#ThatWanakaTree,** late winter 2020*

Wānaka is also the site of the popular airshow called Warbirds over Wānaka. WOW is one of the few opportunities Kiwis have to see nasty little fighter jets in action (the RNZAF no longer has any) along with the vintage Spitfires, of which there are no less than four airworthy examples in the country, along with a whole host of flying machines old and new, prosaic and fantastic.

You can also drive to Hāwea and up the east side of the lake on the Timaru Creek Road past the Te Araroa Trail and tracks on the Timaru River, after which it becomes the Dingle Burn Station road as far as Dingle Burn Station and the Dingle Burn Peninsula Track. On the west side, you can also drive from the

Neck along the west side of Lake Hāwea on Meads Road past the common start of the Kidds Bush Nature Walk and Sawyer Burn Track as far as Hunter Valley Station. Various other huts, tracks and four-wheel drive roads continue north on both sides of the lake, on up into the Hunter River catchment.

The Blue Pools and the Gillespie Pass Circuit

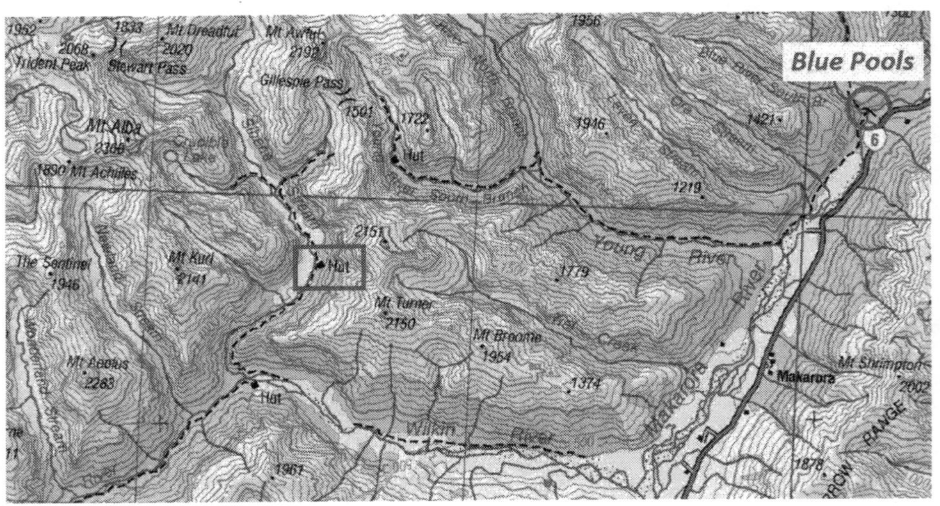

The Blue Pools and the Gillespie Pass Circuit. *This map shows the Siberia, Wilkin and Young Valleys with Gillespie Pass between and the Blue Pools' location at top right, with label and locating circle added for this book. Siberia Hut is indicated, similarly, with a rectangle. Note, further, Mount Dreadful and Mount Awful (!) at top left, and the Crucible Lake to their south. Background map by LINZ via NZ Topo Map, 2020.*

The Blue Pools are a gorgeous gem. They are not the only blue pools in New Zealand, made blue by depth and clarity of water. But they are very accessible from the Haast Pass road, near

Makarora, whereas other pools of this sort are often more of a hike.

One of the Blue Pools, near Makarora

As for the Gillespie Pass Circuit, I will be describing it in more detail in my blog. But just for the moment, I should say that I cheated a bit by getting a helicopter ride from Makarora, on the highway, to a place called Siberia Hut, which is marked on the more detailed map above with a rectangle.

Not a name to inspire much confidence in one's likelihood of keeping warm, Siberia Hut is located below Mount Dreadful and Mount Awful, which make it sound like the hike was going to be some epic journey out of *The Lord of the Rings*– but then, the lovely little Crucible Lake was also nearby. In fact, it was a gorgeous day at the time, as you can see!

The Wilkin River from the helicopter

Crucible Lake

Gillespie Pass

This chapter is expanded in the following blog post:

a-maverick.com/blog/from-haast-to-wanaka

An additional resource from the NZ Automobile Association

aa.co.nz/travel/editorial/full-spectrum-from-lake-hawea-to-jackson-bay

CHAPTER TWENTY-SIX

Matukituki Valley and Mount Aspiring/Tititea

The Wānaka/Queenstown area, showing the Matukituki Valley including its upper branches. *Background imagery ©2019 DigitalGlobe, Maxar Technologies, Landsat/Copernicus; Map data ©2019 Google. Additional information added.*

MY first tramp into Mount Aspiring National Park was with the Upper Clutha Tramping Club, a group of older farmers based out of Wānaka. All of them were between 70 and 85 years old, so I was easily the youngest of the group! They were good people though – I think farmers are friendlier than the professionals I've met in other tramping clubs. They also seemed to co-exist better than another club I had recently left, whose members spent more time complaining than tramping!

We began our tramp into the Matukituki Valley from the Raspberry Creek Carpark, which is an hour's drive up the Matukituki Valley from Wānaka. It was an incredible drive, too, up a half-unsealed road with Rob Roy Peak and Mt Aspiring on the right, and another set of mountain ranges to the left which include the Treble Cone skifield, near the entrance to the valley system. The road is sealed as far as the turnoff to Treble Cone and unsealed thereafter.

Treble Cone and Diamond Lake and the Coming Ski Trail to Cardrona

Near the start of the road into the Matukituki Valley, just west of Wānaka and Glendhu Bay, there's the tiny Diamond Lake, which confusingly has the same name as another Diamond Lake near Glenorchy.

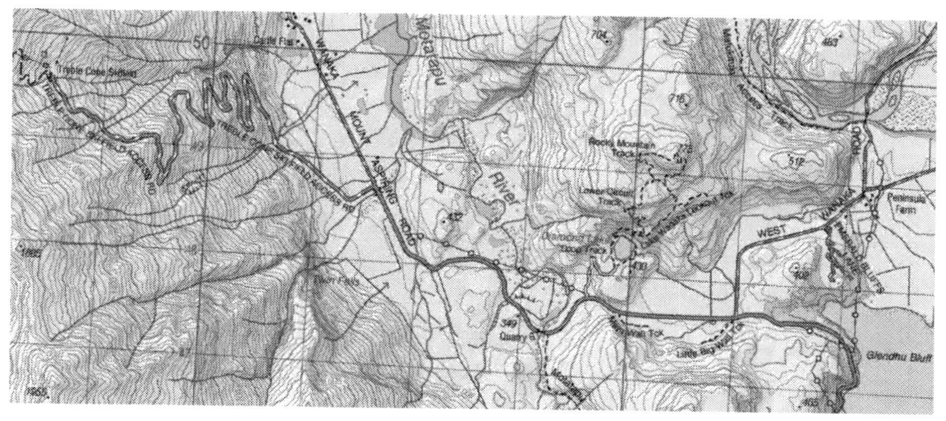

Lake Wānaka (far right), Diamond Lake (right of centre) and Treble Cone (left). *Map by LINZ via NZ Topo Map, 2020.*

The Diamond Lake near Wānaka is a lovely little round lake, somewhat shaded, with a big bluff and some tracks around it that used to support ice skating championships but no longer does so, thanks to global warming.

Just a little further up the road, on the left, is the access road up to Treble Cone skifield. This has amazing views down into the valley and is worth visiting even if you don't want to ski!

There are plans to build a 60 km cross-country ski trail, with six huts, through the Mahu Whenua Conservation area between Coronet Peak skifield, visible from Queenstown International Airport, and Treble Cone. This will be amazing when it is completed. Presumably you'll be able to hike it in summer as well.

Travelling further up

Once we parked our cars and entered the valley, we made our way towards Aspiring Hut, which used to be managed by the

New Zealand Alpine Club along with the French Ridge Hut (which is just below the Bonar Glacier on the approach to Mt Aspiring). The other hut in the valley is Liverpool Hut, tucked in below Mt Liverpool, and they are now all under DOC management.

The Matukituki Valley is an ancient place, first used by early Māori as a hunting ground for native birds such as tūī and kākāpō. These Māori were the first to name Mt Aspiring (3,033 m or 9,951 feet), calling it Tititea, which means 'steep peak of glistening white'. The valley was later settled by Europeans for farming, and its natural features were recognised nationally in 1964 when the Mt Aspiring National Park was created. Colloquially, Mt Aspiring/Tititea is also known as 'The Matterhorn of the South' because of its prominence and dogs-tooth-like shape when seen from certain angles.

From the Raspberry Creek carpark, we tramped up the valley through grassland flats and across small bluffs to Aspiring Hut, a short nine-kilometre hike of about two hours. To get to the other huts in the valley, you need to hike to Pearl Flat, which is another short leg of five kilometres, and then the track forks off towards Liverpool Hut, French Ridge and the head of the West Matukituki Valley, one of the two upper branches of the Matukituki Valley.

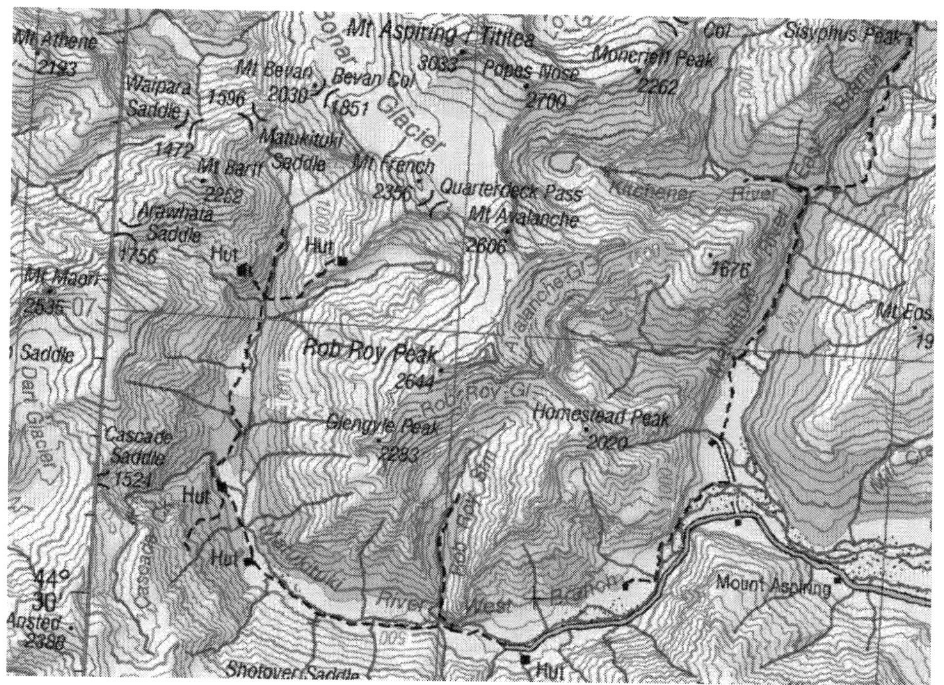

The Upper Matukituki Valley *with Mt Aspiring / Tititea, Rob Roy Peak, the Cascade Saddle and other features, including French Ridge (not named) below Mt French. LINZ via NZ Topo Map, 2020.*

Another striking feature of this area is Sharks Tooth Peak, which rises to 2,096 m and is particularly impressive from the Raspberry Creek carpark.

However, for my first tramp into the valley with the Upper Clutha Tramping Club, we went up towards the Cascade Saddle from Aspiring Hut.

The track forks off in two directions, with one leading deeper up the valley towards Pearl Flat and the other huts, and the other towards the Cascade Saddle, which links the Matukituki with the Rees-Dart Tracks. This route climbs above Mount Aspiring Hut and over a high alpine pass into the Dart Valley, stopping at the Dart Hut on the Rees-Dart. It's a long hike, too, people should expect it to take about ten to twelve hours to complete.

Despite this, many people trek without a pack and only sometimes remember to bring water. I've met many backpackers walking in sandshoes and without the appropriate gear coming over the Cascade Saddle – it amazes me how unprepared some people are!

My father Brian, in the Matukituki Valley

Another Matukituki Valley scene

This time, instead of taking the Saddle, I carried on from Aspiring Hut to the new Liverpool Hut, which was an incredible walk despite being quite steep and slippery in parts. It is a beautiful place with incredible views, and I got a good shot of Mt Aspiring and Mt Liverpool.

After I finished there, I wasn't quite ready to end my tramp. I decided instead I would climb Mt French, and then headed down the valley to find the French Ridge Track.

Very popular with day-trippers, and only part-way along the valley, is the Rob Roy Track, which goes part of the way up the glaciated Rob Roy Peak.

The flanks of Rob Roy Peak, with the Rob Roy Glacier visible

So, all in all, you can get close to the mountains and enjoy great views in the Matukituki Valley, at every level of adventurousness from driving up to the Treble Cone Skifield or wandering around Diamond Lake, to hiking the Rob Roy Track or even climbing Mount Aspiring/Tititea!

I list some blog posts with more images at the end. But first, here's a postscript on the pitfalls of hiring mountain gear.

PS: The pitfalls of hiring mountain gear!

I learned the hard way that it's best to have your own crampons. Hired crampons can sometimes fall apart disastrously due to ill-treatment by previous hirers and general wear and tear. I had such a pair come apart on me on another occasion when I tried to get up Mt Aspiring/Tititea, with an alpine guide named Murray Ball, an incident which received some coverage in the media (Debbie Jamieson, 'Would-be climber alarmed hired crampons fell apart', *Southland Times* / Stuff.co.nz, 11 December 2013; the incident is also mentioned in a *Wilderness* (NZ) article that I talk about further below.)

Though I had paid a lot of money to be guided, the window of opportunity to climb the mountain closed in the time it took for my guide to achieve a field repair of the crampons.

I laid a complaint with the New Zealand Small Claims Tribunal but only received back the crampon hire fee, which was a pittance, and not compensation for money effectively wasted on the guiding fee (which was very much greater) since I was not now able to get to the top, and a holiday spoiled.

***Clockwise from top left**: the beginning of my planned Mount Aspiring/Tititea climb; Kea at Colin Todd Hut; Murray doing his best to fix my failed crampons; looking towards Mounts Barff and Liverpool*

The summit of Mount Aspiring/Tititea – we were so close!

The crampons, which I still believe were defective and could have killed me

Blog posts with more images

I've got a blog post about the Matukituki, including a link to a historic film, here:

a-maverick.com/blog/prelude-to-aspiring-or-what-to-do-when-theres-no-snow-in-paradise

See also this blog post, which expands on the current chapter:

a-maverick.com/blog/matukituki-valley-and-tititea-mt-aspiring

CHAPTER TWENTY-SEVEN

French Ridge

MY tramp up to French Ridge Hut was quite difficult, as the track was coated with spiny plants native to New Zealand called speargrass, which gets very slippery underfoot when it snows. The track was also filled with mountaineers who, like me, wanted to climb Mount French. I had brought my ice axe along and wanted to practice my skills with it on the mountain.

Photo showing French Ridge Hut, under my ice axe

The French Ridge Track forks off to the right from Pearl Flat in the Matukituki Valley, and was around a 3.2-kilometre walk from the Liverpool Hut where I'd come from. From the flat, trampers ford the Liverpool stream or cross over on a swing bridge to the track and climb for a few hours through bush and subalpine terrain to reach the French Ridge Hut.

The hut offers spectacular views of the nearby Mount French, named after WWI Field Marshal John French, who was, rather ironically, said to have been afraid of heights (hat tip Danilo Hegg, 'Mt French, 2356m', in southernalps.wordpress.com).

The climb is only a five to six-hour return trip from French Ridge Hut, heading up towards Quarterdeck Pass and then along a snowy ridge to the summit. Although not a prominent peak itself, Mount French is an incredible viewing platform for the nearby Mount Aspiring and Bonar Glacier, and is often climbed by mountaineers in consolation for not making it to these. The views back down into the valley are really good as well.

For a blog post which expands on the present chapter, see

a-maverick.com/blog/french-ridge

CHAPTER TWENTY-EIGHT

Queenstown: Tourism Capital

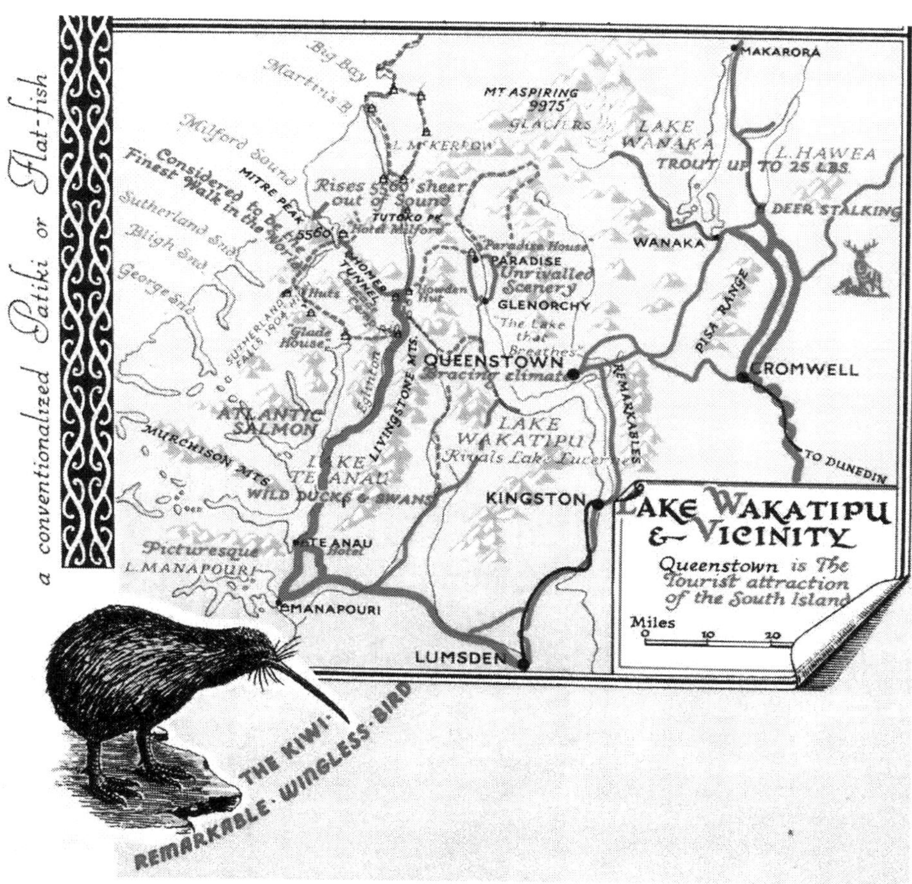

***Map of the Lake Wakatipu Region dated 1946,** a detail from a larger 'Tourist Map of New Zealand' drawn for the NZ Government Tourist Board, on display at the Auckland Public Library in April 2018. Crown copyright reserved.*

QUEENSTOWN is nearly two hours south of Auckland by jet, two hours that make a difference. Auckland has palm trees and looks like Fiji. Queenstown looks more like Norway.

The town is on a long lake called Lake Wakatipu, which stretches 80 km or 50 miles from Kingston at one end to Glenorchy and Kinloch at the other. Queenstown is part-way between.

As the map on the previous page suggests, Queenstown lies at the heart of what has been for perhaps a hundred years and more the most touristy part of New Zealand: a landscape of skifields, tramping tracks and amazing mountain scenery. In spite of its remoteness, Queenstown boasts an international airport, receiving planes from Australia as well as other parts of New Zealand.

Since people arrived in New Zealand, the area has always been something of a gateway to an important hinterland. For old-time Māori, Lake Wakatipu was an accessway between the West Coast, with its waters of pounamu, and communities further east. There were also permanent pā, or villages, in what's now the Queenstown area. The main ones were Tāhuna at Queenstown and Te Kirikiri on what is now the site of the Queenstown Gardens, the great park on a finger of land that extends into the lake from the centre of the town and forms a sort of breakwater on the Queenstown's lakeshore harbour. Tāhuna means shallow bay or cove, and Te Kirikiri means the sandy or gravelly area.

Māori legend has it that the lake is the impression in which the body of a giant was burned. A rhythmic rising and falling of the lake's level over several minutes, which is actually a very slow swell triggered by the wind, was attributed to the slow beating of the giant's heart.

***Wind, steam and speed:** a photograph of the Wakatipu lake steamer Earnslaw under way in 1975, from the New Zealand Maritime Record*

Since the 1860s, four significant steam-powered vessels have plied the lake: the *Antrim* (in service from 1868 until 1905), the Ben Lomond (1872-1951, known as the *Jane Williams* until 1886), the *Mountaineer* (1879-1932) and the *Earnslaw* (1912 to the present). In 1969 the Earnslaw was acquired from the Railways

Department by a company called Fiordland Travel. These days, Fiordland Travel is called Real Journeys, and it's huge.

As for downtown Queenstown, it provides the heritage experience, too. The section of street now known as the Queenstown Mall has not changed very much since the days when people held long poses for Victorian-era photos, though it's not so muddy these days.

Lower Ballarat Street, now the Queenstown Mall, 1878, with the Ben Lomond, known at that time as the Jane Williams, in the background. *Te Papa Tongarewa (the Museum of New Zealand), photograph by William Hart, Hart, Campbell & Co. Purchased 1943. Registration number C.014174. At the time of writing, you can download a 21 MB version of this striking image for free from collections.tepapa.govt.nz/object/18969.*

Visible in the photograph above, Eichardt's Private Hotel is still there at the waterfront end of the left side of the street, and so is the building on the far left of the photo, although most of its façade is now hidden by modern café clutter. But you can still see the '1872' date at the top.

According to the hotel's website, Eichardt's was the first building to have electricity in Queenstown, a system installed under the tenure of Julia Eichardt, who managed it as a sole female proprietor between the death of her husband Albert in 1882 and her own death ten years later.

Not too far away from Queenstown is the even more historic gold-mining settlement of Arrowtown where the Lakes District Museum and Art Gallery is located, along with many old cottages and an old-timey streetscape.

Before the area became as dependent on tourism as it is now, sheep and gold were the mainstays of the colonial economy, along with the extraction of a tungsten ore called scheelite. But even in those days, as the 1946 map attests, there was enough visitor traffic to make Queenstown New Zealand's tourism capital. Along with nearby Milford Sound and lakes Wānaka and Te Anau, the townships of Glenorchy, Kinloch and Arrowtown, and the aptly named Paradise Valley, were all popular destinations with old-time visitors along with Lake Wakatipu itself and "the grandeur of its scenery, which some travelers assert is equal to that of Switzerland." (Israel C. Russell in *The American Naturalist,* July 1876).

The Paradise Valley

At Full Stretch?

But in the present age of international jet travel, which has been crimped by Covid but will surely bounce back, Queenstown is nonetheless far busier than it was in earlier times and in some ways, now, a case study for mass tourism's more negative impacts. Which is not to detract from the argument that you should still go there!

Blog posts, with more information and images

I have a heap of blog posts about Queenstown and its environs on my website! Namely:

Queenstown: Tourism Capital.

a-maverick.com/blog/queenstown-tourism-capital

Ten things to do in Queenstown, and around:

a-maverick.com/blog/queenstown-10-things-to-do-town-around

Christmas in New Zealand, including a late snowstorm that very nearly made it white:

a-maverick.com/blog/xmas-in-new-zealand

Travelling back in time on Queenstown's twin-screw lake steamer, the TSS Earnslaw:

a-maverick.com/blog/history-travelling-time-tss-earnslaw

Paradise: The Real Top of the Lake:

a-maverick.com/blog/paradise-the-real-top-of-the-lake

Lockdown in Queenstown:

a-maverick.com/blog/lockdown-in-queenstown

A blog post that describes the suburban Arawata Track in its second half:

a-maverick.com/blog/leper-colonies-or-lockdown-for-covid-19

A blog post about Otago history:

a-maverick.com/blog/looking-behind-the-scenery-striking-historical-gold-in-new-zealand

Bobs Cove: An amazing bay on Lake Wakatipu, close to Queenstown:

a-maverick.com/blog/bobs-cove-sacred-pool-maori-mine-pakeha-instagrammable-today

Amazing Arrowtown: A colonial time capsule:

a-maverick.com/blog/amazing-arrowtown-new-zealands-colonial-time-capsule

The history of the Coronet Peak skifield from the 1950s to now:

a-maverick.com/blog/changing-times-coronet-peak-ski-club-commercialism-climate-change

A misty day out in the Remarkables mountain range:

a-maverick.com/blog/a-misty-day-out-at-the-remarkables-matchstalk-figures-amid-the-snow

Cross-country skiing at Snow Farm, Part One:

a-maverick.com/blog/adventures-snow-farm-nordic-skiing-downunder-part-one

Cross-country skiing at Snow Farm, Part Two:

a-maverick.com/blog/adventures-snow-farm-nordic-skiing-downunder-part-two

CHAPTER TWENTY-NINE

Up to the Place of Light, down the Water of Tears

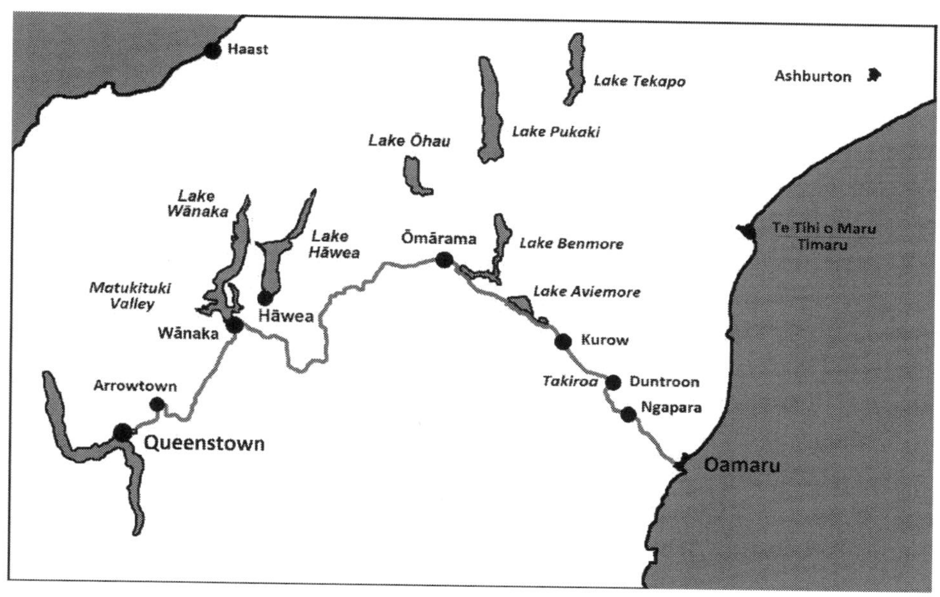

THIS chapter is about a great tour that takes you from Queenstown to Oamaru via the Lindis Pass and the towns of Cromwell, Ōmārama, Otematata, Kurow and Duntroon. Just before Duntroon, it passes by the Takiroa Māori rock drawings site as well.

Between Queenstown and Cromwell, you go through the Kawarau Gorge, and then north along the shores of Lake Dunstan. Cromwell itself has quite an attractive historical district. After that, the first really notable thing you come to is the lovely Lindis Pass.

Lindis Pass landforms

Near the pass, I got out of my car and explored the Lindis Valley.

That was at about half-past seven at night. An hour later there was a real nuclear-bomb sunset.

I drove on through Ōmārama to Buscot Station, my accommodation for the next few days. It's a friendly place, run by a man named Tony Gloag.

I spent some time wandering around Ōmārama, a nice little tourist town with lots of signs advertising places to stay and things to do.

The sign doesn't yet show the tohutō or macron over the first two vowels in Ōmārama.

One of the things this district is famous for is gliding. Westerly winds blowing over the nearby mountains create both updrafts and downdrafts. Gliders can remain aloft over Ōmārama for hours by returning to the updrafts. Several world records for distance and time aloft have been set over Ōmārama. And the area is very scenic as well, so it's not as if the pilots or their passengers would get bored. You can see more about this rather special local attraction on the website of Gliding New Zealand.

Another must-see is the Cappadocia-like Clay Cliffs, which a recent newspaper article describes as being roughly ten kilometres from Ōmārama, "off SH83 onto progressively smaller roads . . . beside the impressively braided Ahuriri River." (Pamela Wade, 'World Famous in New Zealand: The Clay Cliffs, Omarama', 8 April 2018 on stuff.co.nz.) Perhaps because the Clay Cliffs are up a back road, they're easy to miss. But don't miss them!

Also down a back road are the Wairepo Kettleholes, in the Ahuriri Conservation Park. Wairepo means 'swampwater' in Māori: a clue to why this area is interesting to the nature-lover, even if it isn't quite as spectacular to look at.

Kettleholes, or kettle holes, are holes in the ground created by gigantic blocks of ice, like icebergs but sitting on the land, which occupied the site in the Ice Age and melted subsequently. When it rains heavily, the runoff from the land nearby flows into the kettle holes, which thus act as cisterns. Of course, these days, they're also pretty much filled up with mud and silt. The holes now have marshes on top. The result is an ecologically significant system of permanent wetlands. A permanent oasis, in what's otherwise a fairly arid region where the grass isn't always green or lush by any means.

Kettle holes help to stop large areas of the 'big sky country' of the North American plains from drying out too much. This has been important for the ecology of the original prairie grasslands and for subsequent agriculture as well. One agglomeration of kettle holes spans three Canadian provinces and the Dakotas, and spills over into three adjoining US states.

And so, Wairepo is a lush spot in an otherwise rather bony landscape.

Sign announcing the Ahuriri Conservation Park. *Ironically, the prairie growing on its edges is something new in ecological terms, having been self-assembled from plants introduced by the colonist. The original ecology wouldn't have been anything like this.*

The Department of Conservation has a great brochure on all the things you can do in the vicinity of Ōmārama: you can download it here.

The Place of Light

Ōmārama is said to mean 'the place of light'. The name comes, perhaps, from Te Ao Mārama, an oratorical expression translated by the phrase 'the world of life and light', and the name of the commune established by the 1870s protest leader Te Maihāroa near the site of the present-day town of Ōmārama.

It's a name that accidentally gained a new significance in the mid-twentieth century when Ōmārama became a hydro village: a base for the massive Waitaki hydroelectricity/irrigation scheme.

From Ōmārama east to the sea, my road trip would run parallel to a massive river called the Waitaki, and to several dams and artificial lakes on its upper reaches.

Meaning 'Water of Tears', the Waitaki separates the historical provinces of Otago and Canterbury. The lower reaches of the Waitaki are so big and so difficult to bridge that two main roads simply run parallel to it, one on the Otago side and another on the Canterbury side. You cross from Canterbury to Otago well inland where the river finally narrows a bit, at Kurow.

The Waitaki hydroelectric and irrigation system was built over a longer period: first on the lower Waitaki in the 1930s, then at Benmore in the 1950s, and finally on the Upper Waitaki headwaters in the 1970s. The Upper Waitaki Scheme was, for a time, the largest ongoing hydro construction project in the world.

All pretty epic for little old New Zealand! It's fair to say we don't do things on that scale anymore. "Think big" was an expression coined for such projects in the 1970s; borrowed perhaps from a famous quote attributed to the architect Daniel Burnham, who helped to shape Chicago in the days when it was still a frontier boomtown.

Down the Water of Tears

After Ōmārama, I headed down the hydro-rich Waitaki Valley.

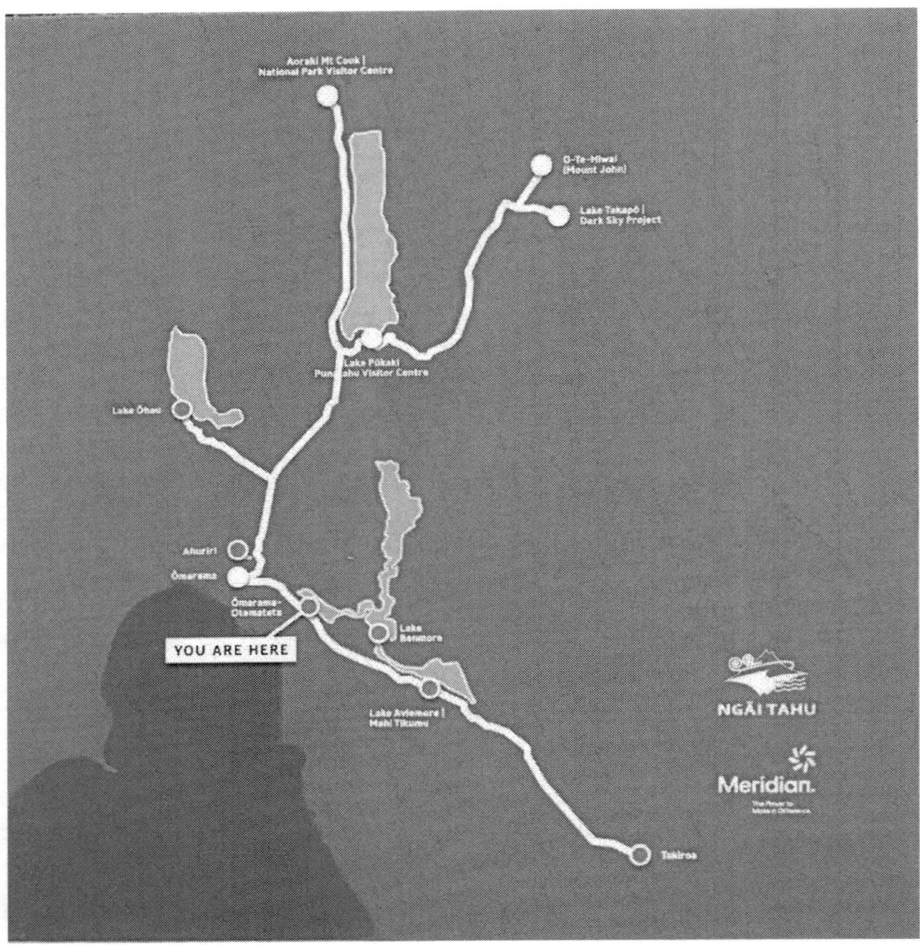

On this display map by Meridian Energy and Ngāi Tahu, *Ōmārama is spelt in the proper fashion.*

The people who built the dams took the view that their new lakes would be good for recreation and getting in touch with (admittedly modified) nature, as well as the more utilitarian purposes of power and irrigation. There are just as many signs pointing to boat ramps, holiday parks, and managed ecological wetlands, as there are to interesting engineering exhibits.

Overleaf, I've included a photo from the Benmore Dam looking down into the headwaters of Lake Aviemore, or Mahi Tikumu.

Looking into Lake Aviemore/Mahi Tikumu from the Benmore Dam

I passed through Kurow, which is famous as the town where New Zealand's 1930s welfare state was piloted by among the hydro workers by a group of local reformers that included Arnold Nordmeyer, a future leader of the New Zealand Labour Party.

Here, too, displays also dealt with Māori issues from the time of the evictions in 1879 and included the photograph that appears in chapter 2, above.

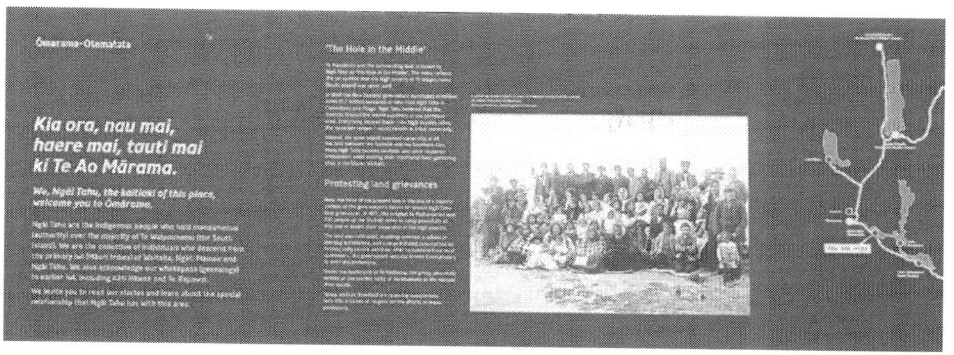

***Another section of a display on the Waitaki River,** describing the trail-of-tears evictions of Te Maihāroa and other South Island Māori from land they sought to keep.*

The Ngāi Tahu iwi have a website called Kā Huru Manu cultural mapping. This includes a page on the role of the lake regions as mahinga kai, or food gathering areas.

kahurumanu.co.nz/ka-ara-tawhito/waitaki

There are also very detailed displays about these cultural issues and grievances up at Lake Pūkaki, which is part of the Waitaki hydroelectric power system and was doubled in size in the 1970s, inundating many cultural sites which now only exist on old yellowing maps.

The region around the upper Waitaki lakes such as Pūkaki and Tekapo, known in English as the Mackenzie Country after the nineteenth-century sheep stealer and folk hero James Mackenzie who hid his flocks of stolen sheep in this area, is known in Māori as Te Manahuna. That is the term used on the display captions.

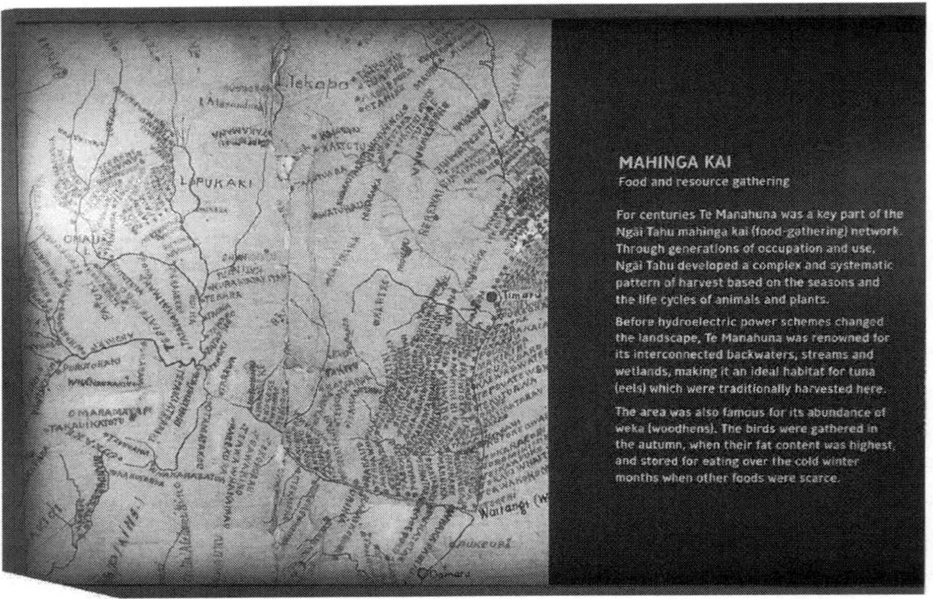

The caption and the map from the display above, at Lake Pūkaki, are magnified on the following pages.

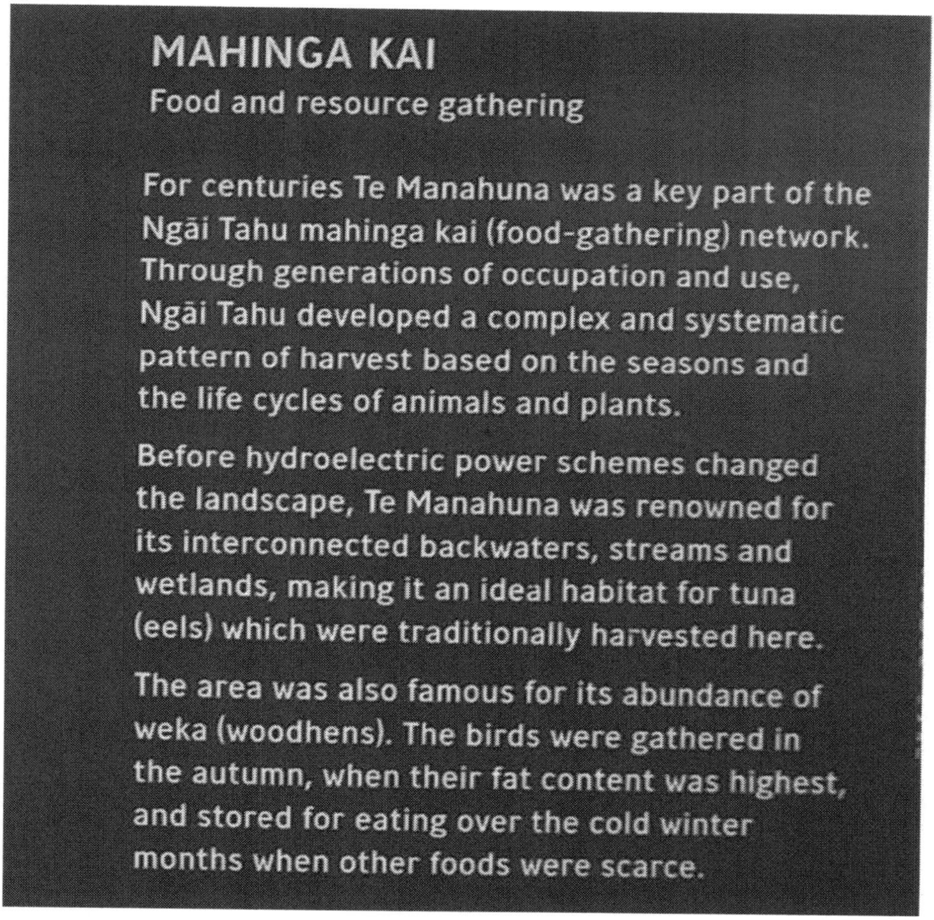

MAHINGA KAI

Food and resource gathering

For centuries Te Manahuna was a key part of the Ngāi Tahu mahinga kai (food-gathering) network. Through generations of occupation and use, Ngāi Tahu developed a complex and systematic pattern of harvest based on the seasons and the life cycles of animals and plants.

Before hydroelectric power schemes changed the landscape, Te Manahuna was renowned for its interconnected backwaters, streams and wetlands, making it an ideal habitat for tuna (eels) which were traditionally harvested here.

The area was also famous for its abundance of weka (woodhens). The birds were gathered in the autumn, when their fat content was highest, and stored for eating over the cold winter months when other foods were scarce.

On the next page there's another display from Lake Pūkaki, showing the travel routes favoured by Waitaki Māori.

NGĀ ARA TAWHITO
Traditional travel routes

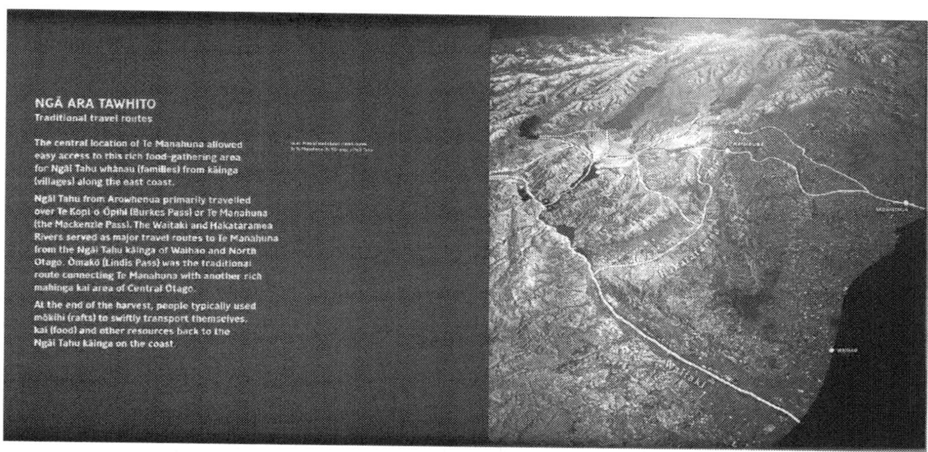

And here are the left and right sides of that display in more detail, once again. The map was provided officially by Ngāi Tahu.

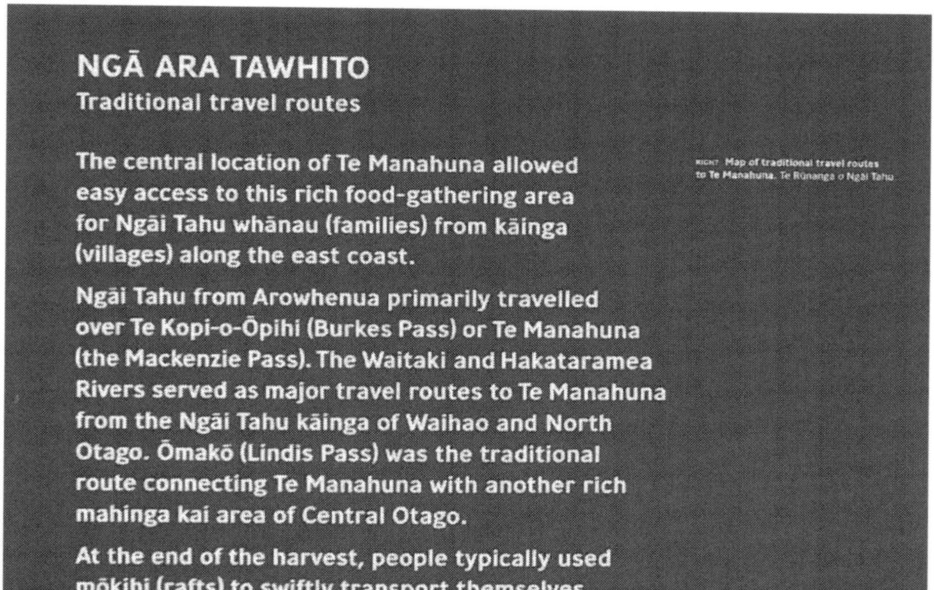

NGĀ ARA TAWHITO
Traditional travel routes
The central location of Te Manahuna allowed easy access to this rich food-gathering area for Ngāi Tahu whānau (families) from kāinga (villages) along the east coast.
Ngāi Tahu from Arowhenua primarily travelled over Te Kopi-o-Ōpihi (Burkes Pass) or Te Manahuna (the Mackenzie Pass). The Waitaki and Hakataramea Rivers served as major travel routes to Te Manahuna from the Ngāi Tahu kāinga of Waihao and North Otago. Ōmakō (Lindis Pass) was the traditional route connecting Te Manahuna with another rich mahinga kai area of Central Otago.
At the end of the harvest, people typically used mōkihi (rafts) to swiftly transport themselves, kai (food) and other resources back to the Ngāi Tahu kāinga on the coast.
RIGHT Map of traditional travel routes to Te Manahuna. Te Rūnanga o Ngāi Tahu

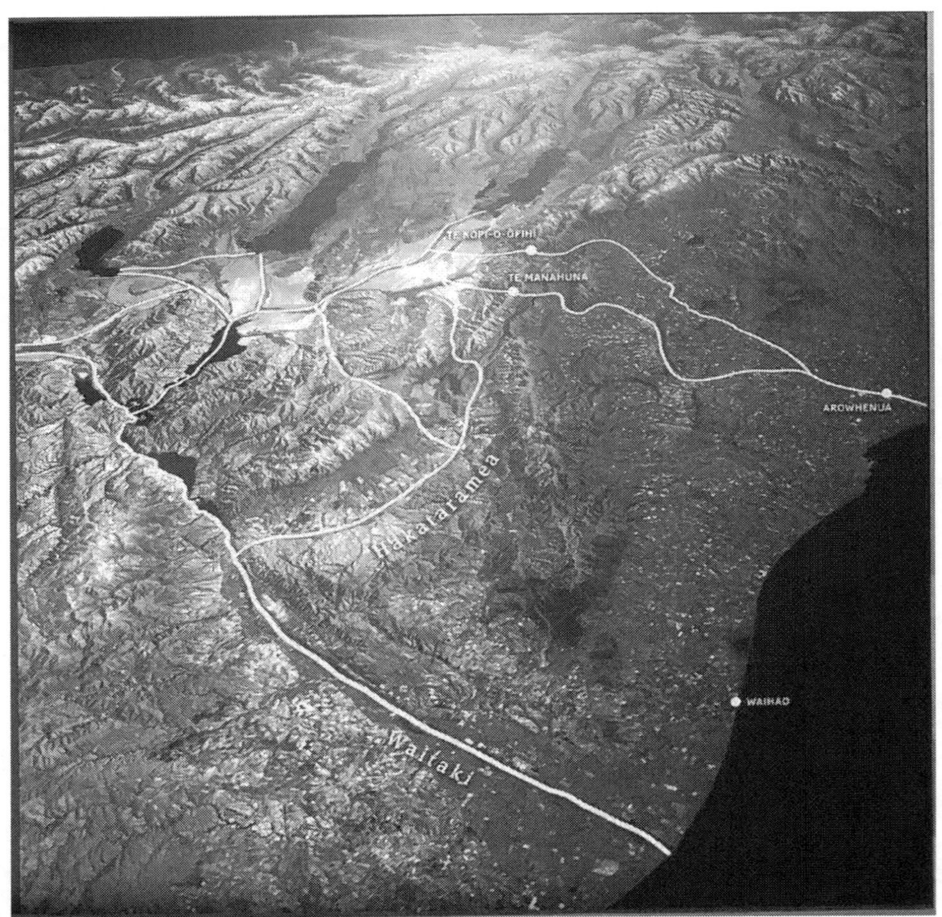

On the facing page, the last display to be reproduced here shows photographs of eels being trapped and transferred to get around the hydroelectric dams, and, at top right, preserved by the traditional method called pāwhara tuna.

In Māori, tuna means eel. The English word tuna, meaning a powerful ocean fish that English-speaking people are most likely to encounter in a can, has a totally different origin.

There' a great online *New Zealand Geographic* article about the Waitaki, about both its cultural and historical significance and its hydroelectric significance, called 'Waitaki: Water of Tears, River of Power'.

The Proposed Waitaki Whitestone Geopark

The whole Waitaki region is also under consideration to be designated a geopark, a UNESCO designation similar to World Heritage and identifying an unusual or distinctive landscape. In the case of the Waitaki, the hoped-for geopark will cover 7,200 square kilometers from the coast to the mountains. It is based on the fact that the area is dominated by white limestone known locally as whitestone, with strange outcrops and caves eroded by water: technically, a 'karst' landscape. According to a PDF flier on the website of the groups lobbying for the geopark, as of the time of writing,

"The karst landscape and its 'whitestone' are integral to the identity of the Waitaki district. The first people to the area found shelter in limestone caves, leaving now treasured rock art. Waitaki's largest town, Ōamaru, is renowned for fine limestone architecture. Today, the Vanished World Centre celebrates the fossils that emerge from the Geopark's whitestone."

Here is the website, which also has an app:

whitestonegeopark.nz

Duntroon and the Takiroa Rock Drawings Site

Heading on down further, I came to the Takiroa rock drawings site.

MAORI ROCK
DRAWINGS
300 m
ON RIGHT

TAKIROA
ROCK ART
SITE
We, the Ngai Tahu Whānui,
The descendants of
Kahui Tipua, Rapuwai,
Hawea, Waitaha,
Mamoe, and Tahu,
The kaitiaki,
the guardians of this place,
Welcome you to Takiroa
Nau mai!
Haere Mai!

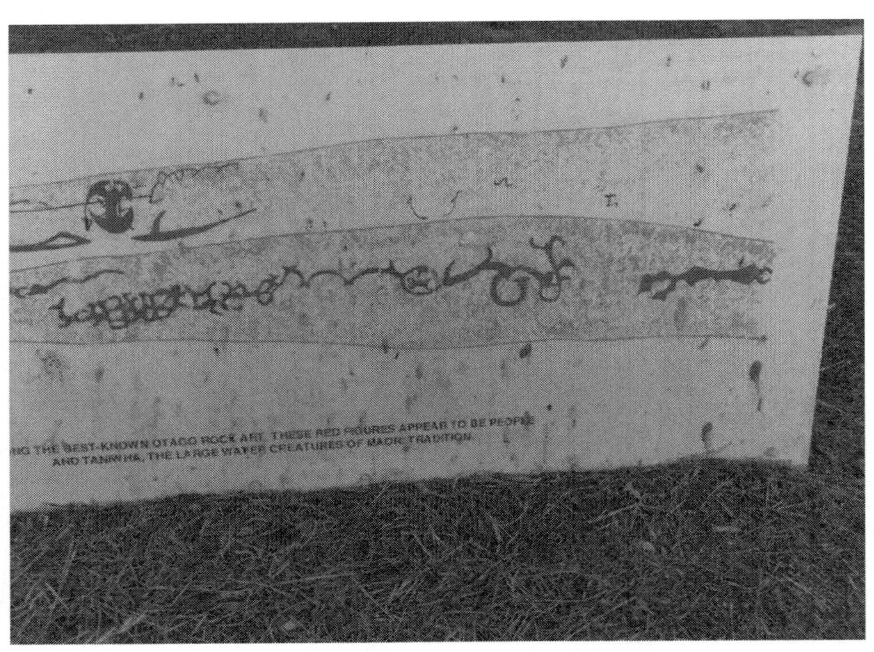
THE BEST-KNOWN OTAGO ROCK ART. THESE RED FIGURES APPEAR TO BE PEOPLE
AND TANIWHA, THE LARGE WATER CREATURES OF MAORI TRADITION.

From there it was a short trip to Duntroon, where the main attraction is the Vanished World Centre, a geological museum with lots of exhibits of the way the Waitaki Valley used to be. Which, for a long time, was the bottom of the sea, as limestone arises out of the crushing-together of the skeletons and shells of sea creatures.

The centre's website includes a guide to the Vanished World Trail, a self-driving route that takes in important sites outside the museum as well:

vanishedworld.co.nz/the-vanished-world-trail

Just lately, I heard of the discovery, in the nearby Kyeburn River, of fossilised footprints of the large flightless birds, now extinct, known as the moa. This is very much the sort of thing the Vanished World deals with, though it seems that these footprints will go to the Otago Museum in Dunedin. There's a video interview with the local guy who found them, who seems to be quite a character.

odt.co.nz/regions/central-otago/moa-footprints-found-river

Duntroon to Oamaru: Take the Ngapara Route

From Duntroon to Oamaru, you should definitely take the back-country route through Ngapara.

This route leads leads past major limestone outcrops that include the Elephant Rocks, Island Cliff and the Valley of the Whales, which I mentioned in the Oamaru chapter and which is definitely in the need of the kind of protection UNESCO Geopark status would confer.

nzgeo.com/stories/valley-of-the-whales

The Waitaki's Cycling Trails

The website of the Alps 2 Ocean trail, which begins at Mount Cook Village, and finishes at Oamaru, is alps2ocean.com

In addition to the Alps 2 Ocean cycling trail, there are also local cycling trails at Waimate and Oamaru. The following link includes the Waimate trails as well as the Oamaru ones:

mapmyride.com/nz/oamaru-otago

Blog Post and App

I've got a blog post which covers the same ground as this chapter, and more, with more imagery:

a-maverick.com/blog/place-of-light-water-of-tears

And you might want to get the app!

TOUR 7: Otago's Dry Interior

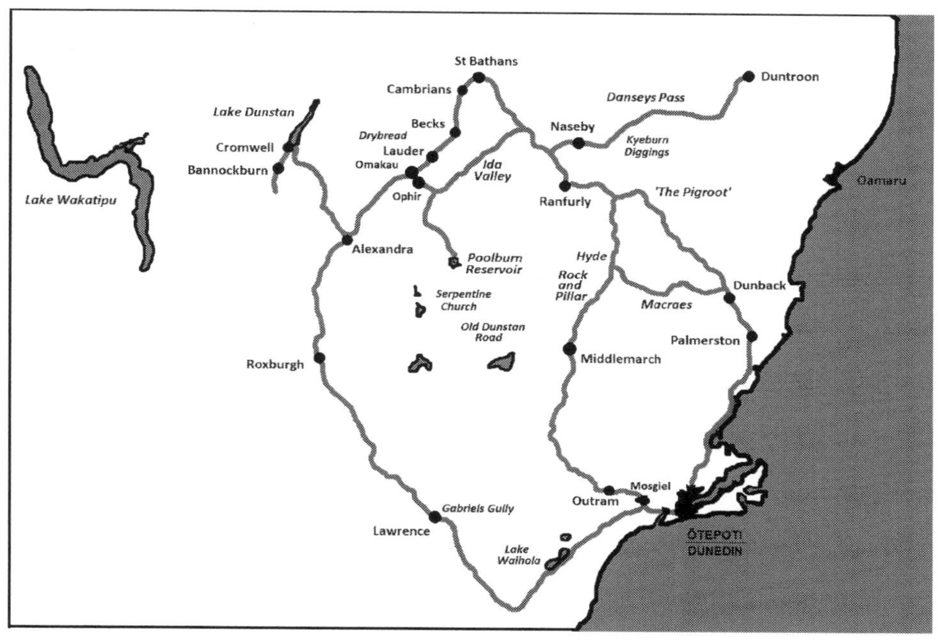

CHAPTER THIRTY

Otago's Dry Centre

BETWEEN Queenstown, where I live, and Dunedin, there's an aridly picturesque region called Central Otago.

Central Otago is a rain-shadow region, kept dry by the blocking effect of the high mountains around Queenstown. It looks a lot like Outback Australia or parts of the Middle East that I've been to. Some call it a desert, though there are a few too many trees and shrubs for that to be literally true.

Though the average year-round temperature isn't high in Otago as compared to Outback Australia or the Middle East, it gets pretty hot under a blue summer sky in Central all the same—and in Queenstown too, once it has been summer for a while.

The Bannockburn area

Here are a couple of photos I've taken in the Bannockburn area, which is the part of Central Otago closest to Queenstown.

Welcome to
Heart of the Desert

Look up 'Bannockburn area' on DOC's website for a list of things to do in and around Bannockburn, including the Bannockburn Sluicings Track

History Perfectly Preserved

Central Otago towns are mostly quite historic by New Zealand standards, with whole streets of stone buildings erected in the 1860s and 1870s for want of timber; buildings that nobody has ever had the heart to demolish.

From Queenstown, if you are headed east to Dunedin, you drive past Cromwell and Clyde (which is below a large modern 1980s dam, the Clyde High Dam) and through Alexandra, before going either via a northern route or a southern route to Dunedin. It's a good idea not to drive past Clyde and Cromwell but actually to turn into them as these towns are really historic and picturesque.

***Cromwell:** The old P & T office, in the town's historic precinct*

Such towns are open-air museums of the early settler's way of life. There are lots of books about Otago history by the way, such as this one, of which the cover depicts a historic bridge in Alexandra (the stone piers are still there).

'Historic Otago' by Gavin McLean, *published by David Bateman, Auckland, 2010, ISBN 978-186953-777-7. Fair review claimed.*

On the following page, there's a map pertaining to the section that it faces, 'Dawdling to Dunedin on the Pigroot Trail'.

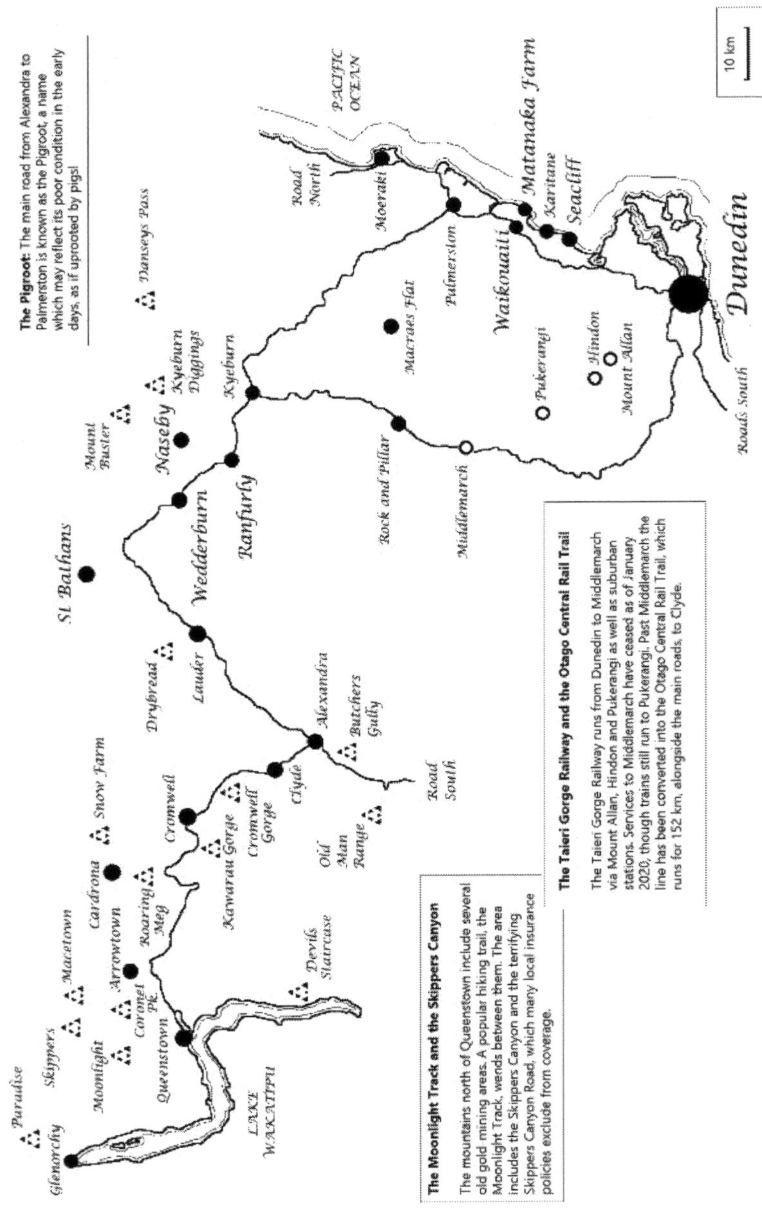

Paradise
Glenorchy
Skippers
Macetown
Moonlight
Coronet Pk.
Arrowtown
Cardrona
Snow Farm
Queenstown
Roaring Meg
Cromwell
Kawarau Gorge
Cromwell Gorge
LAKE WAKATIPU
Devils Staircase
Clyde
Old Man Range
Alexandra
Butchers Gully
Road South
Drybread
Lauder
St Bathans
Wedderburn
Ranfurly
Mount Buster
Naseby
Kyeburn Diggings
Kyeburn
Danseys Pass
Rock and Pillar
Middlemarch
Macraes Flat
Pukerangi
Hindon
Mount Allan
Road North
PACIFIC OCEAN
Moeraki
Palmerston
Waikouaiti
Matanaka Farm
Karitane
Seacliff
Roads South
Dunedin
10 km
The Pigroot: The main road from Alexandra to Palmerston is known as the Pigroot, a name which may reflect its poor condition in the early days, as if uprooted by pigs!
The Moonlight Track and the Skippers Canyon
The mountains north of Queenstown include several old gold-mining areas. A popular hiking trail, the Moonlight Track, wends between them. The area includes the Skippers Canyon and the terrifying Skippers Canyon Road, which many local insurance policies exclude from coverage.
The Taieri Gorge Railway and the Otago Central Rail Trail
The Taieri Gorge Railway runs from Dunedin to Middlemarch via Mount Allan, Hindon and Pukerangi as well as suburban stations. Services to Middlemarch have ceased as of January 2020, though trains still run to Pukerangi. Past Middlemarch the line has been converted into the Otago Central Rail Trail, which runs for 152 km, alongside the main roads, to Clyde.

Dawdling to Dunedin on the Pigroot Trail

A long stretch of the northern road bears the colourful name of 'the Pigroot'. One theory is that in the 1860s and 70s, the stagecoaches and bullock-carts transporting gold and miners to and from the diggings near Queenstown chopped up the then-unsealed road so much that it looked like it had been rooted by pigs!

If you are feeling energetic you can cycle from Middlemarch through to Clyde by way of the Otago Central Rail Trail, 152 km of disused railway line. This involves cycling along the western half of the Pigroot after you reach Kyeburn, till Clyde.

I've mentioned the rail trail in some detail already in the Dunedin chapter, but here is its webpage again: **otagocentralrailtrail.co.nz**.

As elsewhere in Otago, there's a Scots bias to the placenames here. But there are still plenty of Māori placenames, all the same. For instance, the Māori name for much of northern Otago is Maniototo, which means 'plains of blood'. Not actual blood, but rather the red tussock that's native to this semi-arid land and which normally gave it a rather red appearance overall, though in the following photo the sign is in reddish tones while the land has greened up from recent rains.

If you are driving between Queenstown and Dunedin and not on a cycling holiday, the slowest but most scenic way is to take the Pigroot right through to Palmerston and come down the coast through Waikouaiti.

Heading east on the Pigroot, I turned left up a side road to St Bathans. It was November, but there was still snow on the mountains. A sign prominently advertised the Vulcan Hotel, est. 1863.

The Vulcan looked a lot like the more famous Cardrona Hotel, established in the same year.

Clearly, this was the standard look for miners' inns at the time.

It was pretty quiet when I was there, but a lot of these places really swell in the summertime, when they cater to rail trail tourists. Who are thirsty, obviously enough.

St Bathans is an old gold-mining town. There are a couple of lakes, Blue Lake and Grey Lake, which didn't exist prior to the 1860s but were created by the activities of the gold miners.

Blue Lake, St Bathans

The chief method of mining in this district was to aggressively sluice the easily eroded hillsides with jets of high-pressure water.

And that's basically how the lakes were carved out. You can go boating and swimming on the lakes, and there's quite a nice campsite.

There are a number of other old buildings and halls in the township, apart from the Vulcan Hotel.

St Bathans would probably be a ghost town, if it weren't for the fact that the accidentally created lakes now bring in quite a bit of tourism. All the same, only a literal handful of people live there all year round.

There is a heap of interesting places around this area, including the Ida Valley (on the rail trail), Drybread, where a colonial cemetery is being excavated, and Cambrians, a little settlement where the handful of people who live there are restoring the native forest.

A little further on down the Pigroot I turned up a side road to the town of Naseby, where there used to be twenty pubs, of which the Ancient Briton and the Royal are the only two survivors now.

The town also has other historic buildings and generally tons of charm.

Like St Bathans, Naseby's also some way off the Pigroot. But it seems to have a bit more critical mass.

(By the way, what's with names like Cromwell and Naseby? The latter bears the same name as the site of the greatest victory of Oliver Cromwell's New Model Army against the cavaliers of King Charles I. Do names like this imply that some of the miners were less than fulsomely loyal to Queen Victoria? Come to think of it, down by Ophir there's the Daniel O'Connell Bridge, after the Irish nationalist of the same name. I wonder if any royal tour's ever gone through these parts.)

You can continue up the side road from Naseby to Kyeburn Diggings where there are no longer any miners but still a surprisingly large pub, hotel and restaurant called the Danseys Pass Hotel (est. 1862), also known as the Danseys Pass Coach Inn, and then on to Danseys Pass via a road that is, from the Inn onward, simply a bedrock ledge in places. The road's very scenic, but whoever's driving is advised not to look at the scenery. A bit like the Skippers in other words, though not quite as bad. Heavy vehicles, campervans and caravans are not allowed because they cause problems for people coming the other way on narrow sections. And according to the international Dangerous Roads website, "if there's any hint of bad weather, you should not be up here." On the other hand, there are a great many trails that lead off the road into a rocky wilderness on both sides, the Oteake Conservation Park, a paradise for mountain bikers. And to reiterate, it is scenic.

dangerousroads.org/australia-and-oceania/new-zealand/1081-danseys-pass-new-zealand.html

You might also want to look up the Oteake Conservation Park on DOC's website, for a page and a brochure on this attractive area.

Through Danseys Pass you travel on to Duntroon on the Waitaki River, the subject of the previous tour.

The Dunstan Heritage Trail and the Lake Dunstan Trail

The Dunstan Heritage Trail runs through the middle of Central Otago from Dunedin to Alexandra, in an almost straight line for 175 kilometres. It was the preferred route of the goldminers from roughly 1862 onwards, though it is rough and exposed. The remains of old inns exist along the way.

Also known as the Dunstan Trail for short, the Dunstan Heritage Trail is more elevated and adventurous than the Otago Central Rail Trail and leads through a real wilderness of tussock grass and weird rocky outcrops sculpted by the wind. Because of its elevation and exposure, it's closed from the first Tuesday in June till the end of September.

Dunstan Heritage Trail Sign, *at Moa Creek*

Roadhouse at Moa Creek, *on the Dunstan Heritage Trail. Some of the other ones, now disused, on less accessible parts of the trail are more picturesque!*

The trail leads past the Poolburn Reservoir, one of several reservoirs on a barren, rocky plateau southeast of the Ida Valley. The Poolburn Reservoir is accessible by a road from Moa Creek and the Ida Valley that is drivable in an ordinary vehicle provided it has good ground clearance, but the road is pretty rough, being another one of the ones that's just a bedrock slab in places. Past the Poolburn Reservoir, heading east, the road takes the form of a four-wheel-drive road, and it has gates.

The Dunstan Trail is also known as the Old Dunstan Road for much of its length (today's road diverges slightly from the original trail in places). It doesn't get much publicity, because the whole route runs through the middle of nowhere in exposed and dangerous locations, and it has got just about zero commercial potential.

The Poolburn Reservoir, *a* Lord of the Rings *filming site. The road shown is one of the better sections of the Old Dunstan Road.*

It's strictly for the hardcore adventure cyclist, basically.

The Dunstan Trail should not be confused with the Lake Dunstan Trail, which runs for 52 kilometres up the side of Lake Dunstan from Cromwell. These two trails have almost the same name, yet they are completely different!

Here are a couple of websites on the Dunstan Heritage Trail, and the Lake Dunstan Trail, respectively:

kennett.co.nz/archives/ride/dunstan-trail

centralotagonz.com/tracks-and-trails/lake-dunstan-trail

The Southern Route

Between Alexandra and Dunedin, you have the choice of the Pigroot route or a southern route, through Roxburgh. Both skirt around a vast semi-desert through which the Dunstan Trail passes, but which has never been pierced by a road of the kind that's suitable for all vehicles.

The further south you go in Otago, the less barren the landscape tends to become, until you are in the fertile plains of Southland, north of Invercargill. All the same, the southern route through central Otago, from Alexandra to Dunedin via Roxburgh, following the Clutha or Mata-Au River most of the way, still goes through some pretty bony terrain itself.

From Alexandra as far as the Roxburgh Dam, the highway is paralleled by trails in the Roxburgh Gorge (flooded by the dam) and on the adjacent Flat Top Hill Conservation Area, where there are all kinds of weird stone outcrops shaped by the wind once more, a common sight in other parts of central Otago as well, but seldom so visible from a main road as here.

To the west, the Flat Top Hill Conservation Area overlooks a locality called Fruitlands, through which the main road passes and which was an area of early settlement and gold mining. There are lots of relics in that area including the old stone buildings of Mitchell's Cottage in the hills further west, and, just to the east of the main road, a number of ruined stone cottages that look like they belong in Ireland or the Scottish Highlands.

Below the Roxburgh Dam, the valley of the Clutha / Mata-Au is flat and fertile. Along with Fruitlands this is a major fruit-growing area, yet the orchards in the river valley just serve to remind us how much of the area really is a wilderness. When you zoom out on the map, the river valley just looks like a thread.

Driving up and down it actually conveys a misleading impression of fertility.

Past Beaumont, the main road (SH 8) leaves the river valley and heads toward a town called Lawrence, next to the famous Gabriel's Gully. This was one of the first places where gold was discovered in New Zealand, in 1861. The strike soon led to an internationally significant gold rush, a worthy successor to the then-recent strikes in California and Australia and a forerunner to South Africa and the Yukon.

The winnings of Gabriel's Gully, and others like it, paid for a lot of fancy architecture in a hitherto wooden and ramshackle colony, and also helped to locate New Zealand more firmly on people's mental maps of the world. Before the gold rush the response to any mention of New Zealand was likely to be "Where's that?" Admittedly that is still a fairly common response, but not as common as it used to be.

From Lawrence, you reach the town of Milton and then head north on State Highway 1 past Lake Waihola and Mosgiel, to Dunedin.

And no, Waihola is not a misprint. It's another of those Hawai'ian-sounding names, a local variant of the more standard Waihora, meaning shallow waters; a name which is also one of the Māori names of Lake Ellesmere, further north, in Canterbury.

Lake Waihola

Here are some blog posts that cover the same ground as this chapter and extend on it, with more imagery:

a-maverick.com/blog/otagos-dry-centre

a-maverick.com/blog/xmas-in-new-zealand

a-maverick.com/blog/the-old-gold-road-dawdling-dunedin-pigroot-trail

a-maverick.com/blog/looking-behind-the-scenery-striking-historical-gold-in-new-zealand

a-maverick.com/blog/amazing-arrowtown-new-zealands-colonial-time-capsule

Plus, a further resource:

centralotagonz.com

TOUR 8: The Southern Scenic Realm

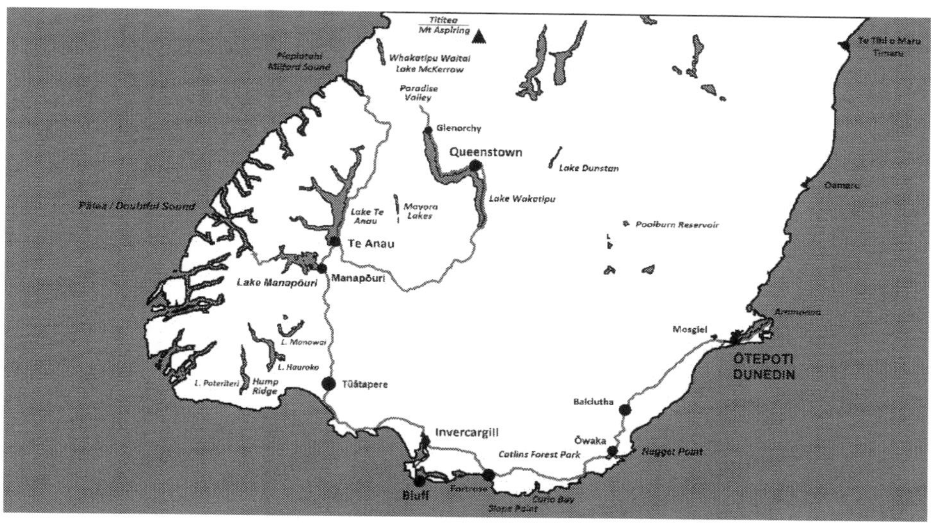

CHAPTER THIRTY-ONE

Milford Sound/Piopiotahi, and its Road

When getting there really is half the journey

NEW ZEALAND'S most famous tourist attraction is Milford Sound, known in Māori as Piopiotahi. Its mile-high craggy ramparts, by some counts the highest sea-cliffs in the world though they aren't strictly vertical, are what make it so famous.

Milford Sound/Piopiotahi. *Mitre Peak/Rahotu, in the middle, is 1,690 metres high, more than a mile. This is the head of the sound. The painting overleaf shows its seaward end.*

Evans, Frederick John Owen (Sir), 1815–1885. New Zealand—Middle [South] Island. Entering Milford Sound in H M S Acheron—Captn J. Lort Stokes 1850. *Ref: B-062–019. Alexander Turnbull Library, Wellington, New Zealand.* /records/23251765

Milford's called a sound, but it's really a fiord, carved by a glacier just like the ones in Norway and for that matter in southern Chile, Alaska, Greenland and other formerly glaciated places.

The name Piopiotahi means 'single piopio', an extinct songbird, one of which is said by Māori to have flown to the distant fiord to mourn the death of the Polynesian demigod Māui. The name Milford comes from Milford Haven, in Wales.

At the head of the sound there is a small tourist township and a harbour with five different boats serving the tourists.

The last time I was there I took one of the boats to Harrison Cove, partway along the sound, where there is an air-conditioned viewing chamber ten metres under the water: an experience which I really enjoyed. Thanks to abundant, tea-coloured freshwater runoff that floats on top, the surface water of the sound screens out nearly all of the light of day. And so, once your eyes have adjusted to the gloom, the viewing chamber allows you to see deep-water species that hide from the light and would normally only be found at crushing depths. This almost unique facility is called the Milford Discovery Centre and Underwater Observatory.

The cruise in a tall-masted boat is another good option. And there are kayaking and diving expeditions as well.

You can get special deals if you book at least three days beforehand.

Why you should take your time on the road

The sound is on the end of a long road from Te Anau, known as the Te Anau Milford Highway or the Milford Road. This is a final section of State Highway 94 and is, therefore, also marked with a shield labelled 94 on most maps.

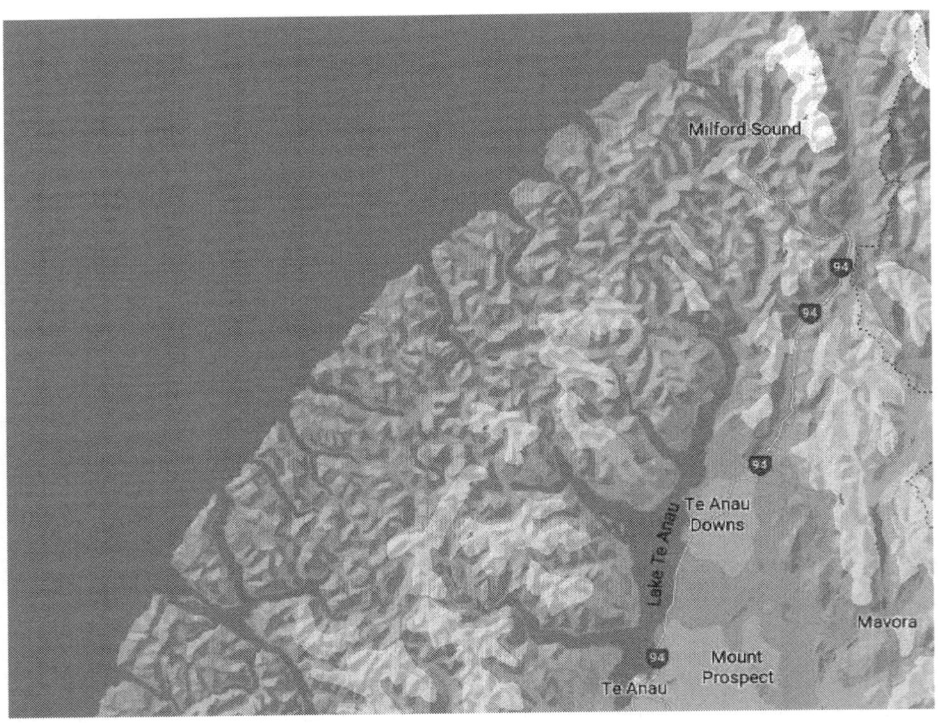

The Milford Road, a final section of SH94. *Map data ©2021 Google.*

People generally go to the sound for a day and come back. Or, alternatively, they walk the Milford Track, the subject of the next chapter.

But you can also spend a week or so in the area just doing day trips off the Milford Road: which is actually one of the most scenic roads in the world in its own right.

A further advantage of spending a week in the area and doing other things on the Milford Road is that you can get the weather you want at the main attraction, Milford Sound/Piopiotahi: and perhaps even a fine day and a wet day, both magnificent in their own way. On the fine day you can see more, but on the wet day the waterfalls are bigger.

What is the Road like?

Between Te Anau Downs, where SH 94 leaves the shores of Lake Te Anau, and the sound, there is another world awaiting you. According to the government website 100% Pure New Zealand, as of the time of writing,

"The first major highlight is the Eglinton Valley, which was once filled with glacier ice. The valley has steep rock sides and a flat, golden tussock floor - it's a surreal place. Further along the road are the Mirror Lakes - on a still day they display a perfect reflection of the Earl Mountains. Then you'll come to the Avenue of the Disappearing Mountain, where an optical illusion causes the approaching mountain to get smaller rather than larger. When you reach Lake Gunn, stretch your legs on the nature walk - an easy 45 minute loop track.

"The Homer Tunnel signals your descent to Milford Sound. This tunnel, which is hewed from solid granite, took nearly 20 years to complete. From mouth to mouth it measures 1270 metres. Before you reach Milford, get some fresh air on the 20 minute walk that leads to The Chasm - a spectacular waterfall where the Cleddau River has scoured its way through solid rock."

The website adds that the Milford Road is a winding mountain road and takes much longer to drive along than you might think. East of the Divide, it follows the course of the Eglinton River and its headwater lakes, Lochie, Fergus and Gunn; to the west, it drops into the valley of the Hollyford River / Whakatipu kā Tuka, and, once through the Homer Tunnel, into the spectacular, vertical-sided Cleddau Valley on the way to the sound. Each of these three valleys is progressively more rugged, from scenic in the Eglinton to epic at the Cleddau Valley and Milford Sound / Piopiotahi end.

Day Walks along the Milford Road, and at the Sound

Short walks, from Te Anau Downs to Milford along the Milford Road include the whole or part of the way on the following tracks, some more difficult than others:

- Lake Mistletoe Track
- Boyd Creek Track and Walk, famous for an abundance of moss. Gets difficult if you go far.
- East Eglinton Track ("challenging")
- Dore Pass Route ("challenging")
- Hut Creek Track ("difficult")
- Mistake Creek Track ("difficult")
- Lake Gunn Nature Walk

- Key Summit (via a section of the Routeburn Track)
- Lake Marian Track (from a couple of km up the Hollyford Road)
- Falls Creek Route
- Gertrude Valley Track, which is followed by a more difficult route to the Gertrude Saddle
- The Chasm
- Grave-Talbot Track, which can be shortened to a stroll on the Gulliver River
- Tutoko Valley Track
- Milford Foreshore Walk
- Milford Sound Lookout Track

Some of the most beautiful day walks in New Zealand are in this area, notably Lake Marian, the Gertrude Valley and Key Summit

Accommodation

There are nine campsites along the Milford Road. From Te Anau Downs, these are:

- Walker Creek
- Totara
- Mackay Creek
- Deer Flat
- Knobs Flat
- Kiosk Creek

- Smithy Creek
- Upper Eglinton
- Cascade Creek (at the south end of Lake Gunn)

All nine campsites are publicly owned apart from Knobs Flat, a commercial venture with nice cabins where you can also have showers for NZ $5. A tenth campsite called the Lake Gunn Campsite is marked on maps, at the north end of Lake Gunn. But as of the time of writing it has been closed for the last few years, and the Cascade Creek campsite has been enlarged instead.

The campsites range from ultra-basic fishing spots to highly serviced, though none have powered sites for caravans as far as I am aware. I parked my caravan at Upper Eglinton. But Cascade Creek is the best-serviced campground in my view, with two outdoor cooking facilities, outdoor fires, and several toilets and water tanks with water from the roof. It's only a 45-minute walk from Lake Gunn as well. But all nine campsites are close to the river (the Eglinton) and some of them also have magnificent views as well. Some have outdoor fireplaces and there is usually a toilet: simply have a look at the links!

All nine campsites are also on the eastern or Te Anau side of the Divide, that is, the main divide of the Southern Alps. At the Divide, there is the Divide Shelter, and there also is the Homer Hut near the eastern end of the Homer Tunnel. But there are no campsites between the Divide and Milford.

At Milford Sound you can stay at the Milford Sound Lodge for NZ $30 per night, for a powered site, in a car or campervan. The Self-catering Lounge, kitchen and bathroom facilities are excellent. There is not much of a fridge though. There are other upmarket options in units. Dorms will be built in a few years, apparently.

The dinner options are quite steep, NZ $40 for a main. However, the local café has more reasonably price healthy options, breakfast and lunch have cheaper options.

At the other end of the road, the Lone Moose Backpackers caters for those who like fixed accommodation or want some R and R at Te Anau Downs. There are also many choices of accommodation back in Te Anau township itself.

Here is a blog post, with more photos, which expands on the present chapter:

a-maverick.com/blog/ milford-road-why-spend-day-milford-sound-piopiotahi-can-spend-week

CHAPTER THIRTY-TWO

Tramping the Milford Track and Feeling Very Scottish

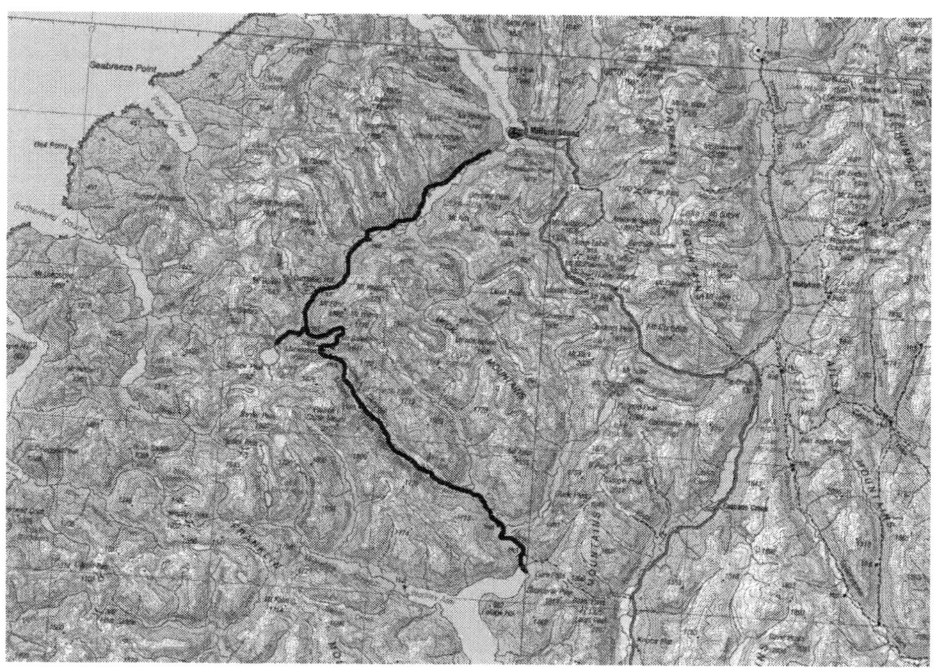

The Milford Track, *marked in black and normally accessed via a boat service on Lake Te Anau (at bottom), runs up the Clinton River, through the Mackinnon Pass and down the Arthur River to Milford Sound/Piopiotahi, with a side trip to Sutherland Falls. Background map LINZ via NZ Topo Map, 2021.*

I did the Milford Track a few years ago with the Wakatipu Tramping Club, after the close of the Great Walks season

(October-April), during which the tracks are busy and hut bookings are required.

The first month after the close of the season is when a lot of locals do the walks, because there's still coal and wood left in the huts!

We stayed at a motor camp in Te Anau and had to catch a boat the next morning at Te Anau Downs, about a 45-minute drive from the town.

Te Anau is a very interesting place, with only two thousand permanent residents. Nestled on the eastern shores of Lake Te Anau, the township of Te Anau is a very popular tourist destination because of its proximity to Milford Sound, the Kepler Track, and other spectacular walks. However, it does have a 'shoulder season' – a period before the high numbers of travellers start to come in, when the town is quieter.

The town has a wonderful movie theatre called the Fiordland Cinema, which was especially constructed for the locally-filmed movie *Ata Whenua – Shadowland*, its title reflecting the Māori name for the region.

The boat ride from Te Anau Downs was a lot of fun and the scenery around Lake Te Anau looked incredible from out in the water.

We landed at Glade Wharf after about an hour on the boat, and strolled along river flats to Clinton Hut, five kilometres from the wharf. This part of the journey passed quickly. All walkers on the track spend their first night at Clinton Hut.

From Clinton Hut, we tramped on to Mintaro Hut on Lake Mintaro, past the more glamorous but expensive Pompolona Lodge and a number of shelters: a walk that took us around six hours. That was where we spent our second night.

The track got steeper the next day, as we climbed towards the beautiful Mackinnon Pass, the highest point on the track.

Mackinnon Pass bears the name of the Scottish explorer Quintin McKinnon, whose first and last names have both been written down in various ways. Like much of the South Island the pass has a real Scottish-highlands feel to it as well. It put me in touch with my father's-side roots for a moment, even if his native town of Dundee is on the other side of the world!

I loved the pass: even though it was cloudy, the view of the entire mountain range was really impressive. Then, we tramped downhill to Dumpling Hut, past the Quintin Lodge and an airstrip. A hike which was, in total, six or seven hours from Mintaro Hut.

We all wanted to see Sutherland Falls, named after another Scotsman, but found them to be taped off with a safety warning advising that the track to the falls was in poor condition and therefore closed. This we ignored on the assumption that, on a Great Walk, such a precaution was probably conservative and aimed at the inexperienced in any case. All the same we were caught on the way back by a DOC officer, who gave us a right talking to!

After our adventure at Sutherland Falls, we continued on to Dumpling Hut where we spent the night. Our final day on the

Milford Track was the eighteen-kilometre tramp to Sandfly Point, passing the impressive Mackay Falls near the Arthur River, and the equally mesmerising Giant Gate Falls beside Lake Ada. At Sandfly Point, the track runs into Milford Sound, also known as Piopiotahi: from the bay you can see the magnificent Mitre Peak / Rahotu rising over the fiord. As we caught a short boat ride past Mitre Peak to finish our tramp, it wasn't hard to see why it is perhaps the most iconic mountain in New Zealand.

The Milford Track

At the Quintin McKinnon Memorial Cairn on Mackinnon Pass. *As you can see, mistiness was the norm.*

For a blog post with a lot more images, see:

a-maverick.com/blog/tramping-milford-track-feeling-very-scottish

For a further resource, see DOC's page on the Milford Track.

CHAPTER THIRTY-THREE

The Hollyford Track

Where the hunters gave me venison

IT was autumn when, fresh from the summer tramping season, I decided to hike the beautiful Hollyford Track in Fiordland National Park. It was an epic four-day journey with a pre-booked jetboat ride back along the lengthy finger lake known as Lake McKerrow, or Whakatipu Waitai, to shorten the return trip.

I tramped the nine kilometres up from the end of the Lower Hollyford Road to the beautiful Hidden Falls, a walk of about two to three hours, and went on the nearby Pyke River swing bridge, the longest swing bridge in the National Park.

I spent the night at the Hidden Falls Hut, and woke early to see a beautiful low-lying fog blanketing the valley – what a majestic sight for only my second day on the Hollyford!

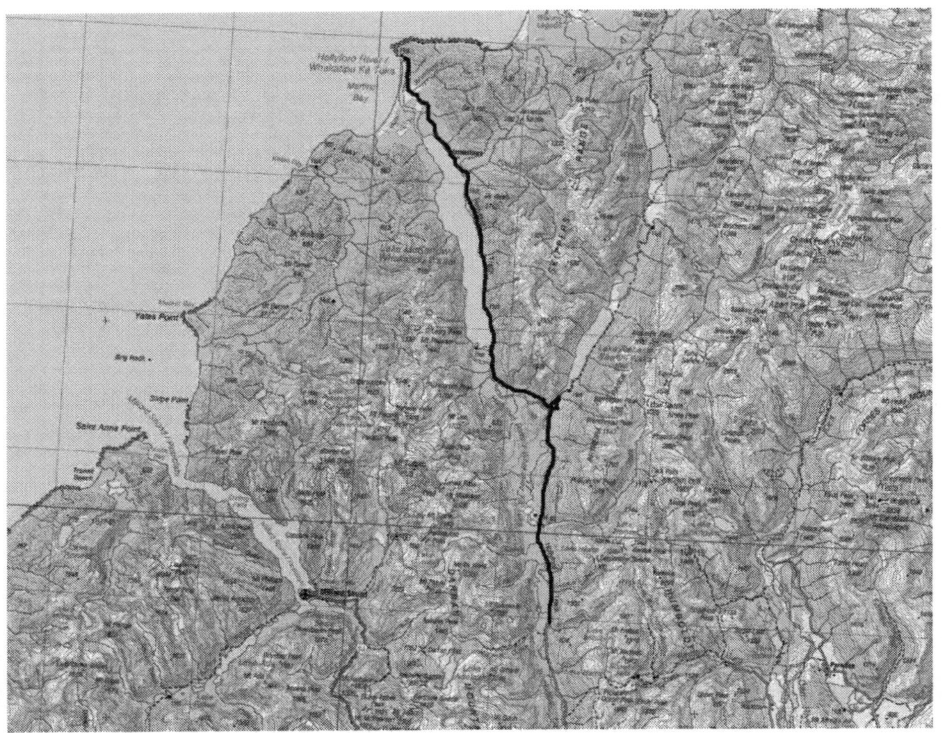

***The Hollyford Track.** The Track, marked in black, goes down the lower Hollyford Valley and along Lake McKerrow/Whakatipu Waitai to Martins Bay, north of Milford Sound/Piopiotahi. Background: LINZ via NZ Topo Map, 2021.*

Following the path of a long-gone glacier, the Hollyford Valley cuts its way through the Darran Mountains area and out to the Tasman Sea, showing much of New Zealand's natural beauty in one walk.

The Hollyford Track is the only major track in Fiordland that can be walked all year round in good weather, though sections can become impassable and dangerous in wet weather.

You can read more in an extended blog post, including how I got free venison, on

a-maverick.com/blog/hollyford-track

CHAPTER THIRTY-FOUR

Gertrude Saddle

A Rock-Climber's Paradise

I had an adventure of quite a different kind when I went tramping and climbing in the Gertrude Valley in the Fiordland National Park. Nestled underneath the Darran Mountain Range, the valley is reached from a carpark that turns off the Milford Road just before the eastern entrance to the Homer Tunnel.

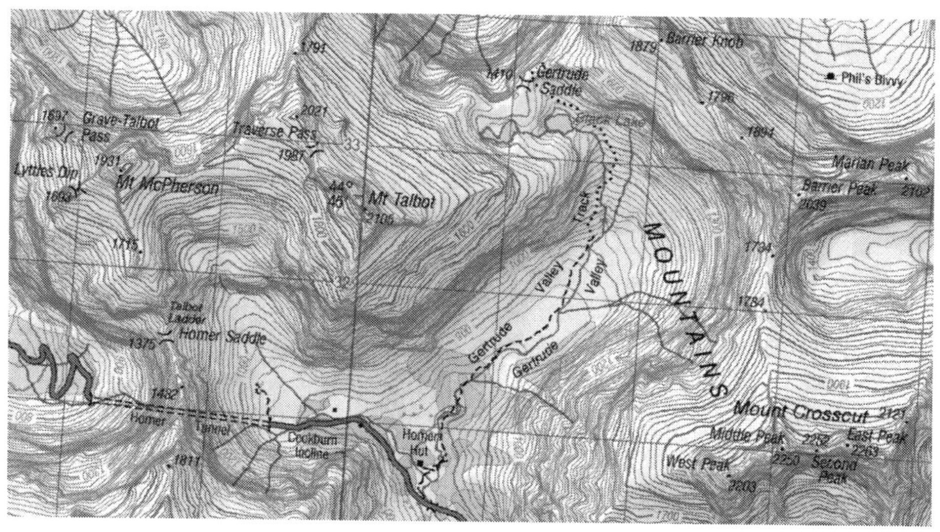

Gertrude Valley and Saddle in relation to the Homer Tunnel, on the Milford Road. *LINZ via NZ Topo Map, 2021.*

The Homer Hut is close to the carpark. Many rock climbers stay at the Homer Hut because the nearby Darran Mountain Range is a great area for rock-climbing.

Gertrude Saddle

The Darran Mountains include the Gertrude Saddle, which is reached by way of the Gertrude Valley Track. The views of the

Gertrude Valley and part of Milford Sound/Piopiotahi from here are terrific! For more on my adventures on Gertrude Saddle, including how I ended up in the middle of a party of Americans in this remote spot, and some notes on the hazards of this area as well, see the following blog post:

a-maverick.com/blog/gertrude-saddle-rock-climbers-paradise

CHAPTER THIRTY-FIVE

The Romantic Routeburn

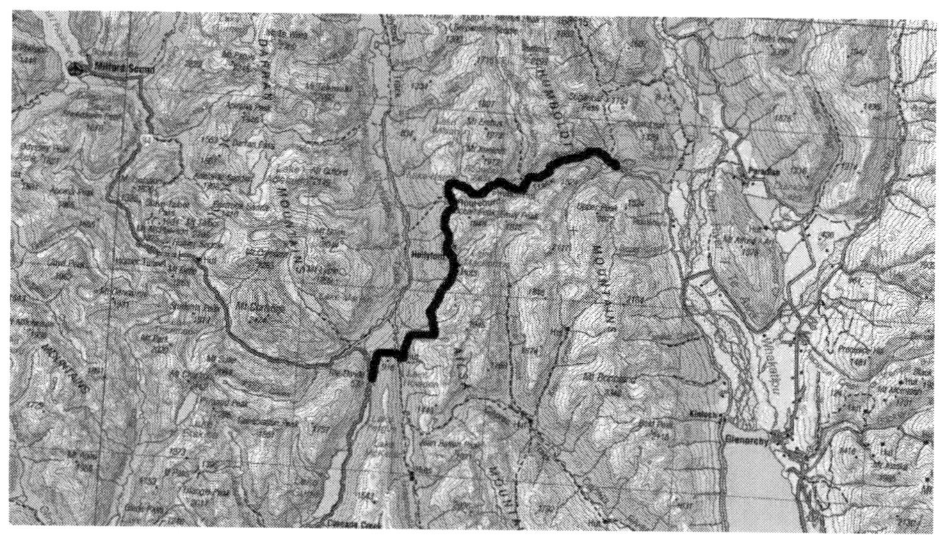

The Routeburn Track (in black), *showing local relationships to Milford Sound (top left) and the head of Lake Wakatipu (bottom right). Background map from LINZ via NZ Topo Map, 2021.*

THE Routeburn Track is one of New Zealand's ten official Great Walks (soon to become eleven). In World Heritage surroundings, the Routeburn Track was also reputedly named one of the eleven top trails in the world by *National Geographic Adventure* magazine in 2005. It leads from the headwaters of Lake Wakatipu to the Divide, on the road to Milford Sound.

The whole 32-kilometre track can be done as a multi-day hike, but sections of the track are also very accessible to day-walkers.

Alpine flowers (top); Darran Mountains from Harris Saddle (bottom)

Also dubbed 'the ultimate alpine adventure' the Routeburn Track boasts unrivalled views of the Southern Alps to the east and the Darran Mountains to the west.

In the warmer part of the year, the Great Walk season, the adventure includes hikes through high-altitude meadows in which flowers such as South Island Edelweiss are often in bloom.

For more, including many more photos, see my blog post on:

a-maverick.com/blog/romantic-routeburn

CHAPTER THIRTY-SIX

Lake Marian

Camping and looking at the Routeburn

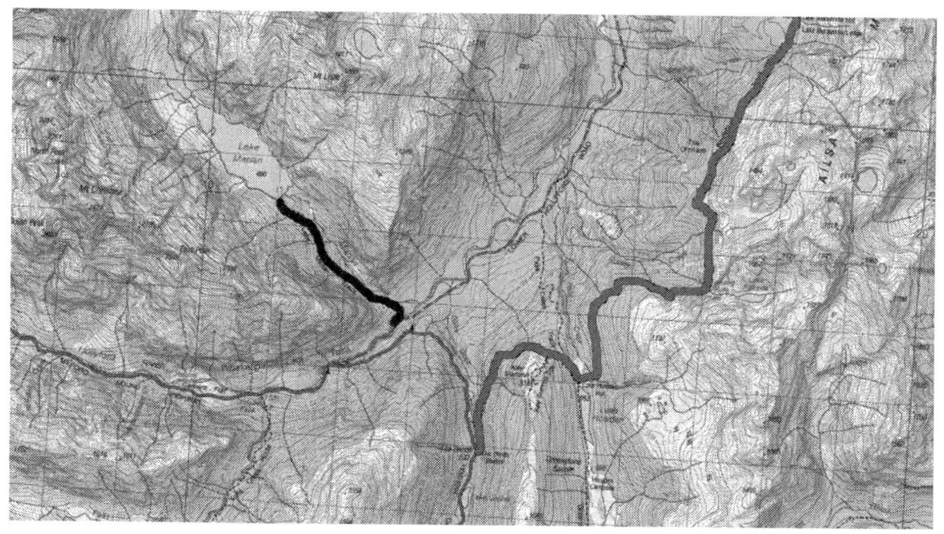

The Lake Marian Track (left, in black) in relation to the road to Milford Sound and the western part of the Routeburn Track (right, in grey). LINZ via NZ Topo Map, 2021.

THE Lake Marian Track has lately become very popular as well, although tourist numbers are down at present because of Covid (so, if in NZ already, you should go there!). The track begins from Marian Carpark, one kilometre down the unsealed Hollyford Road from its intersection with the Milford Road, some ninety kilometres out from Te Anau. It now has a wooden gantry only 20 minutes in, from which you can admire the Marian

Falls, which are really more like rapids. Even if you don't do the rest of the track, you can still walk to the gantry.

***At Lake Marian,** looking toward the Ailsa Mountains where the Routeburn Track is (top) and toward the Darran Mountains (middle and bottom).*

Once at the lake you can camp overnight. There is more birdlife there now than there used to be, what with the conservation and trapping being done on the Routeburn: it is so great to see.

There are good views over toward the mountainous terrain of the Routeburn Track, from which you can also glimpse Lake Marian, from Key Summit at least.

For more, see:

a-maverick.com/blog/lake-marian-camping-looking-routeburn

CHAPTER THIRTY-SEVEN

Rees-Dart

Toward the most beautiful glacier

The Valleys of the Rees and the Dart *surround the Forbes Mountains, north of Glenorchy at the head of Lake Wakatipu. LINZ via NZ Topo Map, 2021.*

IT was cold, and boggy underfoot, as a few friends and I began our tramp up the Dart River on the great Rees-Dart Circuit near Glenorchy.

Partly inside the South Island's World Heritage area, the Rees and Dart Valleys were first used by the Ngāi Tahu people of Murihiku/Southland and Otago for hunting moa and collecting greenstone.

Alongside its English name, the Dart River has an official Māori name which also appears on maps, Te Awa Whakatipu, meaning the river that drains into Lake Wakatipu.

The route runs up the beautiful, initially flat-bottomed river valley of the Dart/Awa Whakatipu and joins with the Rees River in quite different country, at the Tititea/Mount Aspiring National Park boundary, before looping back to Lake Wakatipu down the Rees.

It's at that upper point that you can also go still further up the Dart/Te Awa Whakatipu to the Dart Glacier, or over the Cascade Saddle Track into the Matukituki Valley if you want.

With a return day trip to the Cascade Saddle, the Rees-Dart Circuit normally takes five days.

Despite its accessibility and the fact that the lower parts are mostly an easy stroll, this track gets quite 'gnarly' further up, with some steep bits that beginners would find scary, and it pays to read what Tramping New Zealand has to say about the Rees-Dart Circuit. That web page, in the box following on the next page, has some pretty good photos too!

tramping.net.nz/routes/rees-dart-track-mt-aspiring-national-park

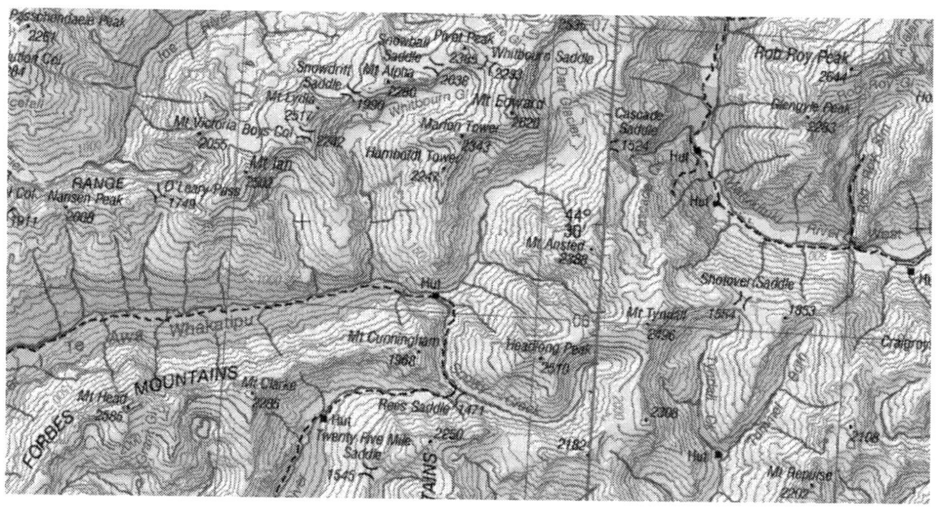

The Dart Glacier (top centre-right) and Cascade Saddle in relation to the Forbes Mountains. *This is a closer view on NZ Topo Map, 2021. The Cascade Saddle route into the Matukutuki Valley does not actually go over the Cascade Saddle and is visible on a still closer view.*

The Dart Glacier and its terminal moraine

The lonesome Cascade Saddle Toilet

For more, see:

a-maverick.com/blog/rees-dart-most-beautiful-glacier

CHAPTER THIRTY-EIGHT

Caples-Greenstone

More birds galore

The Caples-Greenstone Circuit loops around the Ailsa Mountains, *the clearly defined massif west of Lake Wakatipu in this view. Source: Google Maps Terrain View, Map Data ©2017*

A MODERATELY demanding tramp winds its way through the beautiful Caples and Greenstone Valleys, which come together by the shore of Lake Wakatipu and are also united in the hills by the subalpine pass of McKellar Saddle, which offers incredible views of the surrounding landscape.

There is plenty of native wildlife on the track, and when I first did it a few years ago, we were lucky enough to see falcons, kea, mōhua, and plenty of other birds.

The tracks, which form a loop in the same way that the Rees and the Dart do, can be hiked from either the Lake Wakatipu end near Kinloch and Glenorchy, or from The Divide on the road to Milford Sound/Piopiotahi.

The Divide also is one of the end points for the nearby Routeburn Track and many exhausted Routeburn trampers are picked up there, although some choose to extend their hike and carry on through the Caples-Greenstone for a longer tramp.

Even without an extension onto the Routeburn, the Caples-Greenstone is still a significant four-day journey.

On the other hand, tramping.net.nz ranks the Caples-Greenstone as an easier option than the otherwise similar Rees-Dart Circuit.

Caples Valley (top); Mount Christina from the McKellar Saddle (bottom)

For more, see:

a-maverick.com/blog/caples-greenstone-track-more-birds-galore

CHAPTER THIRTY-NINE

Kepler Track

Just divine views

THE Kepler Track begins on the shores of Lake Te Anau – the largest body of fresh water in the South Island of New Zealand – and winds its way through the spectacular Fiordland National Park.

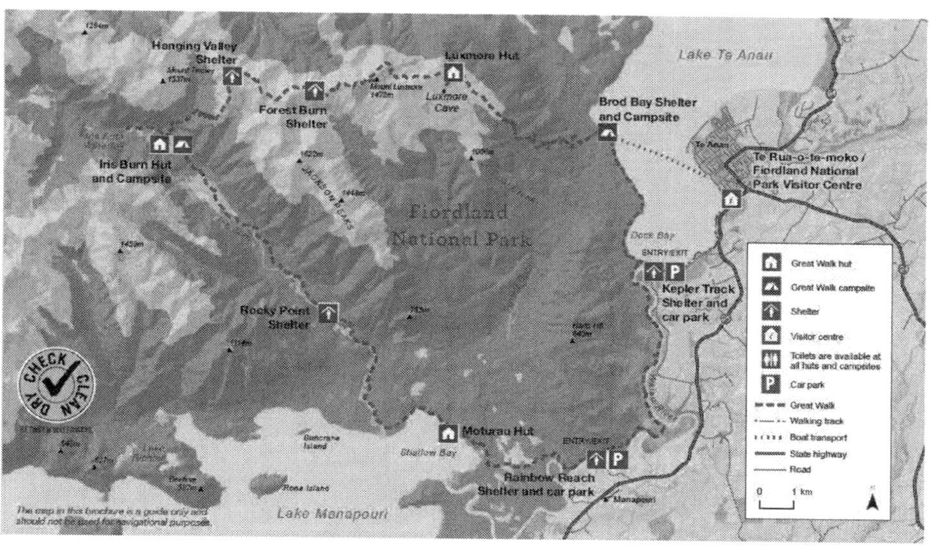

The Kepler Track, a loop between Lake Te Anau (top right) and Lake Manapōuri. *From* Kepler Track *(brochure), Wellington, Department of Conservation, October 2020*

Looping for some sixty kilometres up alpine heights and alongside two beautiful lakes, the track starts and ends only five kilometres from the town of Te Anau, at the Kepler Track carpark.

According to the official Discover New Zealand website newzealand.com, what's unique about the Kepler Track is that it was designed from scratch:

> "Unlike many other multi-day walks, which evolved from Māori greenstone trails or pioneer exploration routes, the Kepler Track was custom-made, built for pleasure, rather than necessity.
>
> "Opened in 1988, the track was carefully planned to show walkers all the best features of Fiordland - moss-draped beech forest, prolific bird life, tussock high country, huge mountain ranges, cascading waterfalls, vast glacier-carved valleys, luxuriant river flats and limestone formations. The track's construction makes for easier walking. Most streams are bridged, boardwalks cover boggy areas and the very steep sections have steps. Walk the Kepler and you'll see everything that's marvelous about this exquisite corner of the world." (Quote as of the time of writing.)

The Kepler Track certain does make for magnificent views of the mountains and of the two large lakes that it loops between!

The Kepler Track, *with views of the Murchison Mountains and Lake Te Anau*

For more, see:

a-maverick.com/blog/kepler-track-just-divine-views

CHAPTER FORTY

Off the Beaten Track at Manapōuri

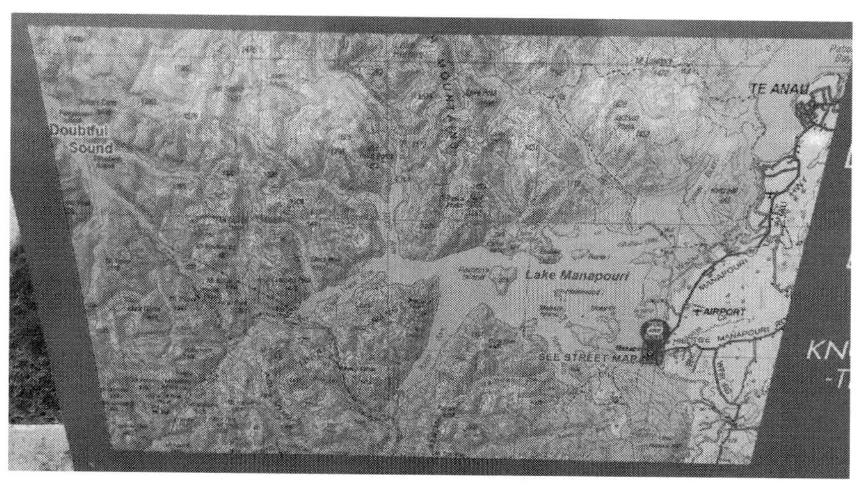

A local signboard map in Manapōuri township

ONE spring, just lately, I hired a campsite at a place called the Manapōuri Motels and Holiday Park.

Spring's a good time to go travelling in New Zealand, as there isn't much pressure.

In fact, I was one of only three people camping there!

The Manapōuri Motels and Holiday Park is on the main street of Manapōuri. Well, there is pretty much only one street in Manapōuri township.

The office and camp shop are both in a sort of European chalet style, next to an old-style phone box of the kind that disappeared from New Zealand streets in the 1980s.

And it's got all these smaller chalets for people to stay in.

The Morris Minor automobile collection, which is another distinctive feature of the holiday park, belongs to Aaron Nicholson, one of the sons of the founders, and his wife Pauline.

Things to do

There are some local walking tracks south-west of Manapōuri township that lead past, and up, the spectacular sugar-loaf peak known as the Monument, which towers 290 metres or just under a thousand feet above the level of the lake.

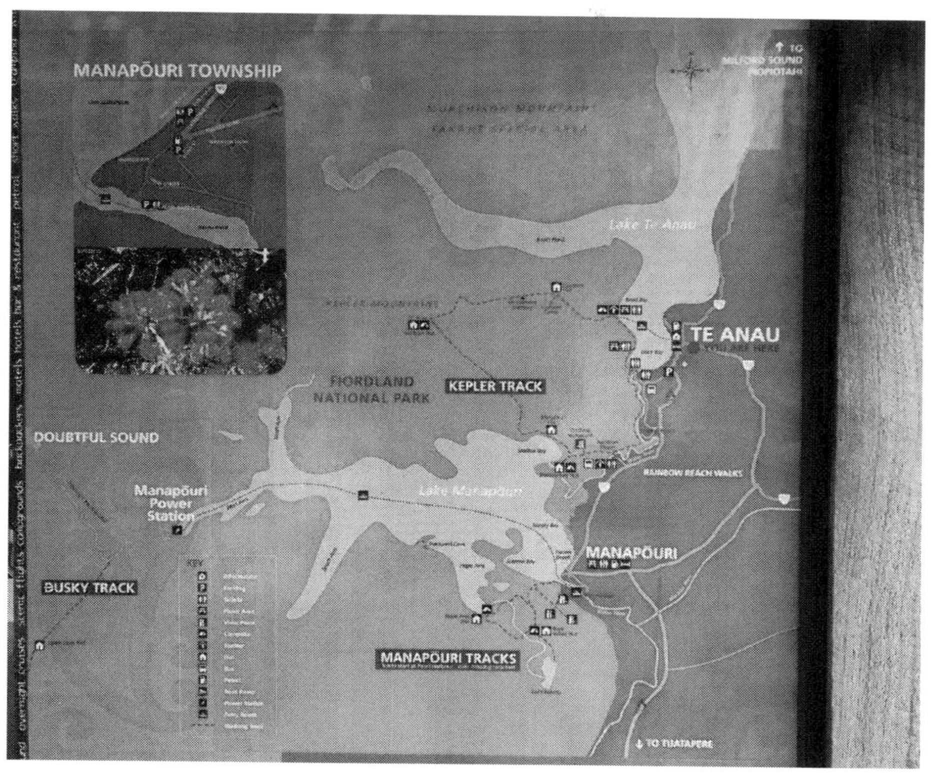

Track near Manapōuri and Te Anau, on a local signboard

Along with the tracks, the map on this signboard also points to the Manapōuri Power Station. There's a ferry route to the station and a road from there to Doubtful Sound, the subject of the next chapter, and to the Dusky Track, which I talk about a few chapters further on as well.

Looking northward, you can see the Kepler Mountains from Manapōuri township. Well, they're hard to miss, really.

Looking westward, you can see the sun set over some other mountains.

With everything then getting lit up again at dawn!

Lastly, if you head east from Manapōuri on the Manapōuri Hillside Road, and then south and then west again on the Lake Monowai Road, you can either continue to Lake Monowai or head up the Borland Road into what's generally known as the Borland country.

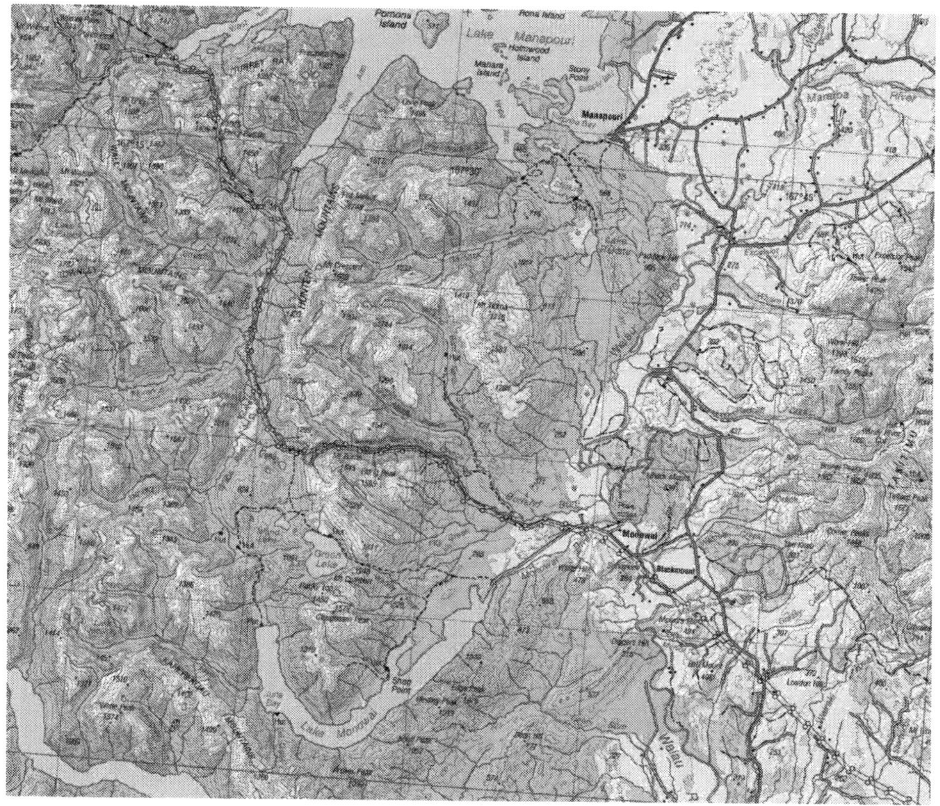

The Borland Country lies between Lake Manapōuri (top) and Lake Monowai (bottom). *The noticeable, apparently grey line through the Borland country is formed by superposition of the power lines from the Lake Manapōuri power station over the Borland Road and, at top left, the Wilmot Pass Road. LINZ via NZ Topo Map, 2021.*

This terrain was formed by what's perhaps the biggest onshore landslide in recent geological times, 27 cubic kilometres from the Hunter Mountains some 13,000 years ago.

There are lots of interesting walks and tramps in the Borland country, with a good-quality lodge with accommodaton for over a hundred in the form of the Borland Lodge. And the road itself is incredibly scenic, apart from the fact that you are accompanied by high voltage power lines nearly all the way.

For the Borland Road was constructed for the hydro workers at the western end of Lake Manapōuri, to which it leads at the head of the South Arm. The Borland Road doesn't make it to the to the West Arm, where the road over the Wilmot Pass is consequently isolated from the rest of New Zealand's road network.

According to DOC's website, as of the time of writing, source emphasis:

> The Borland Road is unsealed, narrow and steep in places, and subject to slips, washouts, snow, ice, high winds and fallen trees.
>
> It is usually fine for walking, mountain biking, 4WD vehicles and some other vehicles (depending on conditions).
>
> It is not suitable for campervans, caravans or trailers. Vehicles are not allowed off the main road.
>
> There are **no** fuel, communication (including cell phone coverage) or emergency services along its length, therefore only those properly equipped should attempt to negotiate the road.

Which sounds exciting, and as though you should also check your insurance or car hire terms.

The Borland Road penetrates much further into 'deep Fiordland' than any other part of New Zealand's ordinary road network, and yet not many people even know it exists. Though as I say, you do have to share it with the power pylons unless you're prepared to head off down one of the bush tracks.

The address of the Borland Lodge is 347 Borland Road. But presumably that's before you get to the gnarly bit.

For more, see my blog post:

a-maverick.com/blog/off-beaten-track-manapouri

CHAPTER FORTY-ONE

No Doubts about Doubtful Sound

Vintage New Zealand Government tourism poster displayed at Auckland Public Library, April 2018. *Crown copyright reserved.*

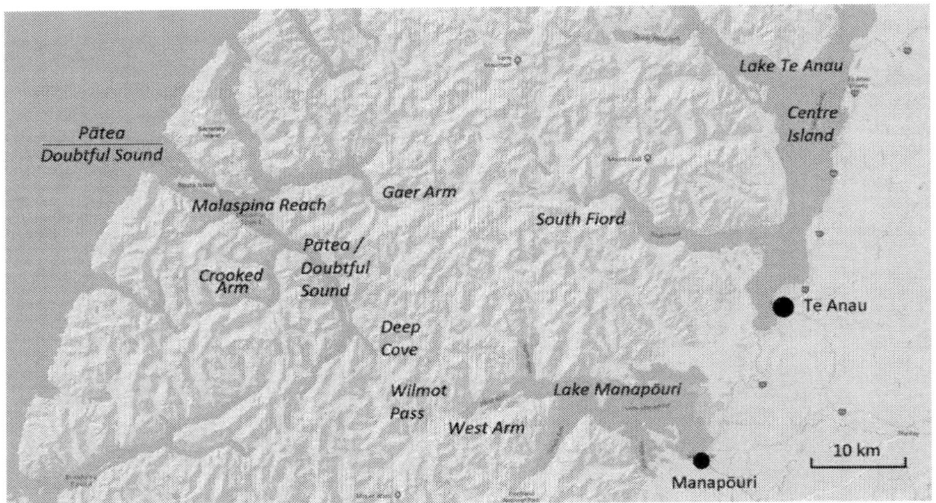

Doubtful Sound/Pātea and the Lakes to its East. *Background map data ©2019 Google.*

DOUBTFUL SOUND, known in Māori as Pātea, meaning 'quiet place', lies to the south of Piopiotahi/Milford Sound. In this part of Fiordland, the fiords of the sea reach toward the western arms of Lakes Te Anau and Manapōuri. The two saltwater and freshwater systems nearly join together, but not quite. If they were linked, we would have equivalents of Norway's huge Søgne and Hardanger fjords in New Zealand. Even as it is, Doubtful Sound/Patea is 40 km (25 miles) long.

You get to Doubtful Sound/Pātea by first crossing Lake Manapōuri and then catching a bus over the isolated Wilmot Pass.

It's hard to get to this fiord, but worth it when you do.

Here are some photos of the trip across Lake Manapōuri. There isn't any tourist-boat jetty on the lake. Instead, you start out on the Waiau River just south of Manapōuri town, from a place with the interesting name of Pearl Harbour. The other Pearl Harbour, obviously.

The Waiau River drains Lake Manapōuri. You head upriver a short distance and then you are on the lake, hooray!

Lake Manapōuri has lots of islands, which you can see in the last photo, and in this one.

The lake historically had two other Māori names, Roto-ua or rainy lake, and Motu-rau, which means 'hundred islands'.

In those days, it wasn't called Manapōuri, a name that translates as 'sorrowful prestige', a phrase much less obvious in its significance than plain old rainy lake or hundred-island lake.

According to a letter by the frontier historian James Cowan, published in the September 1937 issue of the *New Zealand*

Railways Magazine, Manapōuri (then spelt Manapouri) is in fact a nonsense name. It was the product of a mixup on the part of settlers who knew a bit of Māori, but not much:

> "When I obtained the original name from the old men of blended Ngai-Tahu and Ngati-Mamoe in Southland in 1903, they explained that Manapouri was a pakeha corruption of Manawapopore, meaning the violent throbbing of the heart, as after great exertion or under intense emotion. Moreover, the name, they said, did not rightly belong to the lake at all, it was mistakenly transferred to Moturau by an early surveyor from the North Mavora Lake, lying in the mountains between Lakes Wakatipu and Te Anau. Manawa-popore was in the first place the name of an ancestor, and was given to that hill-girt lake in ancient times. Some of the pioneer surveyors misunderstood the Maoris they questioned."

Cowan's story, or a version of it, seems generally accepted today as the explanation for how Lake Manapōuri got its name: one which, Cowan allowed, "for all its garbled construction is a name of music and beauty, perhaps the most euphonious lake name in New Zealand." As for the hundred islands bit, the ever-thorough Cowan added that "I believe the number is thirty-four, besides half-a-dozen which are really only rocks."

Anyhow, proceeding further along Manapōuri as I suppose we must now call the rainy, island-studded lake, we sped past increasingly epic-looking mountains that pressed in from the sides.

The power station takes water from Lake Manapōuri at an elevation of 178 metres, or nearly six hundred feet above sea level, and discharges it into Deep Cove.

We crossed the Wilmot Pass to Deep Cove. I didn't get much of a view going over as the weather was bad. I got a good view coming back, though.

Eventually we got to the end of the fiord, where it joined the open sea.

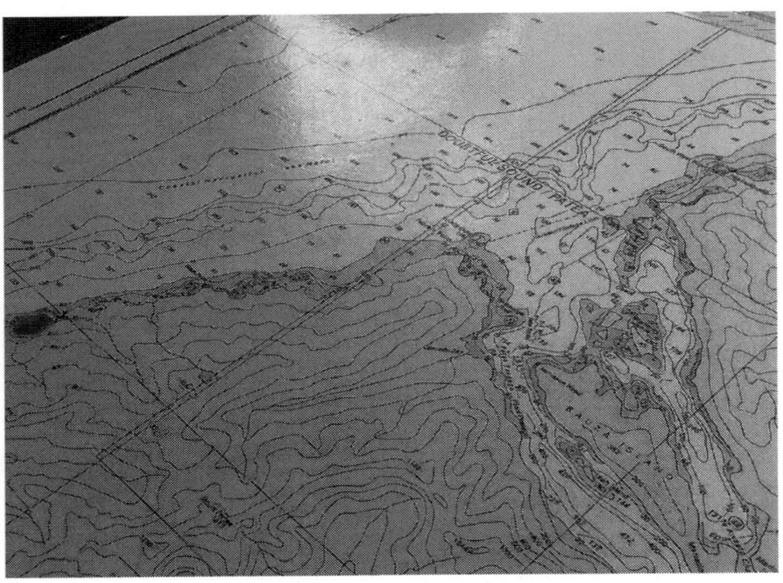

Doubtful Sound is about four hundred metres deep for most of its length, shallowing to about a hundred metres near the entrance, after which the coast drops away to about a thousand metres and then two thousand metres, just like that.

Captain Cook named the sound Doubtful Bay because all these rocks made it look a bit dubious.

The islands that are a bit easier to clamber onto have an abundance of seals on top! The main species here is the kekeno (New Zealand fur seal).

We tied up in a sheltered spot where we were served a lovely and social dinner: another highlight of the overnight trip!

The next day we departed from our quiet anchorage at the mouth of Doubtful Sound / Pātea. It was a beautiful sunny day, not like the day before.

Wow, I said, just wow.

Here's a sort of river of cloud that I saw near the entrance to the sound. Very strange!

We sailed back up the sound.

And into the tranquil and sheltered Crooked Arm, to get some images of still water and listen to the birdsong.

Crooked Arm

Paddling about in the Crooked Arm was also a good chance to get some better photos of the tall-masted ship. It was operated by Real Journeys, one of three firms that operate cruises on Doubtful Sound right now, the others being Fiordland Cruises and Go Orange.

In the main fiord, on an earlier visit, my editor Chris snapped some rather shocking images of a smoke-belching cruise-liner.

Chris also made a video of several scenes filmed along the way, including a lucky shot of a leaping dolphin in the Crooked Arm. That's in one of the blog posts referenced at the end of this chapter.

On my trip back over to Lake Manapōuri I got a clear view of the Wilmot Pass. Wow again!

And so, back to Manapōuri via the power station, which is oddly unobtrusive as nearly all the works are underground. We went into a small building and looked at some information displays about how the station was built in the 1960s, and the associated environmental controversies.

Perhaps you've heard of the legend about a king who sleeps in a hollowed-out mountain. Well, the Manapōuri power station really is inside a hollowed-out mountain. Though it runs night and day, and certainly doesn't sleep.

For more on this amazing fiord, see three of my blog posts:

a-maverick.com/blog/no-doubts-about-doubtful-sound

a-maverick.com/blog/doubtful-sound-revisited

a-maverick.com/blog/doubtful-sound-revisited-part-2

CHAPTER FORTY-TWO

Tūātapere Hump Ridge

The best sunsets in the South Island

THE Tūātapere Hump Ridge Track, New Zealand's newest Great Walk (2019), is near the town of Tūātapere, west of Invercargill. The track is managed by Tūātapere Humpridge Track, a charitable trust set up via a partnership formed between DOC and the local community. The trust offers a range of tour packages such as guided tours and helicopter rides, and it is well worth consulting its website, shown above, even if you are just a more ordinary sort of tramper.

A three-day loop track along the south coast of New Zealand, the Hump Ridge Track (for short) covers fifty-five kilometres of beaches, forests and subalpine terrain. The track is shown in black in the map that follows.

It's also possible, in this area, to tramp over the Hump Ridge by quite a different course, varying from a four-wheel drive road to a poled route, to get to Poteriteri Hut on Lake Poteriteri, the biggest lake in New Zealand without road access.

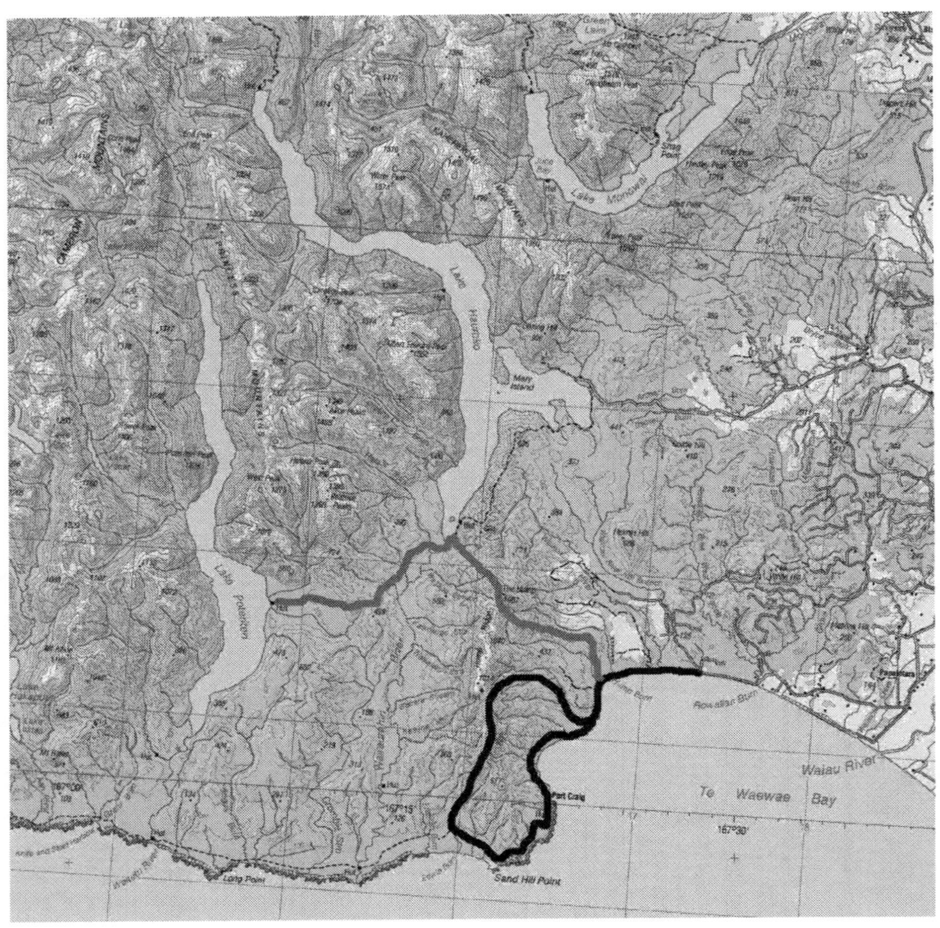

The Tūātapere Hump Ridge Track (black) and the 4WD Road/Track/Route to Poteriteri Hut (grey). *LINZ via NZ Topo Map, 2021. The three big lakes shown are, from west to east, Poteriteri, Hauroko and Monowai.*

The night before the tramp, I stayed in Tūātapere at a backpackers' hostel. Unfortunately, just as I was trying to get to sleep, the local youth began doing burnouts outside my window in their cars. There were people partying on the street and in the hostel until four o'clock in the morning.

After a patchy night's sleep, I started the track and soon met a cigarette-smoking businessman from Hamilton who threw his cigarettes in the bush as he was tramping. I also met and tramped with a Dutch girl who had been tramping around New Zealand for four months. The sunset on the first night was so beautiful, and you could even see Rakiura/Stewart Island in the distance. As well as witnessing the stunning views, walkers on the track can also cross some of the world's tallest wooden railway viaducts.

Hump Ridge Sunset

Hump Ridge

After completing the Hump Ridge Track, I returned to the same hotel in Tūātapere. The owner refunded my first night's fees and then gave me a free night and a lift to Invercargill the next day, which was a great example of southern hospitality and more than made up for my issues on the first night.

Once in Invercargill, I met the DOC manager responsible for volunteer hut wardens, who took me shopping. Here I was to get the food I needed for my next adventure: a two-week stint at the Port William Hut on Rakiura/Stewart Island at the start of the North West Circuit Track.

For more, see my blog post:

a-maverick.com/blog/tuatapere-hump-ridge-track

Additional Resources:

Tūātapere Humpridge Track: **humpridgetrack.co.nz**

The Southland App, by Advocate Communications

CHAPTER FORTY-THREE

46 South going on 47: Invercargill and the Bluff

I figured I needed to get some cheap bits and pieces for my car. I also wanted to do some shopping for good sandals and get a pedicure for my bunioned feet, as Queenstown is notoriously expensive for that sort of thing.

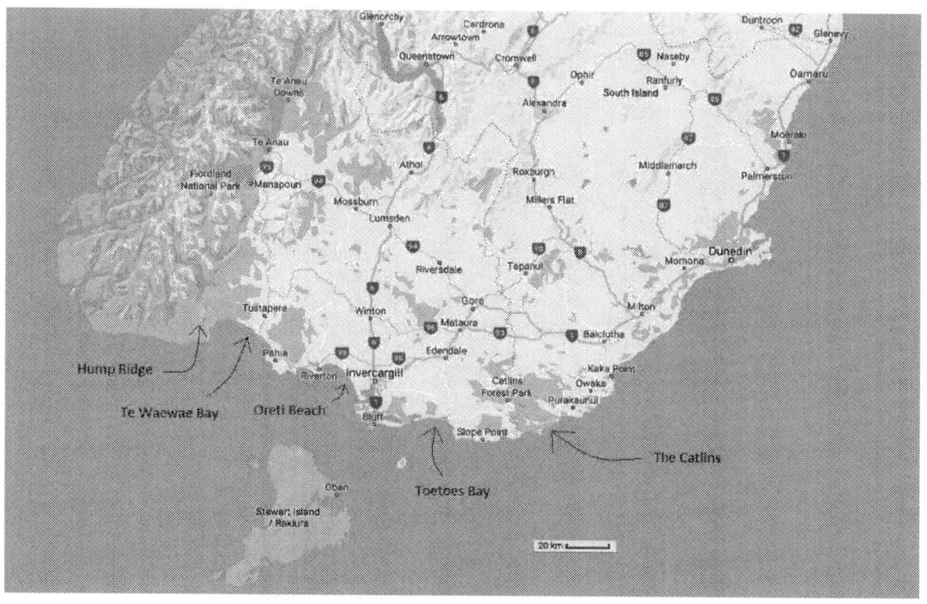

I travelled to Invercargill by driving south from Queenstown on State Highway 6. State Highway 1 continues southward to Bluff*. I've added the names of some other local attractions. Map data ©2019 Google.*

And so, to Invercargill: a city honoured in the internationally popular brass band tune known as the Invercargill March.

Everything in the South Island often seems to be a bit old fashioned and slow to anyone from Auckland, and this is just as true of Invercargill, a city where the traffic stops if it looks like you want to cross the street, and where the motto on the Invercargill Town Hall and Theatre reads 'For the Common Good', a very old-fashioned idea by Auckland standards.

Invercargill Town Hall and Theatre

'For the Public Good'

Formal gardens surround the downtown area, which has a wealth of such old buildings.

Information Panel for Queens Park, Invercargill *(which connects to the town belt). Note the rather grand and formal layout centred on a dead-straight Coronation Avenue. The entrance to the left is guarded by the Feldwick Gates.*

A satellite view showing most of Invercargill. The name of Queens Park has been added. *Clearly visible also is the Invercargill Town Belt (of parkland). Imagery ©2019 CNES/Airbus, DigitalGlobe, Landsat/ Copernicus, Map data ©2019 Google.*

Gerrard's Private Railway Hotel, Invercargill. *Public domain image by Karora, 26 April 2008, via Wikimedia Commons.*

Invercargill might not do bungy jumping and skiing, but it's still the gateway to the wilderness of southern Fiordland where the Tūātapere Humpridge Track is located; the coastal wilderness of the Catlins east of the city; the lengthy beaches of 26-km long Oreti Beach where Burt Munro used to race 'The World's Fastest Indian' and the similarly lengthy beaches of Te Waewae Bay_and Toetoes Bay; the town of Bluff (most southerly on the New Zealand mainland); Slope Point, the southernmost point on the South Island; and Stewart Island/Rakiura further to the south, a large island that is now one of a handful of international Dark Sky Sanctuaries.

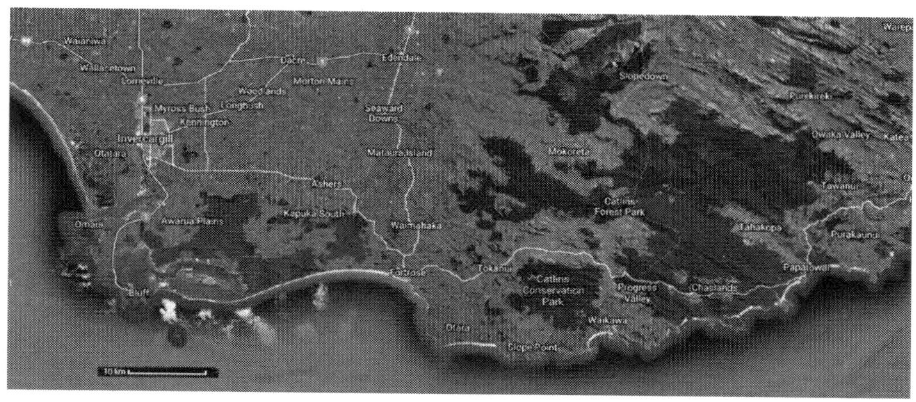

Satellite image of Invercargill and Bluff and the coast to the east, *with Toetoes Bay, the third giant beach in this area, to the east of Bluff, past Fortrose. Note also the lengthy dotted north-south trail through Slopedown, Catlins Forest Park and Progress Valley to the sea. Imagery ©2019 TerraMetrics, Map data ©2019 Google.*

All in all, old colonial cities like Invercargill often have a lot of character and public amenity, and need to be kept that way.

On the other hand, anything to do with petrol and motor racing is a big thing in Invercargill, thanks to the influence of people like Burt Munro no doubt. Or to put it another way, Burt Munro didn't race up and down Oreti Beach all by himself. I went to Teretonga Park, the home of (non-beach) motor racing in Invercargill and its surrounding region, which is known as Southland.

There's also Transport World, an absolutely world-class double transport museum founded by the late H W [Bill] Richardson.

There are two individual museums on the Transport World site, Bill Richardson Transport World, which bills itself as "the largest private automotive museum of its type in the world," and Classic Motorcycle Mecca.

The Southland Museum and Art Gallery in Queens Park has closed due to earthquake risk, pending redevelopment.

On the Saturday, I also managed to make enough time to get to Queens Park, where I caught up with about a hundred runners from a club called Invercargill Parkrun.

Demolition World

The next day, my search for car parts led to a place called Demolition World, which turned out to have nothing to do with car parts at all. Instead, it was a re-created town made up of bric-a-brac from the colonial era to the 1960s, stuff that Leigh saved while on-selling more valuable recycling materials, timber mostly.

One of the old signs outside the front entrance promised panel-beating services, so I thought it must be an auto junk yard. It turned out that it was just a sign and that Leigh was a sign collector.

I was so astounded. Demolition World has 50 shops which recreate the past, a church where people are getting married in the old style; a bar with old style bottled beer; a 'dairy' (NZ expression) or corner shop from the fifties with 1950s containers for the products; a circus; a shop with old toys; a blacksmith's shop; a railway station; and old horse-cart; and an old medical centre. It's a work of art.

Demolition World: Leigh, top centre

When I was there the proprietor, a woman named Leigh didn't charge anything other than a 'gold coin' donation (meaning NZ $1 or $2 coins, not real gold).

Blustery Bluff

Then, finally, I went off to Bluff to climb the Bluff Hill and take some more photos.

Bluff Hill is officially Bluff Hill / Motupōhue, the island of vines. It isn't quite an island, as you can see.

Bluff and the natural harbour of Awarua Bay, *plus a part of the amazing beach of Toetoes Bay. The Tiwai Point aluminium smelter lies just across the harbour entrance from Bluff. Imagery ©TerraMetrics, Map data ©2019 Google.*

Here's a webpage for walks on Bluff Hill:

bluff.co.nz/walking-tracks

By the time I got to Bluff the January weather had turned into the opposite of summer, as it often does in these parts, which lie in the latitude of Patagonia and face south toward Antarctica.

Here I am beside a famous sign.

784 km even to Wellington and 1401 km to Cape Reinga at the northern tip of the North Island, *let alone anywhere that's actually in another country*

There's an old gun emplacement on the hill, created just in case anyone ever tried to attack the most southerly urban seaport in the British Empire (they didn't).

The island of vines is also significant in Māori culture. Although South Island Māori faced a harsher environment and were fewer in number than in the North Island, tītī or muttonbirds were regularly harvested from nearby offshore islands and thus helped to sustain human life.

But do come to Bluff—it's so bracing!

Finally, here's a blog post that describes Invercargill and Bluff in more detail, with more pictures and videos:

a-maverick.com/blog/46-south-going-on-47-invercargill-and-bluff

CHAPTER FORTY-FOUR

The Catlins: An overlooked corner of New Zealand

IN the south-eastern corner of the South Island, the Catlins is a remote, yet beautiful, area that includes the island's southernmost tip. It runs from the town of Balclutha at its northern end, to Fortrose in the southwest.

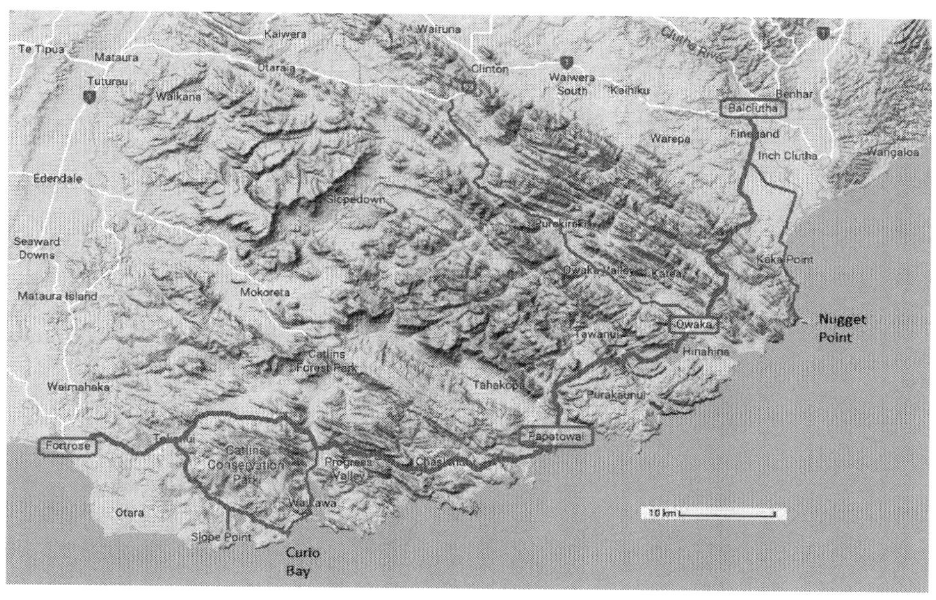

***The Catlins and environs, with highlighted town names and Nugget Point and Curio Bay added to the background map** (©2019 Google). The main coastal road between Balclutha and Fortrose and some of its side roads are also traced out in red.*

The Catlins has a long history of settlement. The area was first populated by Māori tribes, who enjoyed the abundance of food from the sea and forest. The Māori name for the area is Te Ākau Tai Toka, meaning 'the rocky southern shore'. When Europeans arrived in New Zealand, several settlers migrated to the area for logging and farming. One of them, Captain Edward Cattlin, bought land off the Ngāi Tahu chief, Tūhawaiki, a month before the Treaty of Waitangi was signed. Although he only bought a small block of land, Cattlin's modified last name now refers to the whole coastline between the Clutha and Mataura Rivers.

The Place of the Canoe

The name of the village that serves as the Catlins' main tourist hub—Ōwaka—means 'of the canoes' and refers to the fact that Ōwaka was the region's main canoe harbour. It always was the hub of the region, in other words.

The silver canoe at Ōwaka reminds me a little bit of the sculpture called* Sólfar or 'Sun Voyager' in *Reykjavík, Iceland.

The Captain's profession gives you clue as to what the main economic activities were locally. That is, the harvesting of whales, penguins, seals and native timber. These have since given way to a rather low-key tourism industry; so low-key that to this day the permanent population of the Catlins is only about 1,200. A third live in Ōwaka. Fortrose is even smaller.

A rare penguin

I've visited the Catlins several times, including one trip I made with my sister, Maree, where we saw yellow-eyed penguins, or hoiho, on the petrified forest at Curio Bay (more about that in a moment).

The yellow-eyed penguin only exists in New Zealand waters. It breeds in coastal forests and so it is vulnerable to all sorts of threats these days, from deforestation to dogs to the sheer stress of 'walking in a wet suit' from the shore to the forests where it breeds. It's the fourth-largest penguin in the world. And perhaps it is also one of the most raucous as well, for its Māori name, hoiho, means 'noise maker'!

There was only one breeding pair of hoiho at Curio Bay at the beginning of 2019. The scientists are trying to get to bottom of why numbers have decreased from 8 or 9 pairs a few years ago.

Up to my neck in peat

When I was there another time, I went tramping at Papatowai, an inland coastal walk, where I fell into peat. Thank goodness it was summer and not raining, as I certainly would have been worse off in wet weather. Even then, I was up to my neck in peat. Somehow, I made it out and then headed to the coast following a rarely used track, where I cleaned all my clothes in the ocean and made it back to the car.

Aside from the dangerous peat and beautiful views of the coastline, old Māori middens can also be seen along this track. These middens, a word meaning camp remains, can generally be identified by the presence of vast numbers of seashells, in much the same way that later European encampments could be identified by the presence of vast numbers of bottles.

Curio Bay: The petrified forest

In the petrified Jurassic forest, you can still see the grain of the wood, in vertical stumps and fallen logs.

In New Zealand, tree ferns and podocarps still rule many forests including the forests of the Catlins. So, the ecology of the living forest really is closer to the Jurassic, and to the nearby petrified forest, than most other places on earth.

Well, things don't get much weirder than that.

Porpoise Bay

About a kilometre from Curio Bay, Porpoise Bay gets its name because at certain times of the year it contains a pod of Hector's dolphins. The Hector's dolphin is a small dolphin, about the size of a big dog. Like the hoiho, Hector's dolphin is only found in New Zealand waters.

My sister Maree spotting yellow-eyed penguins on petrified wood at Curio Bay, near Porpoise Bay

Nugget Point

The lighthouse at Nugget Point is another spot well worth visiting. You should persevere along the path to the lighthouse, even though it's a bit daunting. From this spot you can also see the coal smoke pollution that hangs over Balclutha at times. There'll be another smudge on the eastern horizon, last night's coal smoke blowing out to Chile. Lots of places in New Zealand have a pollution problem, both in towns and in areas that are intensively farmed. The 'clean green' bit only applies to wilderness areas like the Catlins.

The lighthouse at Nugget Point, with its exposed access-track

My editor Chris said that he'd spoken to a couple of people in a Balclutha pub and that they said they'd always been too nervous to walk to the lighthouse!

Nugget Point is named after a profusion of rocks at its tip, called the Nuggets.

Slope Point: The South Island's southern tip

This really is the end of the line, with gnarly old fence posts, remnants of fences that are slowly falling into the sea. There's an automated light house or beacon there, too.

Looking backward

All in all, visiting the Catlins and its neighbourhood is a bit like going back in time by half a century. Balclutha contains few modern buildings and often smells of coal smoke. And you can stay very cheaply in guest-houses that are right on the beach and practically vacant outside the short summer season. Queenstown, it isn't.

I couldn't think of a better writers' retreat. Maybe that's what they should start selling the region as!

There's plenty more to see and do in the Catlins, which I haven't even touched on as yet, including caves, waterfalls, cold-water surfing and long and adventurous inland hikes through the primeval forest.

For more information, including the best times of year to go and the location of camping spots, cafés, and where to buy fuel, see the tourist website of the Catlins: catlins.org.nz.

The tourist website also includes the option to download a really useful brochure.

Finally, though it's not actually part of the Catlins but just outside it, it's worth mentioning that there's a place called Wangaloa, near Kaitangata on the coast north of the Clutha River mouth. Wangaloa, meaning 'long bay', is another of those Hawai'ian sounding names that you come across in the South Island.

I've got two blog posts about the Catlins, with more details of a later trip by my father and editor:

a-maverick.com/blog/the-catlins-an-overlooked-corner-of-new-zealand

a-maverick.com/blog/the-catlins-continued

Further Resources

nzpocketguide.com/18-attractions-you-cant-miss-in-the-catlins

My Little Local Clutha App

CHAPTER FORTY-FIVE

The Dusky Track . . . An Epic

AFTER being made social secretary for the Auckland Tramping Club, I resigned when I found out that neither I nor any other unattached woman under fifty years old was allowed on one of their tramps to the one of the wildest parts of New Zealand, the landscape around the fiord known as Tamatea/Dusky Sound.

Presumably there had been a scandal at some time and the ageing membership of the club was determined not to allow a repeat. To my mind such policies went some way toward explaining why the membership of this and other tramping clubs was, indeed, an ageing one.

It meant that the ATC was not a place for young people to meet anyone, in direct and obvious contrast to the meet-up groups that the young people were joining! This issue is the subject of a story in the July 2016 issue of the New Zealand outdoor magazine *Wilderness*, 'Smashing Stereotypes' by Hazel Phillips, which also mentions my crampon drama.

For want of a chaperone, I went alone to Fiordland to do one of New Zealand's hardest tramps, even though it is not recommended to go it alone. The Dusky Track was more than back-country, with no maintenance on the track at all at that time, and huts with leaky roofs and full of mice and rats.

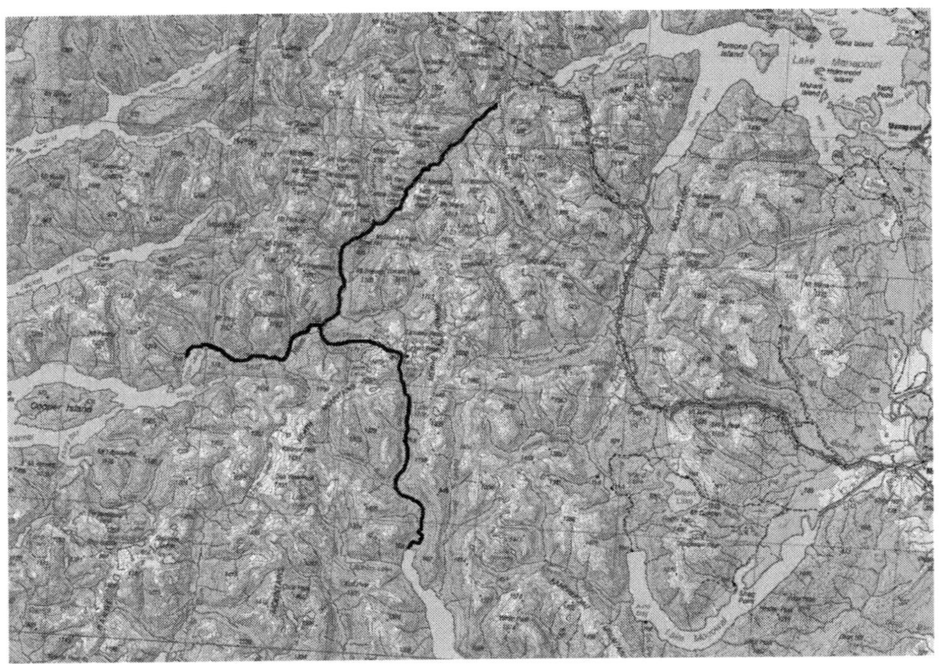

The Dusky Track, *marked out in black, runs northward from Lake Hauroko (bottom) to the Wilmot Pass Road from the West Arm of Lake Manapōuri (top right). This map includes an optional midway detour to Supper Cove. The noticeable, apparently grey line to the east of the Dusky Track is the course of the power lines from the Lake Manapōuri power station over the top of the Borland Road and a section of the Wilmot Pass Road. Background map LINZ via NZ Topo Map, 2021.*

You can do the Dusky Track in either direction. I did it from south to north. In that direction, you get to the Dusky Track by way of a ferry on Lake Hauroko, one of the southernmost big lakes in New Zealand and at 462 m (1,516 feet) max, the deepest. Before boarding the ferry or after you step off at the Lake Hauroko road-end, which can be reached from Southland townships such as Tūātapere. you can also do the 'short but stiff'

Lake Hauroko Lookout Track, which is one of my faves, and the Lake Hauroko Loop Bush Walk. In the other direction, the Lake Hauroko stage would be at the end.

Trailing 84 km through the Fiordland National Park, the Dusky Track is a challenging tramp taking eight to ten days to complete and is rated by DOC as suitable only for experienced groups of trampers.

The Dusky Track is the same length as the Heaphy Track in other words, but takes twice as long to get through; especially if you add the two-day detour west down the Seaforth River to Supper Cove.

There are many walkwires, structures for crossing flooded or deep rivers that are more rudimentary than bridges, around this area of the Fiordland National Park. I try not to use them, if the water is low, for fear of toppling over when I am wearing a heavy pack!

I didn't do the detour to Supper Cove. Nor indeed the whole length of the main route, for I pulled a calf muscle in the end while trying to get through a muddy bit and had to be helicoptered out: my personal locator beacon proving vital at last!

See the DOC page on Dusky Track, and also a few independent blogs which include photos and pass on locally useful tips such as their authors' opinions on how to judge whether areas prone to flooding can be got through on foot or not.

You can read more about my adventure, and a more detailed description of the track, in this blog post:

a-maverick.com/blog/dusky-track

TOUR 9: The South Island's Other Islands

CHAPTER FORTY-SIX

East to the Chathams

IF you've heard of New Zealand, then you probably know that the country has a North Island and a South Island. But did you know there's an east island as well?

More precisely, an archipelago called the Chathams, which are to New Zealand what the Falklands, or Malvinas, are to Argentina. They're mostly rather low, flat, covered in sheep and continentally attached to the rest of New Zealand even though they're hundreds of kilometres out to sea. As you can see!

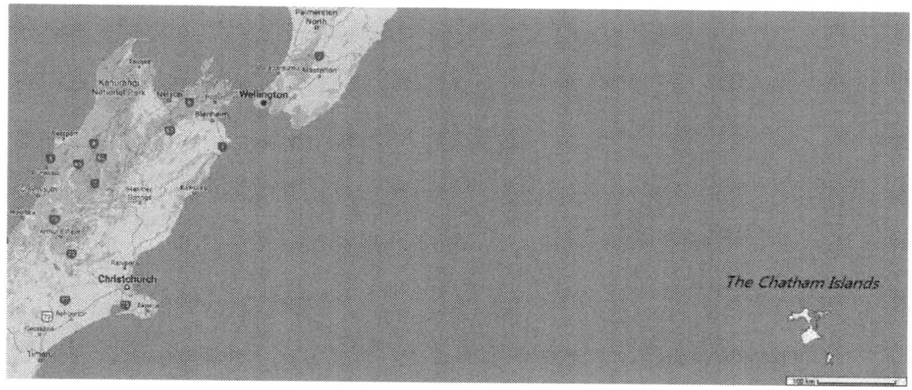

Background map data ©2020 Google

The big island is called Chatham Island or Rekohu, the second largest is Pitt Island or Rangiauria. There are lots of smaller islands as well. The economy revolves around sheep-farming and fishing. There are several fish-factories on the islands, which have a permanent population of about 600. They also get a few tourists, but not many.

Map by GNS Science / Te Pū Ao, 2019

Geologically, the Chathams are part of a great, mostly-submerged continental mass called Te Riu-a-Māui/Zealandia. The North and South Islands of New Zealand are really the main dividing range of Te Riu-a-Māui/Zealandia; which continues for vast distances in all directions under the sea at a depth of a few hundred metres.

In the east, Te Riu-a-Māui/Zealandia ultimately pops up to form the Chathams; an archipelago which is also covered, like Auckland, with many small volcanic cones one or two or three hundred metres high. Some of the offshore islands, like Mangere Island, are also isolated volcanic cones.

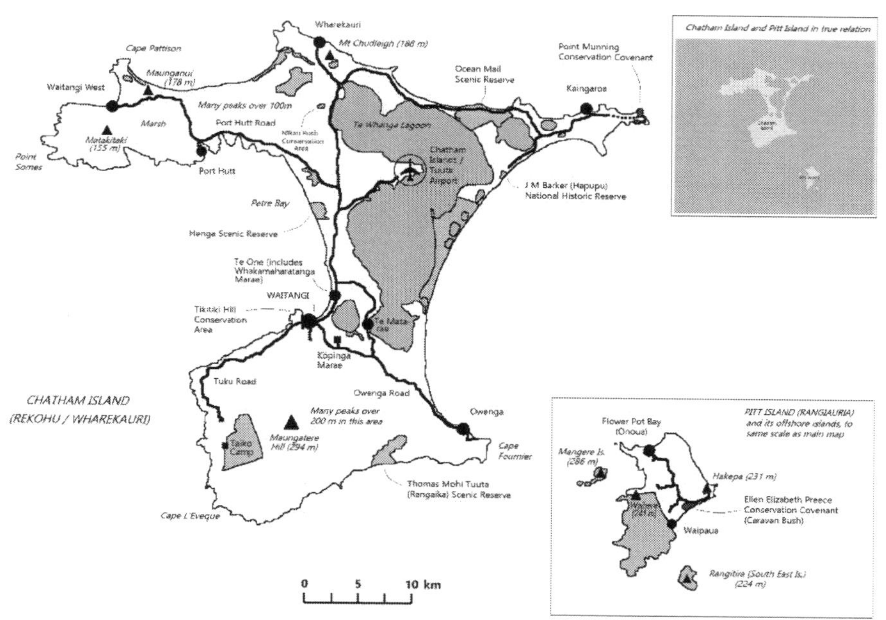

***The Chathams:** Conservation areas and roadways are based on the DOC brochure,* Chatham Islands walks, *November 2018 edition.*

I'd always wanted to go to the Chathams. Why? Because it was there! But it isn't easy, and it isn't cheap. There are goods ships that sail periodically from ports on the North and South Islands, and also an airline called Air Chathams, that flies once a week from each of Auckland, Wellington and Christchurch.

I flew to the Chathams in a Convair 580, a rugged and powerful aircraft of a type that was first designed in the 1940s.

In spite of its age, the Convair can still eat up the distance a lot faster than most of today's twin-prop commuters.

Coming in to land over Petre Bay on Chatham Island/Rekohu

Te Whaanga Lagoon and a couple of smaller lakes

For more, see my blog posts about the Chathams, of which there are four:

East to the Chathams. This post enlarges the current chapter:

a-maverick.com/blog/east-to-the-chathams

There are Moriori, after all! This post describes how claims of the extinction of the islands' indigenous inhabitants were exaggerated:

a-maverick.com/blog/there-are-moriori-after-all

The Museum at Waitangi. The de facto capital of the islands has a fascinating museum:

a-maverick.com/blog/the-museum-at-waitangi

The Lonely Landscape of the Chatham Islands, where the coronavirus probably won't ever arrive. Well, as of the time of writing it indeed has not; and would have to get through the rest of New Zealand first!

a-maverick.com/blog/lonely-landscape-chatham-islands-coronavirus-probably-wont-ever-arrive

CHAPTER FORTY-SEVEN

The Isle of Blushing Skies

Rakiura/Stewart Island and the North-West Circuit Track

Vintage New Zealand Government tourism poster seen at Auckland public library, April 2018. *Crown copyright reserved.*

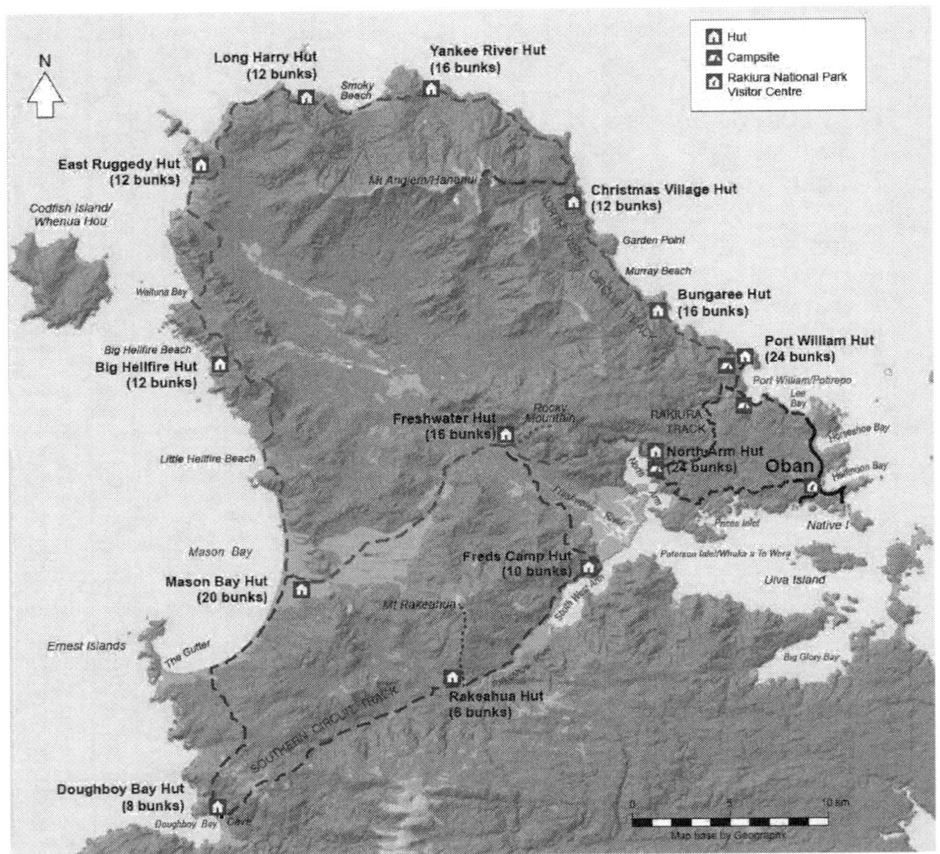

The northern part of Stewart Island/Rakiura, with Codfish Island / Whenua Hou at top left. *From DOC Brochure* North West and Southern Circuit Tracks, Rakiura National Park, *February 2017.*

THE small size of Oban belies its importance as Stewart Island's only town and the entranceway to the North West Circuit Track where I was to be spending a few weeks volunteering as a hut warden.

The Māori name for Stewart Island is Rakiura, which means 'blushing [or glowing] skies' and is far more poetic in my view. It seems to be a reference to long twilights in these subantarctic latitudes, the aurora australis which can sometimes be seen from here, or both.

After catching a ferry over from Invercargill, I met Phil Brooks, the DOC manager in charge of volunteers. He took me through the safety checks, taught me how to operate the radio and detailed what was expected of me while at the Port William Hut, which I was to take charge of.

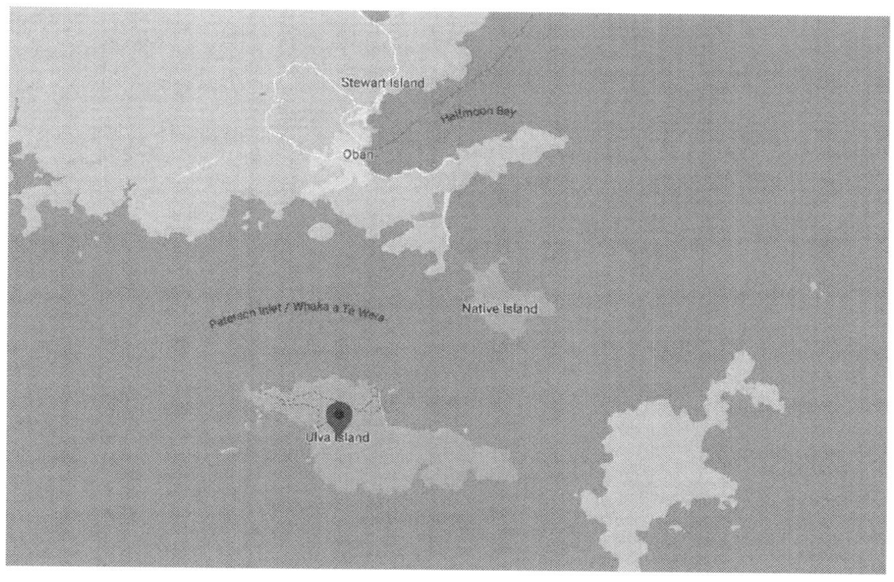

Ulva Island/Te Wharawhara, in relation to Oban. *Map data ©2021 Google.*

Oban is in a bay called Halfmoon Bay, just north of a much larger inlet called Paterson Inlet or Whaka a te Wera. The star of the inlet is Ulva Island or Te Wharawhara, an island that has never been milled and is free of predators, including rats.

Ulva/Te Wharawhara is therefore a little piece of New Zealand as it used to be, or as near as is possible today, and is served by regular ferries as it is an open sanctuary, with walking trails. The island is quite sizable, more than three and a half kilometres long, so there is plenty to see.

As names like Oban and Ulva suggest, names drawn from the Scottish Highlands and Islands, the Scots influence among the settlers seems to have been strong here as well.

From Lee Bay, five kilometres out of Oban, it's a three-to-four hour walk past Māori Beach to Port William Hut at the start of the North West Circuit Track. Bearing a name that rhymes with Fort William, another locality in the Scottish Highlands, Port William has an early European history by New Zealand standards.

An attempt was made at logging, but because of the area's extreme isolation it was hard to get either food shipped to the harbour or logs shipped out, beginning a downward spiral of a flagging industry and dwindling supplies.

As warden at Port William, I had to clean toilets and sweep the hut. I also had to put out campfires at the camp site, a two-hour walk away, as well as collect hut tickets. It wasn't demanding work – but somebody had to be there to do it.

Kiwi are still common on the island, and I also saw sooty shearwaters or tītī landing at night and going into their burrows. It was a magical moment. Three hundred thousand tītī chicks are harvested as muttonbirds annually by Ngāi Tahu: a number which is fully sustainable as there are estimated to be over twenty million of the species nesting around New Zealand, mainly in the Rakiura/Stewart Island area. The chicks are cooked and preserved in their own fat in a semi-dried-out state, just like last week's mutton, albeit with a strong fishy taste. This is a delicacy in the lower South Island, and you can even purchase muttonbird meat in the butchers in Dunedin.

The DOC office on Stewart Island tends to use volunteer rangers, and when it came to the end of my stay, I discovered that the next volunteer had cancelled. I was asked to stay for another two weeks, which I happily agreed to. Most of the time Stewart Island has a cool climate, but during February and March it can be a Pacific Island paradise: hot and sunny and ringing with birdsong of tūī, kākāriki and kererū. When I walked to other huts, I could hear the fishermen's radios mingling with the calls of the birds. It was absolute bliss, and I was more than happy staying longer.

Top to bottom: *Māori Beach; Paterson Inlet/Te Whaka a Wera; Tītī or Sooty Shearwaters*

Myself as Hut Warden

Oban

Beach scene

For more on Rakiura/Stewart Island, see my blog post:

a-maverick.com/blog/isle-blushing-skies-rakiura-stewart-island-north-west-circuit-track

CHAPTER FORTY-EIGHT

Whenua Hou and the Few Kākāpō Left

AFTER my month on Rakiura/Stewart Island, I left for Whenua Hou, also known as Codfish Island, to work on track maintenance. Even in normal times, to stay on the island you have to go through quarantine, which I did in Invercargill. During the process, they checked for foreign grasses in my gear, so I had made sure to purchase new socks and wash down my pack and wet weather gear.

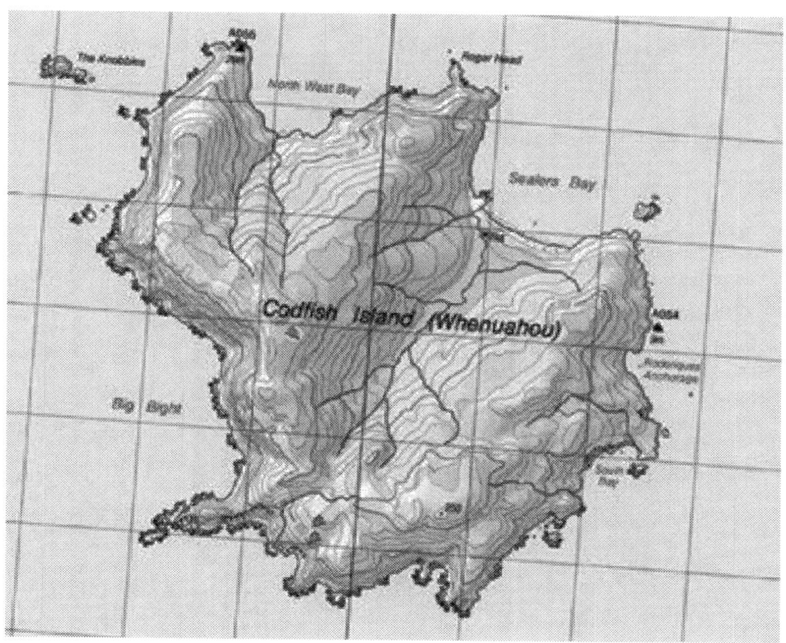

LINZ via NZ Topo Map, 2017

Before departing for the island, I realised I did not know whether I was flying there by aeroplane or helicopter. I was petrified because in the 1990s I had taken a tourist helicopter ride at the Shotover (Queenstown) and I had felt like I was going to fall out of the sky. To my relief, we took a four-seater plane from Invercargill Airport. However, the weather was wet and windy and even the experienced pilot was silently sweating when we took two attempts to land on the beach.

The track maintenance on Whenua Hou was hellish. We were set to work ripping up seventy metres of wire-meshed boardwalk with crowbars and staple-gunning down plastic anti-slip mesh in its place – all this done in the rain, of course! My back just about gave out after doing it for five days.

The kākāpō breeding season on Whenua Hou is a busy affair. It begins with the male kākāpō's booming song, a mating call designed to attract the females. Some males are successful at this, but for the less adept, artificial insemination is also being used. This is essential because some breeding-age males, like Richard Henry's son Sirocco, were hand-reared and now prefer human company to the company of other birds! Poor Sirocco may never mate with another kākāpō but he has other pleasures – he is famous for making out with Stephen Fry's co-presenter's head on a British nature documentary!

During the breeding season, rangers frequent the wooden walkways on the island for about two months, travelling between nests and monitoring the birds. Once they are nesting, volunteers camp outside the burrows and monitor the comings and goings of the parent. There are cameras placed in every nest to monitor the incubation period.

Once the eggs hatch, each chick is like gold. They are weighed, hand-fed and all the growth processes are overseen. I met some of the kākāpō juveniles during the day as they were being weighed. Hand-rearing does occur, but as it can affect their breeding potential later, it is preferable that they are raised in the wild.

The success of a breeding season depends on the growth of rimu berries on the island. These are a key food of the kākāpō, which only breeds in years when rimu berries are abundant ('mast' years).

The rimu is a droopy, cypress-like conifer known to early settlers as the red pine. Its droopy quality also reminded the first Māori of seaweed, an older meaning of the word rimu.

Botanically speaking, the rimu berry is actually a pinecone. Though we normally think of pinecones as hard and woody, some Southern Hemisphere conifers have soft, colourful cones attractive to birds, which eat the cone and spread the seeds in their droppings. These conifers are called podocarps, from the Greek words for 'foot fruit'. And that's the group to which the rimu belongs.

For more on the intertwined life history of the kākāpō and the rimu, see:

meaningoftrees.com/2013/08/06/rimu-dacrydium-cupressinum

Around Whenua Hou you see a lot of rimu berry collection points. Though much effort is made to feed the kākāpō, the rangers tend to lose a lot of weight while on the job!

It is amazing to think that kākāpō once actually lived all through Aotearoa/New Zealand until only quite recently. How anyone could stand by and see a species almost wiped out is unfathomable to me. During the 1890s, one man called Richard Henry (the namesake of the aforementioned kākāpō) attempted to transfer a number of the birds to Resolution Island, where he was working as caretaker. Unfortunately, ferrets and stoats arrived on the island in 1900 and decimated the populations he had established.

After working so hard, I did a lot of hiking around the island and took photographs of yellow-eyed penguins, Sealers Bay, and the view across to nearby Stewart Island.

When it came time to leave, we had to take the helicopter out because the winds were too strong for fixed-wing aircraft. I silently freaked out but let no one know how I felt. To my surprise it was a far calmer ride than the aeroplane. I loved the flight over Stewart Island, and we made a very smooth landing in Invercargill.

Whenua Hou wildlife – penguin and kākāpō

Sealers Bay above and below, *with penguin above – the aptly-named Ruggedy Mountains of Rakiura/Stewart Island can be seen in the distance in both views.*

For more on Whenua Hou, see my blog post:

a-maverick.com/blog/whenua-hou-codfish-island-few-kakapo-left

CHAPTER FORTY-NINE

Te Araroa: The Long Pathway

THE Māori word Araroa translates as 'long pathway' and it is just that. Te Araroa is a continuous, three-thousand-kilometre walking track stretching from Cape Reinga in the North to Bluff in the South (the pathway does not officially extend to Rakiura/Stewart Island but does so unofficially.) Along the way, it explores New Zealand's diverse environment with its plains, volcanoes, mountains, rivers, lakes and valleys.

We are fortunate in New Zealand that the meeting of the tectonic plates causes such a diverse landscape; though unfortunate in that we live with the earthquakes and eruptions that create it, and that are so destructive when they coincide with the location of a city (New Zealand gets earthquakes and eruptions all the time, but most of them happen in remote back country).

In collision, the Australian and Pacific plates created the Southern Alps/Kā Tiritiri o te Moana, a key feature of Te Araroa. And so, Te Araroa becomes a journey, not just through nature and land, but through geological changes that have happened over millions of years.

New Zealand is also the dividing range of the aforementioned, drowned continent of Te Riu-a-Māui/Zealandia. And so, Te Araroa is also New Zealand's equivalent of the Appalachian

Trail, a similarly lengthy trail that runs the length of the Appalachian mountain chain in the eastern United States.

Te Araroa, the Long Pathway. *Sketched here from official sources.*

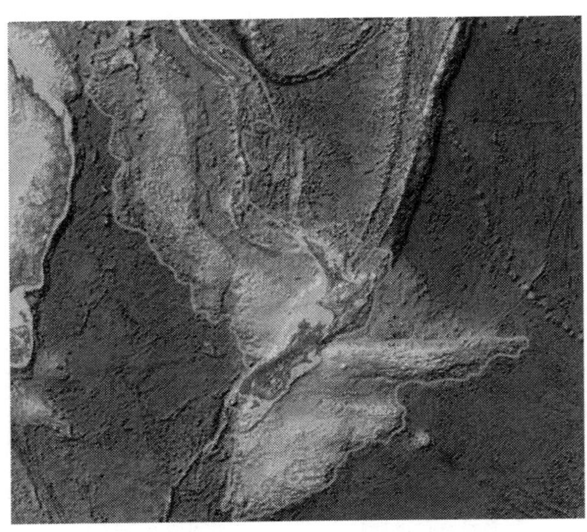

Topographical Map of Te Riu-a-Māui/Zealandia. *US NOAA public domain image, June 2006*

Te Araroa provides some of the best of New Zealand's tramping experiences. It would take five months to complete in full, but it is also possible to complete sections of the trail, which can be done in a few days, a week, or longer. Many of the trail sections are also great day or two-day walks.

Overall, Te Araroa is a very different trail from the traditional backcountry tracks that stick exclusively to the hills, as it connects settlements, townships and cities. Te Araroa is routed in such a way that trampers can be a benefit to the local communities by paying for experiences such as marae stays and other cultural experiences, or by buying food and paying for accommodation. The trail is designed to provide a wide variety of New Zealand experiences to locals as well as foreign visitors.

The Te Araroa trail has more than half a century of history behind it, with the idea of a walk stretching the length of the country being first discussed in Auckland in the late 1960s. In 1975, the New Zealand Walkways Commission was set up with a mandate to form a 'scenic trail' based on the Pennine Way in the United Kingdom, but found it too difficult. DOC tried again in 1995 and made it one of its goals in its Walkways Policy. DOC also proposed giving high priority to a network of countryside tracks crossing private land, as in the United Kingdom.

There are quite a few places in New Zealand where, from a road close to a town or a city, you look up to some ridge and wish you could get up there, or walk along it and look down, and think how good that would be for people's health and fitness – and yet you can't. That attractive range of hills is surrounded by private farmland and 'keep out' signs. Sometimes the farmers will let you across if you ask, sometimes not. In view of indifferent and capricious access nobody bothers to invest in the construction of a trail along the ridge-top even when it is, itself, in public ownership. Most New Zealand tramping has thus tended to be carried out in deep back country, a fact that suits the intrepid but not necessarily everyone else. The public is more or less locked out of many more accessible locations.

Unfortunately, DOC did not have the budget or sufficient co-operation from regional and local authorities to achieve either of the aims just stated.

But today, the Te Araroa Trust (TAT) has at last achieved and indeed surpassed the goal of the great walkway, first set in the 1960s, with this beautiful trail: an achievement that has also expanded the range of accessible locations to tramp. Besides the trust, and the local authorities, there are also many volunteers who have helped to realise this remarkable goal.

There is just one major problem still to be solved, and that is the excessive amount of Te Araroa that actually consists of walking or bicycling along main roads, excessively close to speeding traffic. If this issue can be overcome, New Zealand will have a long trail it really can be proud of.

App Resource:

Atlasguides Te Araroa App: **atlasguides.com/te-araroa-map**

CHAPTER FIFTY

Why not Swap Hiking Boots for Biking Boots?

NEW ZEALAND does not just have fantastic tramping and walking trails, but world class biking trails as well. I'm still making my way through them and they are too good not to mention.

The New Zealand government has spent many millions of dollars in upgrading and creating what they term 'New Zealand's Great Rides'. They are a series of twenty-three cycle trails in the backcountry of New Zealand and they are just that – great rides! These trails are considered New Zealand's premier cycle trails and you can expect them to be slightly busier than some of the others around the countryside. They are mostly off-road in nature. Not having to dodge traffic and pedestrians gives you a good chance to give your undivided attention to the beautiful natural landscapes on offer.

I have done some parts of the Great Rides system, which you can also pick up and leave off where you want. There are various difficulty levels, so there is a trail for everyone and anyone.

I started on one of these trails in Naseby, a small, historical goldmining town in the Central Otago region. The trail I did was about twenty-six kilometres of what I was told was the best scenery and track in the area.

As I made my way along the trail, I met plenty of people from all over the world. I was biking along and would see people on their bikes with their luggage strapped down behind or in front of them. Others even hired bike trailers to carry their luggage.

It was something I thoroughly enjoyed doing and will definitely do more of in the coming years. There's something very leisurely about cycling around New Zealand. When you are away from the road, in particular, it is a very peaceful experience, just gliding along.

Conclusion

WRITING this book, its companion volume *The Neglected North Island,* and the predecessor of both, *A Maverick New Zealand Way,* has made me realise just how much more of New Zealand I need to see, even though I have lived there all my life!

I certainly feel privileged to have done what I have done, with all its trials and tribulations, and I love the mountains, lakes and many walkways in this country. It is important to escape immediate pressures, to 'contemplate the sublime' as philosophers say, and get back to what really matters in life. We also learn to appreciate just what a landscape we are blessed with.

That goes, of course, for the inhabitants of most countries, which have their natural attractions. But I like to think that it applies doubly in beautiful New Zealand. Furthermore, unless we learn to appreciate our nature and protect it, it may not be there forever.

Some say we need to colonise Mars so that a few people will have somewhere to live when the earth is destroyed. I say it is important that we enjoy and protect what we have here, first and foremost.

Acknowledgements and Thanks

I would like to thank my friends and family – you know who you are – and the many people I have met along the way.

I would like to thank my editor Chris Harris, who also drew all the hand-drawn maps not otherwise attributed.

Any further errors or omissions that remain are, of course, all mine.

Other books by Mary Jane Walker

Did you like *The Sensational South Island?* If so, please leave a review!

And you may also like to have a look at the other books I've written, all of which have sales links on my website **a-maverick.com.**

A Maverick Traveller

A funny, interesting compilation of Mary Jane's adventures. Starting from her beginnings in travel it follows her through a life filled with exploration of cultures, mountains, histories and more.

A Maverick New Zealand Way

The forerunner of the present book, *A Maverick New Zealand Way* was a finalist in Travel at the International Book Awards, 2018.

A Maverick Cuban Way

Trek with Mary Jane to Fidel's revolutionary hideout in the Sierra Maestra. See where the world nearly ended and the Bay of Pigs and have coffee looking at the American Guantánamo Base, all the while doing a salsa to the Buena Vista Social Club.

A Maverick Pilgrim Way

Pilgrim trails are not just for the religious! Follow the winding ancient roads of pilgrims across the continent of Europe and the Mediterranean.

A Maverick USA Way

Mary Jane took Amtrak trains around America and visited Glacier, Yellowstone, Grand Teton, Rocky Mountain and Yosemite National Parks before the snow hit. She loved Detroit which is going back to being a park, and Galveston and Birmingham, Alabama.

A Maverick Himalayan Way

Mary Jane walked for ninety days and nights throughout the Himalayan region and Nepal, a part of the world loaded with adventures and discoveries of culture, the people, their religions and the beautiful landscapes.

A Maverick Inuit Way and the Vikings

Mary Jane's adventures in the Arctic take her dog sledding in Greenland, exploring glaciers and icebergs in Iceland, and meeting some interesting locals.

Iran: Make Love not War

Iran is not what you think. It's diverse, culturally rich, and women have more freedoms than you would imagine.

The Scottish Isles: Shetlands, Orkneys and Hebrides (Part 1)

In 2018, Mary Jane decided to tour the islands that lie off the coast of Scotland. She made it around the Orkney and Shetland groups, and to the inner-Hebrides islands of Raasay, Mull, Iona and Staffa as well. She was amazed to discover that Norse influences were as strong as Gaelic ones, indeed stronger on the Orkneys and Shetlands.

Catchy Cyprus: Once was the Island of Love

This is a short book based on Mary Jane's visit to Cyprus, the island that copper's named after and the legendary birthplace of Aphrodite, Greek goddess of love. A former British possession in the Mediterranean Sea, Cyprus is divided into Greek-dominated and Turkish-dominated regions with United Nations troops in between.

Lovely Lebanon: A Little Country with a Big History

"I visit the small country of Lebanon, north of Israel, a country whose name means 'the white' in Arabic because of its snow-capped mountains. Lebanon is divided between Christian and Muslim communities and has a history of civil war and invasion. For all that, it is very historic, with lots of character packed into a small space."

Eternal Egypt: My Encounter with an Ancient Land

In this book, Mary Jane explores Egypt, a cradle of civilisation described by the ancient Greek historian Herodotus as the 'gift of the Nile'. Mary Jane put off going to Egypt for years before she finally went. She's glad she did: there's so much more to Egypt than the pyramids!

The Neglected North Island: New Zealand's other half

In this book, which is the companion to *The Sensational South Island,* Mary Jane explores New Zealand's less touristy North Island. *The Neglected North Island* was judged 'Best Antipodean Cultural Travel Book 2021' by *Lux Life* magazine (lux-review.com).